THE COLLECTED WORKS
OF HERMAN DOOYEWEERD

Series B, Volume 18

GENERAL EDITOR: D.F.M. Strauss

The Roots of Western Culture

Series B, Volume 18

Herman Dooyeweerd

PAIDEIA
PRESS

Library of Congress Cataloging-in-Publication Data

Dooyeweerd, H. (Herman), 1884-1977.
   The Roots of Western Culture
   Herman Dooyeweerd.
   p. cm.

   Includes bibliographical references and index
   ISBN 978-0-88815-353-1 (soft)
   The Roots of Western Culture: Pagan,
   Secular, and Christian Options

   This is Series B, Volume 18 in the continuing series
   The Collected Works of Herman Dooyeweerd
   (Initially published by *Mellen Press*, now published
   by *Paideia Press*)

   ISBN 978-0-88815-353-1

   The Collected Works comprise a Series A, a Series B, and a Series C
   (*Series A* contains multi-volume works by Dooyeweerd,
   Series B contains smaller works and collections of essays,
   Series C contains reflections on Dooyeweerd's philosophy
   designated as: *Dooyeweerd's Living Legacy*, and
   Series D contains thematic selections from Series A and B)

A CIP catalog record for this book is available from the British Library.

The Dooyeweerd Centre for Christian Philosophy
Redeemer College Ancaster, Ontario
CANADA L9K 1J4

All rights reserved. For information contact

©PAIDEIA PRESS 2012
Reprint 2024,
Jordan Station, ON.

Printed in the United States of America

The Roots of Western Culture
Pagan, Secular, and Christian Options

Herman Dooyeweerd

Translated by
John Kraay

Edited by
Mark Vander Vennen and Bernard Zylstra

Newly Edited by
D.F.M. Strauss

Contents

Foreword
General Editor . . . . (ix)

Author's Preface
1959 edition . . . . (xi)

Introduction
The Dutch National Movement. 1
Genuine and Superficial Dialogue 5

Chapter 1
Roots of Western Culture

The Religious Antithesis 7
   The Theoretical Antithesis 7
   The Religious Antithesis 8
   The Religious Ground-Motives of Western Culture 9
   The Religious Dialectic 11
   A Final Warning. 14
Matter and Form. 15
   The Matter Motive 16
   The Form Motive 17
   Dialectical Tension 18
The Roman Imperium 22
   The Motive of Power 23
   Public Law and Private Law 25
Creation, Fall, and Redemption 28
   The Creation Motive 28
   The Scriptural View of Soul and Body 31
   Common Grace 36

Chapter 2
Sphere Sovereignty

Creation and Sphere Sovereignty 41
   Historicism 43
   Two Types of Structure 44
   Sphere Universality 45
   Society and Sphere Sovereignty 48

History and Sphere Sovereignty 50
    Friedrich Julius Stahl 53
    Guillaume Groen van Prinsterer. 55
    Abraham Kuyper 55
Autonomy and Sphere Sovereignty 56
    Biblicism 59
    Barthianism 60

Chapter 3
History, Historicism, and Norms

The Historical Aspect 64
Cultural Power 68
Tradition. 72
Disclosure and Differentiation 74
    Tradition and Culture 74
    Undifferentiated Societies. 76
    Medieval Society 77
    Hitler's Retrogression 79
    Differentiation. 80
    Cultural Economy 82
Individualization and National Identity 83
God's Judgment in History 85

Chapter 4
Faith and Culture

The Structure of Faith. 89
    Might and Right in History 89
    Love of Culture 90
    Faith as the Boundary Aspect 91
    Faith and Revelation. 93
    The Analogies of Faith 94
Faith in a Closed Culture 99
    Example: Mana Belief 102
Disclosure of an Apostate Faith 103
    Example: Egypt 105
Disclosure of an Apostate Culture 105
    Example: The Enlightenment 106
The Radical Challenge of the Word of God 108

Chapter 5
The Great Synthesis

Early Setting 111
   The Temptation of Dualism 113
   Augustine 114
The Roman Catholic Ground-Motive 116
   The Impact of Greek Thought 116
   Thomas Aquinas 118
   The Pretended Biblical Basis 119
The Roman Catholic View of Natural Society 122
   The Social Nature of Rational Human Beings 122
   The Principle of Subsidiarity 124
   Modern Roman Catholic Social Thought 127
The Roman Catholic View of (Supranatural) Christian Society 129
   A Recent Reaffirmation 132
   A Parallel: Faith and Philosophy 134
   Formation of Roman Catholic Political Parties 134
Disintegration of the Synthesis 137
   William of Ockham: Herald of a New Age 137
   Law and Gospel in Luther 139
   Birth of Protestant Scholasticism 141
   Dialectical Theology 143

Chapter 6
Classical Humanism

The Ground-Motive of Nature and Freedom 149
   Dialectical Tensions 152
   Descartes and Hobbes 154
Political Theories of the Modern Age 156
   State Absolutism 156
   Critical Turning Point 159
   Classical Liberalism 162
   Radical Democracy 167
Separation of Science from Faith 170

Chapter 7
Romantic Redirection

The New Personality Ideal 175
Ideology of Community 178
The New Science Ideal 182
Counter-revolution and Christianity 184

Chapter 8
The Rise of Social Thought

Birth of Modern Sociology 189
Distinction between State and Society. 192
Civil Society and Class Conflict. 195
The Class Concept 199
Estates and Classes. 202
Basic Problems in Sociology 205
  Alleged Value-free Character 205
  Causal Explanation versus Normative Evaluation 209
  Dual Structure of Reality. 211
  Ideal Types and Creational Structures 214

Translator's Preface
1979 edition 219

Editorial Preface
1979 edition 223

Glossary
. . . . 225

Index of Persons
. . . . 235

Index of Subjects
. . . . 237

Foreword

A series of editorial articles written by Herman Dooyeweerd (in the weekly paper, *Nieuw Nederland*) during the first three years after the Second World War was compiled by J.A. Oosterhof and published in book form by J.B. van den Brink & Co. in Zutphen, 1959, under the title, *Vernieuwing en Bezinning om het reformatorisch grondmotief* (Renewal and Reflection upon the Reformational Ground-Motive). A second edition appeared in 1963 – with the addition of two paragraphs – one on Groen van Prinsterer, the politician who established the Anti-revolutionary Party and who first employed the expression "sphere sovereignty" subsequently elaborated by Kuyper and Dooyeweerd, and another paragraph on the overestimation of the concept of a "natural community" in sociological universalism.

In 1979 the first English translation of this work appeared under the title, *Roots of Western Culture: Pagan, Secular, and Christian Options*. The work did not include the extensive last part of *Vernieuwing en Bezinning om het reformatorisch grondmotief* where Dooyeweerd discusses the nature of business organizations within modern society.

As the 1979 edition has been out of print for some time now, the Dooyeweerd Centre decided to incorporate it in the Collected Works of Herman Dooyeweerd in its present form. The entire translation has been subjected to a thorough new check against the original Dutch text by the General Editor. In its present form the translated text strictly follows the order in which the text appeared in the Dutch edition. Because the work is based upon a series of articles, Dooyeweerd constantly resumed his explanations with a brief summary of preceding sections, in some instances causing minor, partially overlapping, repetitions in the text. In addition to minor alterations a number of larger sections – sometimes one or more paragraphs – had to be translated for the first time. The page numbers of the 1979 edition have been inserted in the running text and can be found between square brackets. At a later stage a new edition will include the last part of the Dutch text on the nature of business organizations.

Dooyeweerd's own preface (written in 1958 but not taken up as such in the 1979 edition) has been included at the beginning of this edition. Furthermore, the translator's preface and the editorial preface from the 1979 edition are to be found at the back of the volume, after chapter eight.

D.F.M. Strauss
General Editor[1]

---

1 *General Editor's note:* This Volume contains three different kinds of footnotes: (i) those inserted by the *General Editor*, (ii) the notes present in the original Dutch text, and (iii) the notes added by Kraay, Vander Vennen and Zylstra to the 1979 Edition.

Author's Preface
(1959 edition)

Shortly before my departure for North America where I was asked to deliver a series of lectures at a number of universities and other institutions for higher learning, I was asked to give my approval for the publication in book form of the feature articles that I wrote for and which appeared in the weekly newspaper *Nieuw Nederland* some years ago.

I was delighted with this request because it indicated that there remains an interest, in broader circles, in the ideas I had developed in these articles. But for many people it proved to be difficult to obtain copies of the back-issues in which they appeared. Accordingly, it is my hope that this publication in book form will meet the needs of those who have been looking for them.

I wish to express my sincere appreciation to Mr. J.A. Oosterhoff, who during my absence abroad undertook to assemble and adapt the rather extensive material brought together in this book, a laborious task of which he acquitted himself most conscientiously.

The title *Renewal and Reflection*[1] reminds us of the catchword "renewal," which during the first years after the liberation and re-awakening of our fatherland could be heard everywhere. It often drowned out any plea for prior reflection on the foundations and the course that the quest for renewal should take. The manner in which the so-called breakthrough movement supposed it could finally dispose of the "antithesis" in all its significance for temporal life, urgently necessitated a renewed reflection on the meaning and scope of the religious ground-motives that have controlled our western culture in its historical development.

Reflection on these matters continues to be of vital importance today. This is so, because on the one hand the spiritual crisis in which this culture is entangled and the influence of unbiblical dualistic ground-motives on Christian thought can easily blur our awareness of the central, all-of-our-earthly-life-encompassing significance of the antithesis posed by the biblical starting point. On the other hand, this reflection also remains important in order to learn to understand the danger of overestimating the value of Christian forms of organization and of formulated Christian principles that can turn into sinful weapons when the driving force of God's Word is missing from them.

Herman Dooyeweerd
Amsterdam, 1959

---

1 Dutch: *Vernieuwing en Bezinning*.

Introduction

The Dutch National Movement

On May 12, 1945, the Dutch National Movement [*Nederlandse volksbeweging*] made an appeal to the Dutch people in a manifesto which decisively rejected the Christian antithesis[1] as a principle of demarcation for political party formation in the postwar period. It stated this conviction:

> The Second World War signifies the close of an old era and the dawn of a new period for all nations. Economically, socially, politically, and spiritually the world has changed profoundly and confronts the individual and the community with new demands.
>
> In order to promote their own national community and to maintain a worthy place among the nations, the people of the Netherlands need above all a spiritual renewal nourished by the wellsprings of Christianity and humanism, which have always been our sources of strength.
>
> Fundamental to this striving for renewal ought to be respect and responsibility for humankind, which can unfold only in the service of a strong, just, and inspired community (personalistic socialism).
>
> Every area of human life is bound by absolute norms, such as charity, justice, truth, and neighborly love. According to the gospel, these norms are rooted in the will of God. However, they are also grounded in convictions other than Christian. From this follows an unconditional rejection of nation, state, race, or class as the highest corporate good, and likewise of all spiritual coercion as an instrument for the formation of community. [1]

The manifesto particularly stressed this matter:

> The greatest possible consensus among the various religious and political groups is necessary at this time, in order to alleviate our desperate needs, to repair what was laid waste, to stamp out all corruption, to set production in motion again, and especially to base governmental authority upon new confidence. . . .
>
> Our national political life must move along lines of division which are

---

1 *General Editor's note:* The opposition between *belief* and *unbelief*.

different from those of before 1940. Specifically, the Christian antithesis and the Marxist class struggle are no longer fruitful principles for the solution of today's social problems. . . .

A time of open discussion is urgently needed, so that spiritual renewal will become visible also in the political arena.

The appeal was signed by representatives of the most diverse viewpoints and beliefs. Their names alone guaranteed the sincerity and earnestness of this attempt.

One can assume that the manifesto gave expression to the aspirations of many in the country who wish to break down the old barriers that kept our nation divided, a wish stirred most powerfully by the deep distress of a people under enemy occupation. These hopes and aspirations required formulation. The appeal of the Dutch National Movement has indeed given them a specific form. Instead of an *antithesis* between the Christian and humanistic views of life, the appeal recommended a *synthesis*. It called for unification rather than absolute opposition, so that the Dutch national strength, which had been nourished by the spiritual traditions of both Christianity and humanism, might be drawn together again in national unity.

The manifesto indicated that "personalistic socialism" should be the way toward spiritual renewal of our nation. The old antithesis, it argued, must be bridged by the principle that human solidarity and responsibility develop only in the service of a strong, just, and inspired community. According to the appeal, Christians and humanists alike can find themselves in agreement on this common basis. The assumption was that neither the Christian antithesis nor the old Marxist-socialist dogma of class struggle can serve any longer as a fruitful foundation for the solution of today's social issues.

Anyone who would claim the contrary for the Christian antithesis would therefore have to prove that the Christian religion does indeed draw a permanent dividing line of essential significance not only for one's personal faith but for one's whole view of society. Specifically, one would have to demonstrate the meaning of this spiritual antithesis for the solution of the acute postwar problems.

Dealing with this burden of proof will not be an easy task for those who continue [2] to take their stand on the basis of the antithesis. As one option, they might be tempted to duck the issue by putting the onus of proof on the Dutch National Movement. They might ask the latter to explain how specifically its newly enunciated principle will, in fact, provide a fruitful foundation for the solution of contemporary social problems and thus allow the old polarity between Christianity and humanism to be made irrelevant.

However, evading the issue in this way would not be a very convincing approach. After all, one cannot really take cover behind the weak position

Introduction

of one's opponent when sooner or later one will be expected to demonstrate the value of one's own principle in the practice of daily life.

There is, rather, another option. It involves making the case that since the days of Groen van Prinseterer [1801-1876] and Abraham Kuyper [1837-1920] the principle of the Christian antithesis has been a vital driving force. One must make clear to both allies and opponents that Christians have not simply relied on the authority these leaders exercised, but have worked productively with their spiritual heritage. For if the spirit that moved Groen van Prinsterer and Kuyper is no longer alive among their present followers, then a theoretical appeal to the principles they confessed is of no avail. Then we are confronted with a spiritless continuation of tradition which fearfully guards against the budding of new shoots on the trunk of the past. Perhaps the slogans and terms remain the same, but those who voice them are no longer inspired. Their view no longer exudes the sparkle of devout inspiration. The convincing effect of the old slogans disappear, because for those who express them they are no longer a spiritual reality, and because those who are addressed by them cannot fail to detect that the slogans no longer embody any spiritual reality for their advocates.

For surely, the Christian principle is not the permanent possession of a select few who can manipulate it as if it were a collection of magical formulas! On the contrary, it is a dynamic, spiritual force that cannot be halted. Those who confine it within the fixed boundaries of tradition are irrevocably left behind. Those who claim to be led by the Christian principle are placed directly before the face of God who knows our hearts and consumes every insincerity in the fire of his anger. Today the Christian principle fills us above all with a deep concern for the spiritual and physical distress of our nation and of the entire world which passed through the fire of God's judgment.

What then are we to say? Amidst the ruins of our nation's existence and the rubble of western civilization it is hardly fitting for us to beat the drums. Surely, this is not the time for the proponents of the antithesis to sound the battle cry. The antithesis can only be *confessed*, as always, in recognition of the complete solidarity of Christian and non-Christian alike in the sin and guilt of humankind, the same sin and guilt which recently led the world to the brink of destruction.

The antithesis runs right through Christian life itself. Although everywhere, whether in the personal life of the individual, in the life of the Christian family, in Christian organizations and political groups, or even in the Christian church, there have been gratifying signs of genuine vitality, there have at the same time been alarming symptoms of apostasy, discord and schism. These latter symptoms are manifestations of the turbulent spirit of darkness which wages war against the spirit of Christ in the most reprehensible ways.

The antithesis is therefore not a dividing line between Christian and non-Christian groups. It is the unrelenting battle between two spiritual principles that impacts the entire nation and indeed all of humankind. It does not respect any perceived sanctuaries of Christian lifestyles and patterns.

If the Christian idea of the antithesis were to seek its root in and take its nurture from the human person, then it would be a clear invention of Satan, the source of all hypocrisy and pharisaic pride. But if the impact of the antithesis continues to make itself felt as the battle between the [3] spirit of God and the spirit of darkness, then we must each day humbly give thanks to God for his grace in proving his continuing commitment to the world, and confess that we ourselves as Christians cannot take any credit for having brought it about.

How wide is the scope of the antithesis? Is it limited to the secret compartments of the human heart, or does it also draw a principial[1] demarcation line in temporal life? Is it limited to the personal life of each individual or does it also penetrate temporal society in science, culture, politics, and economics? And if the latter is true, is the antithesis then limited to a few "specifically Christian areas," or is its significance *fundamental* and *universal*?

In other words, shall we agree with the Dutch National Movement that the Christian antithesis is no longer a fruitful principle, at least for the solution of contemporary societal problems? Shall we agree that its significance for political and social life has been transient and historical? This is the crucial question.

It is concerning this decisive issue that we will initiate an open discussion with the Dutch National Movement in a series of articles, hopefully for the benefit of the entire Dutch nation. Taught by experience, we have decided to pursue a path different from the ones generally followed in a dialogue of this kind. We hope that the Dutch National Movement will follow us on this path for the sake of the discussion, for we believe that it does not permit either side to evade important issues. Since more than ever before this issue is of fundamental importance for our spiritual development of the nation, more than ever before, the Dutch people have the right to expect clear and explicit answers from those who claim to be able to give spiritual guidance. [4]

---

1 The adjectival and adverbial form of the Dutch words *beginsel* and *principe* ("principle") is *principieel* which as a rule will be translated as *principial* or *principially* (i.e. based on principle).

Introduction

Genuine and Superficial Dialogue

The antithesis was not invented by Groen van Prinsterer and Abraham Kuyper. Anyone who lives the Christian religion and truly knows the Scriptures is aware of that. Still, even among those who confess Jesus Christ as the only Redeemer there is no unanimity about the scope of this antithesis for temporal life. Even worse, it appears that in the discussion about this fundamentally important problem, no method has yet been found to uncover the true underlying nature of this difference of opinion. The result of this is that the discussion, in spite of all the good intentions of those who participate in it, continues to display the character of a *soliloquy*, a monologue of every participant on its own, since it does not really come to a true *dialogue*, a genuine discussion where those who participate indeed contribute to the mutual aim of acquiring a principled clarification of what is understood.

Genuinely fruitful communication is possible only when both points of view are developed jointly and when both sides try to penetrate to the root of their differences. Then the discussion will exhibit the character of a dialogue in which individual people truly cooperate to achieve a mutual clarification of the principles at stake. Only then can the reader begin to reflect on the fundamental question as to which side to join.

It is possible that one can react to such a method by raising the well-known objection which comes from the period before the Second World War: is this type of discussion not far too difficult for the average reader? Is it not more appropriate for a *scientific* discussion than for a popular exposition meant for everyone?

Whoever argues in this way is still the victim of a fatal misunderstanding that constituted one of the greatest obstacles to real contact among the various spiritual currents in our nation before the war.

Surely, then, the first question is this: what should we expect from a discussion about the meaning of the antithesis? Should we merely expect that two opinions are put forward and that each participant is given the opportunity to advance a number of arguments in favor of that participant's point of view? Should we leave the reader with the impression that apparently something can be said for either standpoint? It seems to me that in this way little if anything is gained. This kind of debate remains superficial. The arguments from both sides only give the appearance of meeting on common ground, because the deeper starting points, that determine the argument, remain hidden. As long as these starting points themselves are not placed in sharp and clear light in their opposition to each other, real contact is simply out of the question. It is even conceivable that those who defend their views are not aware of their own deeper points of departure. In that case certainly the whole discussion never moves toward dialogue, and the listener is left in the dark as to the basic principles at stake.

In the second place it is quite wrong to think that the quest for the deepest source of our differences about the antithesis is fitting only in a *scientific* inquiry. The deepest source of our view on life's fundamental issues does not lie in scientific theory, but in the *religious* direction of our lives. This is a matter [5] which concerns every human being and which certainly cannot be delegated exclusively to the theoretical sphere of scholarship.

It may be true that a segment of the reading public prefers not to concern itself with the deepest motives in life and seeks discussion for the sake of entertainment instead of insight. But this attitude is hardly a criterion for distinguishing readers with scientific training from those who have little or none. It is a fact that among scientists, too, there are those who would rather *escape from themselves* and find some kind of "diversion." Indeed, experience tells me that many in academic circles belong to this class. Unfortunately, many view the realm of science as a haven where they think they can escape from themselves by means of the "diversion" of theoretical inquiry which in their opinion is quite unrelated to the deepest root of their life. And precisely the opposite situation is often found among those who are not scientifically schooled; they frequently put the shallowness of the educated to shame.

Whatever the case may be, "spiritual renewal" has become a slogan for the postwar period. We will readily adopt it. If we are to take it seriously, however, we must not be content with *superficiality*, but must look for renewal in *depth*. If the postwar "dialogue" is to contribute to the spiritual renewal of our nation, it must penetrate to that depth dimension of human life *where one can no longer escape from oneself*. It is precisely at that level that we must come to the unmasking of the various views regarding the significance and scope of the antithesis. Only when people have nothing to hide from themselves and from their counterparts in the discussion, will the way be opened for a dialogue that seeks to invite rather than repel.

Anyone who seriously desires to start out along this path will not quickly dismiss my discussion under the pretext that it is too "heavy" to digest for the ordinary reader. If serious investigation is the only way that ultimately promises results, then no effort necessary for a truly mutual understanding of the various standpoints should be considered too great. This road is indeed accessible to every serious reader and not merely to a select company of "intellectuals." *It is the way of self-examination and not the way of abstract theoretical inquiry.* [6]

Chapter 1

Roots of Western Culture

The Religious Antithesis
Taken by itself, the word *antithesis* means no more than "opposition." At an early stage it was given a special meaning in philosophy, particularly in the so-called dialectical way of thinking. This must be considered at the outset, in order to prevent a possible misunderstanding with respect to a discussion of the place of the antithesis.

The Theoretical Antithesis
There are some who hold that dialectical thought does away with every absolute antithesis. According to them, the dialectical method bridges and relativizes whatever is contradictory, including Christianity and humanism. I do not mean to say that this idea is prevalent in the Dutch National Movement, but it undoubtedly claims adherents in certain intellectual circles, especially those oriented toward Hegel.

The dialectical way of thought, which originated in Greek antiquity, is not content with simple, *logically* determined opposites, such as *motion* and *rest*. It attempts to reconcile them in a higher unity. This unity is then understood as the synthesis or connection between a thesis and an antithesis. The great Greek thinker Plato, for example, found the higher synthesis of motion and rest in the idea of "being," arguing that both, with equal right, "are." And it is of course true that in concrete, time-bound reality, motion and rest continually appear together. [7]

Taken in this merely theoretical sense, "antithesis" means no more than setting apart logically what in reality belongs together. In order to obtain a concept of *motion*, it must logically be distinguished from *rest*. Yet this logical *distinction* cannot not lead to an actual *separation*. The key to this antithesis is that it must acknowledge a higher synthesis.

Let me explain further. The consistent reflection of the dialectical method demonstrates that mutually opposed concepts stand together in a mutual relation. In this relation they are each other's correlates; that is, in it one concept cannot exist without the other. Without the thought of something at rest, it is impossible to determine motion, and vice versa.

The premise here is that the opposites which the method resolves in a higher unity are indeed *relative* and not *absolute*. The method must proceed under that assumption. As such it is merely theoretical in character. Certainly the dialectical way of thought is legitimate if, in using the tools of logical contrast, it searches for the higher synthesis of *relative* opposites. When used correctly, the method illustrates that nothing in temporal life is absolute.

The Religious Antithesis

But the case is quite different with the antithesis that has been established in the world through the Christian faith. This antithesis pertains to the relation between the creature and its Creator, and thus touches the religious root of all temporal life.

The religious antithesis does not allow a higher synthesis. It does not, for example, permit Christian and non-Christian starting points to be theoretically synthesized. Where can one find in theory a higher point that might embrace two religious, antithetically opposed stances, when precisely because these stances are religious, they rise above the sphere of the relative? Can one find such a point in philosophy? Philosophy is theoretical, and in its constitution it remains bound to the relativity of all human thought. As such, philosophy itself needs an absolute starting point. It derives this exclusively from religion. Religion grants stability and anchorage even to theoretical thought. Those who think they find an absolute starting point in theoretical thought itself come to this belief through an essentially religious drive. Because of a lack of true self-knowledge, however, they remain oblivious to their own religious motivation.

The absolute has a right to exist only in religion. Accordingly, a truly religious starting point either claims absoluteness or abolishes itself. It is never merely theoretical, for theory is always relative. The religious starting point penetrates behind theory to the sure, absolute ground of all temporal, and therefore relative, existence. Likewise, the religious antithesis it poses is absolute.

To arrive at the true and all-encompassing meaning of this antithesis and, at [8] the same time, to penetrate to the real source of the differences of opinion about the breadth of its reach, it is necessary to take a close look at the *religious ground-motives [religieuse grondmotieven]* of western civilization. These ground-motives have been the deepest driving forces behind the entire cultural and spiritual development of the West.

In every religion one can point to a ground-motive having such a force. It is a force that acts as a spiritual mainspring in human society. It is an absolutely central driving force because, from the religious center of life, it governs temporal expressions and points towards the real or supposed origin of all existence. In the profoundest possible sense it determines a society's entire life- and worldview. It puts its indelible stamp on the culture, science and the social structure of a given period. This applies so long as a leading cultural power can in fact be identified as giving clear direction to the historical development of society. If such ceases to be the case, then a real crisis emerges at the foundations of that society's culture. Such a crisis is always accompanied by spiritual uprootedness.

The religious ground-motive of a culture can never be ascertained from the ideas and the personal faith of the *individual*. It is truly a *communal* motive that governs the individual even when one is not consciously aware of it or acknowledges it. However, such lack of awareness or acknowledgement should not give anyone the misguided idea that this might be an appropriate subject for a scientific (so-called socio-psychological) analysis and explanation. Scientific analysis only deals with the temporal "branches," or ramifications of communal life. It never manages to penetrate to its spiritual root or its religious life-centre. It concentrates on the distinctive contemporary expressions of that society as these are revealed at the time in feelings, ways of thinking, artistic endeavors, moral standards, legal structures and emanations of religious beliefs. Indeed, science itself, in its own starting point, is ruled by a religious ground-motive. Therefore, science can never be neutral with respect to the religious ground-motive out of which it operates.

Directly at work in the religious ground-motive is either the spirit of God or one that denies and opposes him. Each ground-motive is a spiritual force in whose service people place themselves and in which they are participants. It is a community founding spiritual force that is not controlled by people. Rather, it controls them. For it is specifically religion that reveals to us our profound dependency on a higher power to whom or to which we look to find stability and to learn the origin of our existence. We never encounter this higher power as masters but only as servants. These motives acquired their central influence upon the historical development of humankind via certain cultural powers, which, over the centuries, successively gained leadership in the historical process.

The Religious Ground-Motives of Western Culture
The development of western culture has been controlled by several religious ground-motives. The most important of these powers have been the spirit of ancient civilization (Greece and Rome), Christendom, and modern humanism. Once each had made its entrance into history, it continued in [9] tension with the others. This tension was never resolved by a kind of "balance of powers," because cultural development, if it is to be sustained, always requires a leading power.

In classical Greek civilization the leading power was the *polis*, the Greek city-state. It was the carrier of the new culture religion of the Olympian gods. In classical Roman times it was the *res publica,* the Roman commonwealth, and later the emperor as the figure who personified the religious idea of *imperium*. The idea of the *sacrum imperium* (the holy empire) remained in the Byzantine period, having accommodated itself externally to Christianity. The tradition of the "Holy Roman Empire" continued in the Christian rule of Charlemagne and his successors. By that time the Germanic peoples had accepted the heritage of ancient civilization and had adopted the Christian religion. It should be noted that the adaptation of Christianity to the Roman idea of *imperium* at the end of the third century signified a crisis in the foundations of ancient culture.

During the Middle Ages the Roman Catholic Church managed to secure the role of leadership. It established a unified culture, placing all the spheres of life under the dominion of the church.

But in the fifteenth century, after the church's grip on life had weakened during the spiritual decay of the late Middle Ages, the rise of the modern Renaissance movement ushered in the church's downfall and the next great cultural crisis. When the content of the religious ground-motive of the Renaissance was transformed by the emergence of humanism, the classical component of western culture began to tear itself loose from the guidance of the church. Proceeding from a different orientation the great movement of the Reformation at the same time challenged the ecclesiastical power of Roman Catholicism.

Meanwhile, in the countries that remained largely faithful to the church, Roman Catholicism regrouped its forces in the Counter-Reformation. It created room for the absorption of Renaissance culture, just as it had previously adapted itself to classical civilization. In Protestant countries, cultural leadership shifted temporarily to the Reformation.

Gradually, however, a new direction in the development of western civilization became apparent. Both Roman Catholicism and the Reformation were driven back as leading cultural factors by modern humanism. Initially, humanism had aligned itself partly on the side of the Reformation and partly on the side of Roman Catholicism. But in the Enlightenment it broke away completely from the faith of the Christian church. Then it began to display its true colors and became the leading cultural power in the West. Of course, humanism did not eliminate Roman Catholicism and the Reformation as factors in cultural and historical [10] development; they continued to function, partly in an effort to oppose the new worldview that had transformed Christianity into a rational, personal religion, and partly in an effort to synthesize Christianity with the new humanistic ideas that were shaping history. But unlike before, they could not imprint western civilization with the stamp of Christianity. The power struggle for the *spirit* of culture pushed Roman Catholicism and Protestantism into the defensive for nearly three centuries. For the time being the leadership came to rest with humanism.

But in the last few decades of the nineteenth century a general process of decay entered the humanistic worldview. Out of this decay emerged the antihumanistic cultural powers (Marxism, Darwinism, Nietzsche's doctrine of the Superman) which pushed humanism itself onto the defensive. This turn of events heralded a tremendous period of transition in world history and sparked a fierce battle for the spiritual leadership of western culture. Its outcome is still undecided.

The first world war, together with bolshevism, fascism, and national socialism, greatly accelerated the internal degeneration of humanism. Fascism and national socialism battled the humanist "ideology" with their religious "myths of the twentieth century." The reactionary and intensely anti-Christian power of fascism and nazism was broken by the Second World War, at least on the political terrain. Nevertheless, the spiritual crisis that set in long before the war was not overcome. Today the "new age" exhibits the features of spiritual confusion everywhere. One cannot yet point to a definite direction that cultural development will follow in the near future.

In this apparently chaotic stage of transition the West's older and spiritually consolidated cultural powers, Roman Catholicism and the Reformation, have again joined the spiritual fray. This time they fight with modern weapons. Their aim is not just to defend the Christian foundations of modern civilization but to reclaim leadership for a future which is still so unknown and bleak.

The Religious Dialectic
The development of western political systems, social structures, sciences, and arts demonstrates time and time again that all the public expressions of society depend upon spiritually dominant cultural powers.

By and large, four religious ground-motives have determined this development. Three are internally dualistic and fragmentary. Their discord pushes one's posture of life to opposite extremes that cannot be resolved in a true synthesis. We call these extremes "polar opposites" because [11] they are two spiritually "charged" poles that collide within a single ground-motive. Each pole bears the seed of a *religious dialectic*.

To analyze the meaning of the "religious dialectic," we must once again sharply contrast the theoretical and the religious antithesis. By way of orientation, let us briefly recall our earlier discussion.

We observed that the two antitheses are entirely different. We noted that the theoretical antithesis is relative while the religious antithesis is absolute. We concluded that any attempt to bridge an absolute antithesis with the method of the theoretical dialectic rests on the illusion that a higher standpoint exists outside of religion.

The theoretical dialectic is concerned with relative opposites. Insofar as these opposites, in reality, are bound together in a higher unity, they resist any effort on the part of theoretical thought to absolutize them. Thus, for example, the proposition that motion and rest exclude each other absolutely makes no sense; it is not difficult to determine that motion and rest simply make the same temporal reality visible in two different ways. Instead of excluding, they presuppose each other. Their mutual dependence points to a third element in which the two are united, even though conceptually they are mutually exclusive.

The task of theoretical dialectic is to think through a solely logical opposition to its higher synthesis. Therein lies its justification. Whether or not it successfully reaches this synthesis depends upon its starting point, which is governed by a religious ground-motive. We have noted that this starting point of theoretical thought itself is governed by the religious ground-motive of scholarship. In any case it must be conceded that theoretical dialectic, in its search for a higher unity on the basis of *relative* oppositions, is fully justified.

The true religious antithesis is established by the revelation found in God's Word. The key to the understanding of Holy Scripture is given in its religious ground-motive, which consists of the triad of creation, fall into sin, and redemption through Jesus Christ in the communion of the Holy Spirit. What is at stake here is not simply a *theory* which one can theoretically elaborate in a theological system apart from the guidance of God's Spirit. What is primary in the religious ground-motive of Holy Scripture is the motive-power of God's Word through the Holy Spirit, which redirects the religious root of life and which thus permeates all temporal expressions of life.

The radical meaning of God's Word can be revealed to us only by God's Spirit. In abysmal depths it reveals to us at once the *true God* and *ourselves*. God's Word teaches us when it operates in our lives redemptively. Wherever it operates redemptively in this sense, of necessity it effectuates a radical turn-about in our apostasy from God.

It is therefore neither *scholarship* nor *theory*, not even *theology* as a discipline, which can discover the true sense of the religious ground-motive of Holy Scripture. As soon as theology pretends that it can accomplish this, it degenerates into a God-opposing power which resists God's work and renders the religious ground-motive of God's self-revelation powerless by *resolving it into a theory*.

As a science, theology too is totally dependent upon the motivating force of a religious ground-motive. If it withdraws from the driving power of divine revelation, [12] it falls into the clutches of an idolatrous, non-Christian ground-motive.

From the beginning the Word of God stands in absolute antithesis to every form of idolatry. The essence of an idolatrous spirit is that it draws the hearts of people away from the true God who is then replaced with a creature. Every absolutization of what is relative points at the deification of what has been created. It considers self-sufficient that which is not self-sufficient. Insofar as such an absolutization appears in science, it is not science itself but a religious drive that leads theoretical thought in an idolatrous direction. For the direction of scientific thought is always determined by a religious ground-motive.

Therefore, when a religious ground-motive focuses on the deification of something creational, it leads to an absolutization of what is relative. This absolutization calls forth, with inner necessity, some or other correlate of what has been absolutized; that is, those counterparts in reality with which the former is connected and which now claim the same pretended absoluteness as the initial absolutization.

The result is a religious dialectic: a polarity or tension between two extremes within a single ground-motive. On the one hand, the ground-motive breaks apart; its two antithetical motives, each claiming absoluteness, cancel each other. But on the other hand, each motive also determines the other's religious meaning, since each is necessarily related to the other.

Because it is religious, the religious dialectic cannot come to rest in a relation of mere correlativity. The result is that it drives thinking and the practice of life from one pole to the other.

The religious dialectic, in other words, entangles life and theory in a dialectic that is utterly incomprehensible when measured with the yardstick of the theoretical dialectic. Unlike the theoretical dialectic, the religious dialectic lacks the basis for a real synthesis.

In this quest it seeks refuge in one of the antithetical principles within the ground-motive by giving it religious priority. Concomitantly, it debases and depreciates the opposite principle. But the ambiguity and brokenness of the dialectical ground-motive do not give it access to reconciliation in a truly higher unity; reconciliation is excluded by the ground-motive itself. In the end a choice must be made.

Let no one, therefore, try to correct the religious dialectic by way of the theoretical dialectic – the method attempted by the Hegelian school. That approach is an utterly uncritical form of dialectical thought, because at the root of its overestimation of the theoretical dialectic lies a religious dialectic that is hidden to the thinking person. Certainly it is true that the two motives in a dialectical ground-motive are no more than correlates in temporal reality; nevertheless, in the ground-motive they stand in absolute antithesis to each other. The religious drive of an [13] idolatrous spirit absolutizes them both. This religious force can never be controlled or corrected by mere theoretical insight.

Another kind of religious dialectic arises when one attempts to strike a religious synthesis between the ground-motive of Christianity and the ground-motive of either Greek antiquity or humanism. In that event the tension between the two antithetical poles is different from the tension within a strictly idolatrous ground-motive. It originates in the effort to bridge the absolute antithesis by mutually adapting divine revelation and idolatry. Their mutual adaptation requires that both tone down the pure, original meaning of their ground-motives. But the antithesis between them remains in force and continually drives the motives of this apparent synthesis apart.

Those who defend this synthesis often recognize the Christian antithesis to a certain degree, at least in the "spheres" of faith and religion. Generally, however, a distinction is made between the specifically Christian issues of temporal life that directly involve the Christian faith and the so-called neutral issues that do not. Or, by contrast, occasionally a partially Christian ground-motive is structured so that the Christian pole almost completely controls the adapted non-Christian pole. Then indeed the universal significance of the antithesis is recognized. Nevertheless, the antithesis would have been understood differently if the scriptural ground-motive had worked itself through completely. This is the case with Roman Catholicism, which from the outset aimed at assimilating the Greek ground-motive (and later the humanistic ground-motive) to Christianity. The same misunderstanding arises whenever those whose life and thought have been fostered by the Reformation cling to the ground-motive of Roman Catholicism.

The central issue in this religious dialectic is the *pseudo-synthesis* which, time and again, threatens to fall apart into an absolute division or opposition between Christian and non-Christian "areas of life." We must subject all such attempts at synthesis to a thorough investigation, for here, and here alone, lies the real source of disagreement among Christians as to the scope of the antithesis.

A Final Warning
Four religious ground-motives have controlled the development of western culture. We must focus on each in succession, for one cannot penetrate to the core of today's questions on the antithesis until one sees which religious forces have been operative in our culture, and understands how these forces have been central in the resolution of life's practical problems.

Once more I must warn against a possible misunderstanding. We are not about to engage in a learned academic discourse. What is at stake in [14] the issue of the antithesis is the relation between religion and temporal life. This is not a purely theoretical matter of interest only to theoreticians. Since the antithesis touches the deepest level of our existence as human beings, it is a problem that concerns everyone. Those who delegate it to theory shirk their personal responsibility. One cannot escape from oneself behind an impersonal science, for the only answers science gives to the central questions of life are religiously biased.

The antithesis is to be "discussed." Let it be a serious discussion. This is not possible if we are not willing to penetrate to the deepest drives that determine the various points of view. Neither is it possible if anything that seems foreign and strange in the religious motivations of our fellow human beings is brushed aside as being "not to the point" or "of perhaps merely theoretical interest." In a serious dialogue we must faithfully support one another. Perhaps some are not aware of their deepest motives in life; if so, then we must help bring these motives out into the open. We, in turn, must be willing to learn from our opponents, since we are responsible both for ourselves and for them.

Finally, when tracing the religious ground-motives of western culture, we must constantly remember that they concern us personally. We are children of this culture; it has borne, bred, and molded us. By and large, those living in the modern age have not reckoned with western culture's religious ground-motives and their origin. Even in Christian circles these have been taken too lightly. Unfortunately, however, the lack of critical reflection on the religious foundations of cultural development is one of the deepest causes for estrangement among the different spiritual currents confronting each other in our cultural setting. It is essential for the welfare of contemporary culture that the religious roots of its various streams be uncovered and explored.

Matter and Form

The religious ground-motives in the development of western civilization are basically the following:
1. The "form-matter" ground-motive of Greek antiquity in alliance with the Roman *power* motive.[1]
2. The scriptural ground-motive of the Christian religion: creation, fall, and redemption through Jesus Christ in communion with the Holy Spirit.
3. The Roman Catholic ground-motive of "nature-grace," which seeks to combine the two mentioned above.
4. The modern humanistic ground-motive of "nature-freedom," in which an attempt is made to bring the three previous motives to a [15] religious synthesis, concentrated upon the value of human personality.

It is absolutely necessary to consider the Greek ground-motive first, since, despite its modifications, it continued and has continued to this day to operate in both Roman Catholicism and humanism.

---
1 *General Editor's note:* That is, the idea of *imperium*.

Although it was the famous Greek philosopher Aristotle who first coined the term "form-matter," the "form-matter" ground-motive controlled Greek thought and civilization from the beginning of the Greek city-states. It originated in the unreconciled conflict within Greek religious consciousness between the ground-motive of the ancient nature religions and the ground-motive of the then more recent culture religion – the religion of the Olympian deities.

The Matter Motive
Outside of their primeval Greek core, the nature religions contained much that was pre-Greek and even of foreign origin. These religions differed greatly in local ritual and in specific faith content. Reconstructing all the early forms of nature religions is largely guesswork for lack of information, but it is clear that from at least the beginning of the so-called historical age (the age documented by written records), the communal ground-motive of these religions sustained a great influence on Greek culture.

What was at stake in this ground-motive was the deification of a formless, cyclical stream of life. Out of this stream emerged the individual forms of plant, animal, and human being, which then matured, perished, and came to life again. Because the life stream ceaselessly repeated its cycle and returned to itself, all that had individual form was doomed to disappear. The worship of the tribe and its ancestors was thoroughly interwoven with this religious conception. Closely related to this belief was its view of time: time was not linear, as in Newton's modern conception of an ongoing continuum, but cyclical.

Mysterious forces were at work in this life stream. They did not run their course according to a traceable, rational order, but according to *Anangkē* (blind, incalculable fate). Everything that had a life of its own was subjected to it. The divine was thus not a concrete form or personality. On the contrary, the nature gods were always fluid and invisible. The material names used to indicate them were just as undefined as the shapeless divinities themselves. Instead of a unified deity, a countless multiplicity of divine powers, bound up with a great variety of natural phenomena, were embodied in many fluid and variable conceptions of deities. The state of constant variation applied not only to the "lesser" gods (the so-called demons: shapeless, psychical powers) and to the "heroes" (worshipped in connection with the deification of life in tribe and family), but with equal force to the "great" gods such as Gaia [16] (mother earth), Uranus (god of the skies), Demeter (goddess of grain and growth) and Dionysus (god of wine).

In this context it is understandable that the rise of relatively durable, individual forms in nature was considered an injustice. According to the mysterious saying of the Ionian philosopher of nature, Anaximander (sixth century B.C.), these individual forms would "suffer retribution in the course of time." With a genuinely Greek variant on Mephistopheles' saying in Goethe's *Faust*, one could express this thought as follows: "Denn alles, was entsteht,/Ist wert, dass es zugrunde geht" (For all that comes to be/Deserves to perish wretchedly).[1]

On the other hand, it is also understandable that in this nature religion one's faith in the continuity of a divine stream of life provided a certain comfort with respect to the inevitable destruction of all definite, visibly shaped and formed individual life. "Mother earth" sustained this religion; out of it the stream of life began its cycle.

The Form Motive

The newer culture religion, on the other hand, was a religion of form, measure, and harmony. It became the official religion of the Greek city-state, which established Mount Olympus as one of history's first national religious centers. The Olympian gods left "mother earth" and her cycle of life behind. They were immortal, radiant gods of form: invisible, personal, and idealized cultural forces. Mount Olympus was their home. Eventually the culture religion found its highest Greek expression in the Delphic god Apollo, the lawgiver. Apollo, god of light and lord of the arts, was indeed the supreme Greek culture god.

This new religion, which received its most splendid embodiment in the heroic poetry of Homer, tried to incorporate the older religion in its own ground-motive of form, measure, and harmony. It was particularly concerned to curb the wild and impassioned worship of Dionysus, the god of wine, with the normative principle of form that characterized Apollo worship. In the city of Delphi, Apollo (culture) and Dionysus (nature) became brothers. Dionysus lost his wildness and took on a more serious role as the "keeper of the souls."

Early in this period of transition the ancient Greek "seers" and poet-theologians (Hesiod and Homer) sought to convince the people that the Olympians themselves had evolved out of the formless gods of nature. Hesiod's teaching concerning the genealogy of the gods, which deeply influenced subsequent Greek philosophical thought, gave the [17] ground-motive of the older nature religions a general, abstract formulation: the basic principle of all that comes into being is *chaos* and *formlessness*.

But the inner connection between the culture religion and the older nature religions is most evident in the peculiar part played by *Moira*. Originally, *Moira* was nothing other than the old *Anangkē* of the nature religions: inexorable fate revealing itself in the cycle of life. But later it was adapted somewhat to the form motive of the culture religion. *Moira* is re-

---

1 *Goethe's Faust*, trans. and intro. Walter Kaufmann, bilingual ed. (Garden City, New York: Doubleday & Company, 1961), lines 1339, 1340.

lated to *meros*, a word that means "part" or "share." Among the Olympian gods *Moira* became the fate that assigned to each of the three most important deities a "share" or realm: the heavens to Zeus, the sea to Poseidon, and the underworld to Hades (Pluto). This already implied something of design instead of blind fate. *Moira* actually became a principle of order. Its order, however, did not originate with the Olympian gods but with an older, impersonal, and formless divine power. Thus *Moira* still revealed its original dark and sinister self when it decreed the fate of death upon mortals. Even Zeus, lord of Olympus, father of gods and human beings, was powerless before *Moira* (although sometimes Homer designated Zeus as the dispenser of fate). *Moira*, the fate that held death for all the individual forms of life, was incalculable, blind, but nonetheless irresistible.

Dialectical Tension

At this point, where both religions united in the theme of *Moira*, the culture religion revealed an indissoluble, dialectical coherence with the religions of nature. The religion of culture is inexplicable without the background of the nature religions. With intrinsic necessity, the groundmotive of the culture religion called forth its counterpart. *Moira* was the expression of the irreconcilable conflict between both religions. In the religious consciousness of the Greeks this conflict was the unsolved puzzle standing at the center of both tragedy and philosophy. Likewise, the religions of nature continued to be the threatening antipode to the Greek cultural and political ideal.

We have seen that the new culture religion of Olympus and the poetic teachings regarding the origin of the gods sought to reconcile the antithetical motives of the older religions of nature and the newer religion of culture. These attempts failed for at least three reasons, the first of which is decisive.

1. The newer culture religion neglected the most profound questions of life and death. The Olympian gods protected humans only as long as they were healthy and vigorously alive. But as soon as dark *Anangkē* or *Moira*, before whom even the great Zeus was impotent, willed the fate of a mortal's death, the gods retreated: [18]

    But death is a thing that comes to all alike. Not even the gods can fend it away from a person they love, when once the destructive doom *[Moira]* of levelling death has fastened upon him.[1]

2. The Olympian culture religion, given mythological form by Homer, came into conflict with the moral standards of the Greeks. Even though the Olympian gods sanctioned and protected Greek morality, the Olympians themselves lived beyond good and evil. They forni-

---

1 The *Odyssey of Homer*, trans. and intro. Richmond Lattimore (New York: Harper & Row, 1965) 3:236-238.

cated and thieved. Homer glorified deception as long as it expressed the grand manner of the gods.
3. The whole splendid array of deities was far too removed from ordinary people. The Homeric world of the gods suited Greek civilization only during its feudal era, when the relation between Zeus and the others served as a perfect analogy to that of a lord and his powerful vassals. But after feudalism had run its course, the divine world lost all contact with the cross section of the people. Thereafter it found support only in the historically formative Greek *polis*, the bearer of culture. The critical years of transition between Mycenian feudalism and the Persian wars marked a religious crisis. The Greek city-states withstood the ordeal brilliantly. Nilsson, the well-known scholar of Greek religion, characterized this crisis as a conflict between an ecstatic (mythical) movement and a legalistic movement.[1] The first revived and reformed the old suppressed religions, and the second, finding its typical representative in the poet-theologian Hesiod, stood on the side of the Olympian culture religion.

In the light of these reasons it is understandable that the Greeks observed the ancient rites of nature religions in private but worshipped the Olympians as the official gods of the state in public. This also explains why the deeper religious drives of the people became oriented to "mystery worship," for in this worship the questions of life and death were central. Hence it is not surprising that the culture religion in its Homeric form began to lose its strength already in the sixth century B.C. Criticism against it grew more and more outspoken in intellectual circles, and the sophists, the Greek "enlightenment" thinkers of the fifth century, enjoyed relative popularity, although there was a reaction against them in the legal trials dealing with "atheism." [19]

Throughout, the dialectical ground-motive remained unshaken. Born out of the meeting between the older religions of nature and the newer Olympian religion of culture, this ground-motive maintained its vitality even after the myths had been undermined. In philosophical circles it was able to clothe itself with the garments of creeds that answered the religious needs of the times. The old conflict continued to characterize this religious ground-motive; the principle of blind fate governing the eternal flux of all individual forms in the cyclical life stream stood over against the principle of the supernatural, rational, and immortal form, itself not ruled by the stream of becoming.

The same conflict found pointed expression in the Orphic school, founded by the legendary poet and singer Orpheus. This school, basically

---

1 Most likely, Dooyeweerd is referring to chapter 6 ("Legalism and Mysticism") of Martin P. Nilsson's classic book *A History of Greek Religion*. 2nd ed., trans. F.J. Fielden (New York: W.W. Norton & Company, 1964). The book first appeared in 1925.

a religious reform movement, gained great influence in Greek philosophy. Following the old religions of the flux of life, the Orphics worshipped Dionysus. This, however, was a reborn Dionysus. After the Titans had devoured him, the original Dionysus, the untamed god of wine, reappeared in personal form as the twin brother of Apollo, the Olympian god of light. The transfiguration of Dionysus illustrates the sharp distinction in Orphic religion between life in the starry heavens and life on the dark earth, which moved in the cycles of birth, death, and rebirth.

The Orphic view of human nature clearly expressed the internal discord of the Greek ground-motive. At one time, according to the Orphics, a person had an immortal, rational soul. It originated in the heavens of light beyond the world. But at a certain point the soul fell to the dark earth and became imprisoned or entombed in a material body. This imprisonment of the soul meant that the soul was subject to the constant cycle of birth, death, and rebirth. Not until it had been cleansed from the contamination of matter could the soul cease its migrations from body to body (including animal bodies) and return to its true home: the divine, imperishable sphere of starry light. As the Orphic inscription, found in Petelia, declares: "I am a child of earth and of the starry heaven/But heaven is my home."

The ascription of an imperishable sphere of light to the heavens points to the combination in Orphic religion between the culture motive and the so-called uranic nature religion which worshipped the sky and its light giving bodies. Like the older nature religions, the uranic religion did not know of an immortal form. Even the radiant sun rose from the earth and returned to the earth's bosom after it had set. The Orphic movement transferred the Olympian concept of divine immortality to the rational substances of the soul that made their home in the starry sky. The soul had an imperishable form, but earthly bodies, subject to the cycle of the ceaselessly flowing life stream, did not. Clearly, the religious contrast [20] between form and matter determined this entire conception of "soul" and "body."

The Greek motive of matter, the formless principle of becoming and decay, was oriented to the aspect of movement in temporal reality. It gave Greek thought and all of Greek culture a hint of dark mystery which is foreign to modern thinking. The Greek motive of culture, on the other hand, was oriented to the cultural aspect of temporal reality ("culture" means essentially the free forming of matter). It constantly directed thought to an extrasensory, imperishable form of being that transcended the cyclical life stream.

The Greek idea of *theoria* (philosophic thought) was closely linked to the culture motive. The form of being could not be grasped in a mere concept but required *contemplation* as a supra-sensible, luminous figure. This too was a typically Greek tendency which is foreign to us in its original sense. Just as the Olympian gods could only be conceived of as imperishable figures of light standing beyond sense perception, so also could "immutable being" only be conceived of as a radiant form. *Theoria* was always contemplation directed to an invisible and imperishable form of being which contained the divine. From the outset Greek philosophical thought presented itself as the way to true knowledge of god. It tied belief to the sphere of *doxa* (uncertain opinion), which belonged to sense perception.

Form and matter were inseparably connected within the Greek religious ground-motive. They presupposed each other and determined each other's religious meaning. The dialectical tension between them pushed Greek thought to polar extremes and forced it into two radically conflicting directions, which nevertheless revealed a deeper solidarity in the ground-motive itself. The Greek conception of the nature *(physis)* of things, for example, was determined by this tension. The Greeks viewed nature sometimes as a purely invisible form and sometimes as an animated, flowing stream of life, but most often as a combination of both. Likewise, this tension shaped the Greek community of thought and culture. Greek philosophy, which so profoundly influenced Roman Catholic scholasticism, cannot be understood if this ground-motive is left out of consideration. The same holds for Greek art, political life, and morality.

The connection between the Greek religious ground-motive and the Greek idea of the state may serve as an illustration. In the classical age of Greek civilization the state was limited to the small area of the city-state *(polis)*. The city-state was the bearer of the Greek culture religion and hence the Greek cultural ideal. A Greek was truly human only as a free citizen of the *polis*. The *polis* gave form to human existence; outside of this formative influence human life remained mired in the savagery of [21] the matter principle. All non-Greeks were barbarians. They were not fully human since they lacked the imprint of Greek cultural formation.

The ideas of world citizenship and of the natural equality of all human beings were launched considerably later in Greek philosophy by the cynics and the Stoics. These ideas were not of Greek origin. They were essentially hostile to the Greek idea of the state, and they exerted little influence on it. The radical wing of the sophists was similarly antagonistic. Guided by the Greek matter motive, it declared war on the city-state. Even more radically foreign to the classical Greek was the Christian confession that the religious root-community of humankind transcends the boundaries of race and nation.

The Greek ideal of democracy that emerged victorious in Ionian culture was quite different from the democratic ideal of modern humanism. Democracy in Greece was limited to a small number of "free citizens." Over against them stood a mass of slaves and city dwellers with no civil rights.

"Freedom" consisted in total involvement with the affairs of state, and "equality" meant only that ownership of capital was not a prerequisite for full citizenship. Labor and industry were despised and left to workers and slaves. Soon every aristocracy, whether or not meant in a spiritual sense or in terms of property owned, became suspect and liable to all sorts of confining regulations.

The idea of sphere sovereignty was therefore utterly foreign to the Greek mind. Rooted in the Christian view that no single societal sphere can embrace our whole life, sphere sovereignty implies that each sphere in society has a God given task and competence which are limited by the sphere's own intrinsic nature. These limited spheres of power ought to respect each other in their mutual relationships.

The Greek idea of the state, however, was basically totalitarian. In accordance with its religious ground-motive it demanded the allegiance of the whole person. Or rather a person truly became a human being only as an active, free citizen. All of life had to serve this citizenship, because it was only citizenship that bestowed a divine and rational cultural form upon human existence. The Greek state, realized in the "democratic" city-state, was not founded on the principle that the state's authority is inherently limited by its inner nature. Neither was it governed by the principle that an individual has inalienable rights over against the body politic. The Greek had only formal guarantees against despotism.

The Roman Imperium

Greek culture became a world culture when Alexander the Great, the royal pupil of Aristotle, created the Macedonian empire. This empire (the *imperium*), which stretched from Greece to India, had little connection with the small city-state. As it arose, certain eastern religious [22] motives began to mingle with Greek motives. Alexander made use of the Asiatic belief in the divine ancestry of monarchs in order to legitimize and give divine sanction to the Greco-Macedonian world empire. He allowed himself to be worshipped as a *heros*, a demigod, and later as a full god. From east to west, from Greece to India, the worship of Alexander was added to the existing cults. In 324 B.C. Athens decided to include Alexander among the city's deities as Dionysus. The worship of Alexander was the foundation for the religious *imperium* idea, which became the driving force behind the Roman conquest of the world and continued in a christianized form with the Germanic-Roman idea of the *sacrum imperium*, the "Holy Roman Empire," after Rome's fall.

The religious idea of *imperium* lent itself toward a combination with the ground-motive of Greek culture. It was not by chance that Alexander was worshipped as Dionysus in Athens. We noted earlier that the cult of Dionysus expressed the matter motive of the older nature religions, the formless stream of life moving in the cycle of birth, death, and rebirth. It is even likely that this cult was originally imported from Asia. In any case, the fatalistic conception of the cycle of life meting out death to everything that existed in individual form, was eminently suited to a deification of the monarch as the lord over life and death. The monarch soon displayed the same mysterious power as Dionysus, the demon, the dynamic soul of the ever flowing life stream. Carried forward by a deified ruler, the *imperium* became surrounded with a kind of magical halo. Like fighting the inexorable fate of death, resisting the *imperium* was useless. The *imperium* idea was already well established in Hellenistic culture when, after Alexander's death, his world empire broke up into several large realms which eventually yielded to Roman might.

As the Roman empire expanded, it was understandable that the religious ground-motive of Greek culture would influence Roman culture. The Romans had already made acquaintance with the Greeks when the latter conquered southern Italy. The Greeks had established colonies there and had named that part of the Italian peninsula "Magna Graecia." After the Romans occupied Greece itself they adapted the worship of their own gods to Greek culture religion. Moreover, the Roman religion of life, which worshipped communal life in the tribe and clan, had much in common with the older Greek nature religions. In this way, the religious *imperium* idea found fertile soil among the Roman conquerors.

The Motive of Power
The motive of power deeply penetrated the Roman world of thought. Yet it did not become embodied in the person of a ruler until the emperor Augustus replaced the ancient republican form of government. [23] Even then, however, the deification of the office of emperor was first associated with the common Roman practice of ancestor worship. The emperor Tiberius, successor to Augustus, still resisted veneration of a living emperor and allowed worship only of his predecessor. But after him the infamous Caligula dropped this restriction and the existing ruler came to be worshipped as a god.

In the religious consciousness of the Romans, the deification of the *imperium* was the counterpart and antipode to the typically juridical tendency of their ancestor worship. Roman worship was sober and businesslike. It had a stern juridical bent. The gods of the state had their own sphere of competence next to the old gods of home and hearth who represented the continuity of family life throughout the generations. The claims of both spheres regarding sacrifices and worship were precisely defined and balanced.

The religious motive of power and law thoroughly pervaded the old folk law *(ius civile)* of Roman tribalism. This motive rested on a strict juridical delimitation of different spheres of authority. Each sphere was religiously sacred and unassailable. The large patrician clan *(gens)* defined the sphere of authority, centered in the religious communal life of the family. With the head of the clan as its priest, the family deified and worshipped its ancestors. This sphere was carefully distinguished from the sphere of authority belonging to the Roman tribe *(civitas)*, where the public tribal gods maintained an inviolable religious sway. When in the course of time the Roman state as the *res publica* slowly cut itself off from this still primitive and undifferentiated societal structure, the power of the great patrician clans was broken. The clans then dissolved into narrower spheres of authority: the Roman *familia* or domestic communities.

The *familia* was not like our modern nuclear family. Like the old *gens*, the *familia* was undifferentiated. It displayed the traits of many different societal spheres which diverge into well defined communities, such as the family, the state, industry, and the church in a more highly developed culture. One might compare this undifferentiated structure with the lack of specialization in lower animals, such as worms, which do not develop specific organs for the various functions of life. Like the old *gentes* and tribes the Roman *familia* displayed such an undifferentiated character. Each *familia* was a family community, an economic unit, a miniature state, and a community of worship. Above all, it was the embodiment of the religious authority of the household gods, who represented the communion between the living and dead members of the *familia*. The head of the *familia* was usually the oldest male member, the *pater familias*, who wielded the power of life and death over all – over his wife, his children, his slaves, and his so-called clients. He also presided as the priest.

The sphere of authority of the *pater familias* was juridically distinct [24] from the power of the state. It was religiously inviolate and absolute, and the state could not interfere with it. Its territorial basis was the plot of Italian soil on which the *familia* was situated, just as the sphere of authority of the older patrician clan had been territorially based on lands owned by the clan. To this piece of land, which, under solemn invocation of the god *Terminus*, had been ceremoniously marked off with boundary stones, the *pater familias* had the rights of absolute ownership and exclusive use. This ownership was not at all like our modern civil legal right to ownership which is strictly a right to property and does not include any authority over persons. The right to absolute ownership held by the Roman *pater familias* was rooted in the *familias* religious sphere of authority. For those who belonged to the ancestral lands it was an authority that disposed of their life and death. It was exclusive and absolute. In this still undifferentiated form of ownership, legal authority and property rights were indissolubly bound together. The *pater familias*, for example, had power to sell the children and slaves that resided under his jurisdiction.

Roman folk law *(ius civile)* can never be understood apart from the religious ground-motive of Roman culture. For example, this motive permeated the contractual laws of Roman society. The household heads were mutually equal as bearers of power; the one had no jurisdiction over the other. But if one were indebted to another and did not discharge his debt immediately, then a contract *(obligatio)* was established. Originally this meant that the debtor was brought within the religious jurisdiction of the creditor. A prescribed legal formula dictated the severity of punishment. Payment *(solutio)* released the debtor from this sphere of power which, like a magic bond *(vinculum)*, held him captive. If he failed to pay, then his whole person fell to the creditor.

Like ancient Germanic and other primitive folk law, Roman folk law *(ius civile)* was exclusive. It made one's entire legal status dependent upon membership in the Roman *populus*. Banishment from the community resulted in the total loss of one's legal rights. A foreigner too had no rights and could only secure juridical protection by living under the patronage of a Roman *pater familias*, who took such a person into the *familia* as a "client."

Public Law and Private Law
When Rome became an empire, the need arose for a more universal law that could apply to the private interrelations between both citizens and foreigners. This universal law, the *ius gentium*, was what we today would call the civil law of the Romans. It was no longer bound to the religious sphere of authority of the undifferentiated *gens* or *familia*. It raised every free person, regardless of birth or nationality, to the status of a legal subject, a status which endowed that person with both rights and [25] obligations. It created a sphere of personal freedom and self-determination that offered a healthy counterbalance to the jurisdiction of the community (both the state and the *familia*). It was a product of the process of differentiation in ancient Roman society. Certainly the Roman state as the *res publica*, though founded on the power of the sword, had the public good as its goal when it acknowledged over against itself a civil legal sphere of freedom for individual personalities in which those individuals could pursue their private interests.

Public law, then, as the internal sphere of jurisdiction in the Roman state, began to distinguish itself in accordance with its *inner nature* from civil private law. This distinction had already appeared in the old folk law *(ius civile)* but, as long as the Roman community was still undifferentiated, public and private law could not be distinguished in accordance with their *inner nature*. Both were rooted in a religious sphere of authority which, because of its absolute character, embraced the entire temporal life of its subordinates. Both had sway over life and death. The difference between them depended strictly on who or what carried authority. If it was the Roman folk community, one was subject to the sphere of public law; if it was the *pater familias*, one was subject to the sphere of private law. This undifferentiated state of communal life allowed room for neither a constitutional law nor a differentiated civil private law. All law was folk law. Differences within this law were due to differences depending on who wielded authority.

The development of a universal civil law common to all free people presented the Roman legislators with a deeply religious problem. The universal law *(ius gentium)* could not be based on the religious authority of either the old *gens*, the *familia*, or the Roman community. Where then could its ultimate foundation be found? Here Greek philosophy provided assistance with its doctrine of natural law *(ius naturale)*. Natural law resided not in human institutions but in "nature" itself.

Stoic philosophy (influenced by semitic thought) had introduced into Greek thought the idea of the natural freedom and equality of all human beings. It had broken with the narrow boundaries of the *polis*. The founders of Stoic philosophy lived during the period when Greek culture became a world culture under the Macedonian empire. Their thinking about natural law, however, was not determined by the religious idea of *imperium*, but by the old idea of a so-called golden age. This age, an age without slavery or war and without distinction between Greek and barbarian, had been lost by humankind because of its guilt. The Stoic doctrine of an absolute natural law reached back to this pre-historic golden era. For the Stoics, all people were free and equal before the law of nature.

The Roman jurists based the *ius gentium* as a private world law on this *ius naturale*. In doing [26] so, they made an outstanding discovery. They discovered the enduring principles that lie at the basis of civil law according to its own nature: civil freedom and equality of human beings as such.[1] Civil law is not communal law and cannot be made into communal law without distorting its essence. As one would put it today, civil law is founded on human rights. The Roman *ius gentium*, which still legitimized slavery, actualized these principles only in part, but the doctrine of the *ius naturale* kept the pure principles of civil law alive in the consciousness of the Roman jurists.

At the close of the Middle Ages most of the Germanic countries of continental Europe adopted this Roman law as a supplement to indigenous law. It thus became a lasting influence on the development of western law. The fact that national socialism resisted this influence and proclaimed the return to German folk law in its myth of "blood and soil," only proves the reactionary character of the Hitler regime. It failed to see that the authentic

---

1   *General Editor's note:* Dooyeweerd refers here to two articles of the Dutch Civil Code (1838): "article 1: The enjoyment of civil rights is independent from constitutional rights, which are acquired only according to the Constitution"; article 2: Whoever is present on the territory of the state is free and entitled to the enjoyment of civil rights. Slavery and all other forms of serfdom, whatever their nature or designation, will not be tolerated within the realm."

meaning of civil law acts as a counterforce to the overpowering pressure of the community on the private freedom of the individual person. But the process of undermining civil law, which is still with us, began long before national socialism arose.

The Roman *ius gentium* was a gift of God's common grace to western culture. The Roman jurists masterfully developed its form with a great sensitivity to practical needs. Many deepened principles of law so familiar to us today because of modern civil law, came to expression here, such as the protection of good morals, good faith (bona fide), and equity. Nevertheless, the religious ground-motive of Greco-Roman culture continually threatened this blessed fruit of God's common grace. Roman civil law stood at the mercy of the religious motive of power that had governed the development of Roman law from the outset. In its development civil law (the *ius gentium*) remained intimately connected to the Roman world domination. Personal freedom was limited by the demands of empire. Civil law placed the individual person squarely in opposition to the all-powerful Roman state apparatus, which had to take care of the "common good" of the Roman empire.

The Christian idea of the sphere sovereignty of the differentiated areas of life was as foreign to the Romans as it was to the Greeks. How could individual persons maintain their private freedom in the face of the Roman leviathan? It was not by chance that the individual's freedom soon fell victim to the absolute authority of the *imperium*. Certainly, this was not the case when Rome flourished. At that time one found a sharp demarcation between the sphere of the state and the sphere of individual freedom. Essentially, however, this was only due to the fact that the old undifferentiated *familia* managed to maintain itself over such a long period of time. In the *familia* structure lay [27] the ancient division between the absolute and impenetrable religious authority of the head of the household *(pater familias)* and the authority of the Roman state. Throughout the duration of the Roman empire the *familia* continued to protect the freedom of trade and industry. The workshops and plantations in and beyond Italy belonged to the *familia* and therefore fell outside of state interference. Wealthy Romans were thus able to maintain the plantations with great numbers of slaves. This mechanical delimitation of private and public jurisdiction naturally led to a capitalistic exploitation of labor; personal freedom was purchased by the head of the household.

In the days of the Byzantine emperors (beginning in the latter part of the third century A.D.) the Greco-oriental idea of the *sacrum imperium* advanced further. This spelled the end of civil freedom for the individual. The Greeks did not know of the Roman *familia*, and the idea of marking off its religious jurisdiction from that of the state was foreign to them. In this period the only stronghold for the Roman idea of freedom was destroyed. It was replaced by an unrestrained state absolutism, against which not even the *ius gentium* could offer resistance. Trade and industry were forced into the straightjacket of the Roman state structure, which established a strictly hierarchical "guided economy." Everyone became a civil servant. After Constantine the Great accepted the Christian faith, this absolutism even subordinated the Christian church to the state. The church became a "state church." In Christian style, the divine ruler of the world empire called himself "Caesar by the grace of God," but he claimed absolute temporal authority, even over Christian doctrine. The "caesaropapacy" was a fruit of the Greco-Roman motive of power.

Creation, Fall, and Redemption

The second ground-motive which shaped the development of western culture is the motive of creation, fall, and redemption through Jesus Christ in the communion of the Holy Spirit. The Christian religion introduced this motive in the West in its purely scriptural meaning as a new religious community motive.

The Creation Motive

Already in its revelation of creation the Christian religion stands in radical antithesis to the religious ground-motive of Greek and Greco-Roman antiquity. Through its integrality (it embraces all things created) and radicality (it penetrates to the root of created reality) the creation motive makes itself known as authentic divine Word-revelation. God, [28] the Creator, reveals himself as the absolute, complete, and integral origin of all things. No equally original power stands over against him in the way that *Anangkē* and *Moira* (blind fate) stood over against the Olympian gods. Hence, within the created world one cannot find an expression of two contradictory principles of origin.

Influenced by its motive of form and matter (founded in the conflict between the new culture religion and the old religion of life), Greek philosophy could not speak of a real creation. Nothing, the Greeks argued, could come from nothing. Some Greek thinkers, notably Plato, did hold that the world of becoming was the product of the formative activity of a divine, rational spirit; but under pressure from the ground-motive of culture religion, this divine form-giving could only be understood according to the pattern of human cultural formation. With Plato, for example, the divine mind, the demiurge, was the great architectural and artistic force which granted the world its existence. The demiurge required material for its activity of formation. Due to the influence of the Greek matter motive, Plato believed that this material was utterly formless and chaotic. Its origin did not lie in the divine Reason, since the demiurge was only a god of form or culture. The demiurge does not create; it simply furnishes matter with divine form. Matter retains its self-determining function, i.e., the *Anangkē* or blind fate, which is hostile to the divine function of form-giving. In Plato's famous dialogue *Timaeus*, which dealt with the origin of the world, the divine Logos was able to restrain *Anangkē* only by means of rational persuasion.

The same principle was expressed by the great Greek poet Aeschylus. In his tragedy *Oresteia, Anangkē* persecuted Orestes for matricide; Orestes had killed his mother because she had murdered his father. Likewise, for Plato's great pupil Aristotle pure form was the divine mind *(nous)*, but *Anangkē*, which permeated matter, was still the peculiar cause of everything anomalous and monstrous in the world.

The earlier philosophers of nature gave religious priority to the motive of matter (the motive of the formless, ever-flowing stream of life). Plato and Aristotle, however, shifted religious priority to the motive of form. For them matter was *de-divinized*, no long viewed as divine. Nevertheless, the rational form-god was not the origin of matter. It was not the integral, sole origin of the cosmos. Therein lay the apostate character of the Greek idea of god.

The Greek idea of god was the product of an absolutization of the relative. It arose from a deification of either the cultural aspect of creation or that of the flow of life. It thus stood in *absolute antithesis* to God's revelation in the Bible, in opposition to God as the creator of heaven and earth. Consequently, a synthesis between the creation motive of the Christian religion and the form-matter motive of Greek religion is not possible.

God's self-revelation as the creator of all things is inseparably linked with the revelation of who human beings are in their fundamental relationship to their [29] Creator. By revealing that humankind was created in God's image, God revealed humankind to itself in the religious root-unity of its creaturely existence. The whole meaning of the temporal world is *integrally* (i.e., completely) bound up and concentrated in this unity.

According to his creation order, Jehovah God is creaturely mirrored in the heart, soul, or spirit of a human being. This is the religious center and spiritual root of a person's temporal existence in all its aspects. Just as God is the origin of all created reality, so the whole of temporal existence was concentrated on that origin in the core dimension of humankind before the fall into sin. Therefore, human life in all of its aspects and relations, with nothing excluded, ought to be directed toward its absolute origin in a total self-surrender in the service of love to God and neighbor. As the apostle Paul said: "Whether you eat or whether you drink, or whatever you do, do all to the glory of God." [1 Corinthians 10:31. The Revised Standard Version is the translation used here and elsewhere, unless indicated otherwise.]

Scripture teaches us not only that the heart or soul is the religious center of the entire individual and temporal existence of a person, but also that each person is created in the religious community of humankind. In Adam all of humanity was contained in his relationship to God; and in him humankind as a whole departed from God in apostasy. Thus, humankind is a religious community that is spiritual in nature. That is to say it is governed and maintained by a religious spirit that works in it as a central driving force. According to the plan of creation, this spirit is the Holy Spirit, who brings an individual person into communion and fellowship with God.

Not only the temporal existence of human beings, but that of the whole temporal world was concentrated upon the service of God in this religious root-community. God created the human being as *lord* of creation. The powers and potentials which God had *enclosed* within creation were to be *disclosed* by humans in their service of love to God and neighbor. Hence in Adam's fall into sin, the entire temporal world fell away from God. This is the meaning of apostasy. The earth was cursed because of humankind. Instead of the Spirit of God, the spirit of apostasy began to govern the community of humankind and with it *all of temporal reality*.

In contrast to humankind, neither the inorganic elements nor the realms of plants and animals have a spiritual or religious root. It is humankind which makes their temporal existence complete. To think of their existence apart from humankind, one would need to eliminate all the logical, cultural, economic, aesthetic, and other properties that relate them to humankind. With respect to inorganic elements and plants, one would even need to eliminate their capability of being seen. Objective visibility exists only in relation to potential visual perception which many creatures do not possess themselves.

Along these lines the modern materialists, overestimating the mathematical, natural-scientific mode of thinking, tried quite seriously [30] to grasp the essence of nature completely apart from humankind. Nature, they thought, was nothing more than a constellation of static particles of matter determined entirely by mechanical laws of motion. They failed to remember that the mathematical formulae which seem to grasp the essence of nature presuppose human language and human thought. They did not recognize that every concept of natural phenomena is a human affair and a result of human thinking. "Nature" apart from humankind does not exist. In an attempt to grasp "nature" one begins with an abstraction from given reality. This abstraction is a logical and theoretical activity which presupposes human thought.

In a similar fashion the scholastic Christian standpoint, influenced by Greek thought, held that inorganic elements, plants, and animals possess an existence of their own apart from humankind. The scholastics argued that the so-called material "substances" depend on God alone for their sustenance. But in the light of God's revelation concerning creation, this too cannot be maintained. In the creation order objective visibility, logical characteristics, beauty, ugliness, and other properties subject to human evaluation are necessarily related to human sensory perception, human conceptualization, human standards for beauty, etc. Both the former and the latter are created. They consequently cannot be ascribed to God the Creator. God related all temporal things to the human being, the last creature to come into being. Temporal reality comes to full reality in humankind.

The scriptural motive of creation thus turns one's view of temporal reality around. It cuts off at the root every view of reality which grows out of an idolatrous, dualistic ground-motive which posits two origins of reality and thus splits it into two opposing parts.

Jehovah God is integrally, that is totally, the origin of all that is created. The existence of human beings, created in the image of God, is integrally, that is totally, concentrated in the heart, soul, or spirit of human existence. And this center of existence is the religious root-unity of all functions of a person in temporal reality – without exception. Likewise, every other creature in temporal reality is integral and complete. It is not closed off within the few aspects abstracted by the natural sciences (number, space, motion), but in its relation to human beings it is embraced by all of the aspects of reality. The whole of the temporal world (and not just some abstracted parts) has its root-unity in the religious community of humankind. Hence, when humankind fell away from God, so did all of temporal reality.

The Scriptural View of Soul and Body

In the years just prior to the Second World War the question as to how we are to understand the human soul and its relation to the body in the light of God's Word was fiercely debated in Reformed circles. The arguments [31] surrounding this question can be understood only with reference to the absolute antithesis between the scriptural ground-motive and the religious ground-motive of Greek thought.

Perhaps some readers impatiently wonder why I devote so much attention to the ancient ground-motive of the Greeks. If it is true that our modern western culture came forth out of the conflicts and tensions of four religious ground-motives, then it is simply impossible to enlighten the reader concerning the significance of the antithesis for today if it is not made clear that the present can be understood only in the light of the past. The most fundamental doctrines of the Christian religion, including creation, fall, and redemption, are still influenced by the religious ground-motive of ancient Greece. The Greek ground-motive still causes strife and division among Christians today, and it is therefore imperative that we devote our time and attention to it.

We want to put our readers in a position to penetrate to the real essence of the antithesis problem. Furthermore, we want to do it in such a way that they will come to see that the Christian religion itself is compelled to engage in a battle of life and death against all sorts of religious ground-motives. These ground-motives are out to capture people's souls with regard to every fundamental issue of our times.

It is a battle that must be fought not only against those who on principle reject the Christian ground-motive but also against those who time after time try to rob it of its intrinsic strength by "accommodating" it to non-scriptural ground-motives. It is a battle between the spirit of the Christian religion and the spirit of apostasy. It is also a battle that cuts right through the Christian camp and through the souls of individual Christians.

What is the soul? Is this a question that only the science of psychology can answer? If so, why has the Christian church considered it necessary to make pronouncements concerning the relation of "soul" and "body" in its confessions? Perhaps, one might argue, the Church confessions only address the soul's imperishability, the soul's immortality, and the resurrection of the body in the last judgment, leaving the philosophy of psychology to deal with the question as to what the "soul" actually is. This, however, places the Christian church in a strangely contradictory position. What if psychology comes to the conclusion that a soul in distinction from the body does not exist? Or what if psychology gives an elaborate theory concerning the "essence of the soul" that is completely oriented to the ground-motive of Greek philosophy or to the worldview of modern humanism?

Does not the Christian church build on sand if it honors philosophical constructions of the soul predicated upon the concepts of "immortality" and "imperishability?" From its beginning, scholastic theology tried to push the church into this intrinsically contradictory position by allowing the Greek conception of the soul into the Roman Catholic confessions.

But the radical antithesis between the ground-motive of Holy Scripture and the ground-motive of Greek "psychology" [32] cannot be bridged. Any conception of body and soul that is determined by the Greek form-matter motive cannot stand before the face of revelation concerning creation, fall, and redemption.

The question as to what we are to really understand by "soul," "spirit," or "heart" when dealing with our human existence is not a scientific but rather a religious type of question. This is because it is the question that asks where human life finds its religious root-unity. The soul is the religious focal point of human existence wherein all temporal, diverging rays come together before the prism of time breaks up the light from which they originate.

As long as we focus our attention on our temporal existence we discover nothing but a bewildering variety of aspects and functions: number, space, motion, organic functions of life, functions of emotional feeling, logical functions of thought, functions of historical development, social, lingual, economic, aesthetic, jural, moral, and faith functions. But where amongst these functions does the deeper unity of one's existence lie? If one keeps looking only at the temporal diversity of one's functions on the basis of the various aspects of reality as these aspects are investigated by the various academic disciplines, one will never come to true self-knowledge. One's gaze will remain dispersed and confused in the immense diversity of it all. We can obtain genuine self-knowledge only by way of religious concentration, when we draw together the totality of our existence, which diverges within time in a multiplicity of functions, and focus it upon our authentic, fundamental relationship to God, who is the absolute and single origin and creator of all that is.

Because of the fall, however, no person can any longer attain this true self-knowledge. Self-knowledge, according to Scripture, is completely dependent on true knowledge of God, which humankind lost when apostate ground-motives took possession of its heart. Humankind was created in God's image, but when it lost the true knowledge of God it also lost the true knowledge of itself.

The "soul" is the religious focal point of human existence. In it all the diverging beams of light coincide before, from this source, it is refracted by the prism of time. Augustine once remembered that in a certain sense the soul is identical to our relationship with God.

An apostate ground-motive forces humankind to see itself in the image of its idol. For this reason Greek "psychology" could never grasp the religious root-unity of being human and never penetrated to what is truly called the "soul," the religious center of human existence. When the matter motive dominated Greek thought, the soul was seen merely as a formless and impersonal life principle caught up in the stream of life. The matter motive did not acknowledge "individual immortality." Death was the end of a person as an individual being. One's individual form of life was again necessarily destroyed so that the great cycle of life could go on.

With Orphic thought this would come to be seen as a rational, invisible form and substance. It originated in heaven and existed completely [33] apart from the material body. But this "rational soul" (*anima rationalis*, as it would later be called in scholastic theology) was itself nothing more than a theoretical abstraction from the temporal existence of the human being. It was comprised of an abstracted and selective compilation of only some of the many and various functions of a human being, namely only the function of feeling, the function of logical thinking and assessment, and the function of faith. This "rational soul" was seen as the invisible individual form of a human being, which, just like the Olympian gods, possessed immortality. The "material" body, on the other hand, was viewed as being entirely subject to the cycle of life, death and rebirth.[1]

The "rational soul," then, was said to be characterized by the theoretical-logical function of thought. One finds many differences in the development of this philosophical conception. Plato and Aristotle, for example, changed their views throughout the different phases of their lives. I will not pursue this here, but it is important to mention that their conception of the rational soul was inseparably related to their idea of the divine. Both Plato and Aristotle believed that the truly divine resided only in theoretical thought directed to the imperishable and invisible form-world of being. The Aristotelian god was absolute theoretical thought, the equivalent of pure form. Its absolute counterpart was the matter principle, characterized by eternal, formless motion or becoming.

If the theoretical activity of thought is divine and immortal, then it must be able to exist outside of the perishable, material body. To the Greeks the body was actually the antipode of theoretical thought. For this reason, the "rational soul" could not be the religious root-unity of temporal human existence. Time after time the ambiguity within the religious ground-motive placed the form principle in absolute opposition to the matter principle. The ground-motive did not allow for a recognition of the root-unity of human nature. For Plato and Aristotle, just as God was not the Creator in the sense of an absolute and sole origin of all that exists, so also the human soul was not the absolute root-unity of the temporal expressions in human life. In conformity with their Greek conception, the soul's activity of theoretical thought always stood over against whatever was subject to the matter principle of eternal becoming. Greek thought never arrived at the truth, revealed first by Holy Writ, that human thinking springs from the deeper central unity of the whole of human life. Because this unity is religious, it determines and transcends the function of theoretical thought.

Scripture says: "Keep your heart with all vigilance; for from it flow the springs of life" [Proverbs 4:23]. "Biblical psychology" may not denature this to a mere expression of Jewish wisdom or understand it simply as a typical instance of Jewish language usage. Whoever reads Scripture in this way fails to recognize that Scripture is divine Word-revelation which can only be understood through the operation of the Holy Spirit out of its divine ground-motive. [34]

The pregnant religious meaning of what the soul, spirit, or heart of a person actually is, cannot be understood apart from the divine ground-motive of creation, fall, and redemption. We have pointed out that this ground-motive is *integral* (encompassing) and *radical* (penetrating the root of creatureliness) in nature. Those who take their stand upon this inte-

---

1 *General Editor's note:* Plato, in his dialogue *Phaedo*, stresses that the soul exhibits the greatest similarity to the divine, immortal, conceivable, simple indissoluble, constant and "self-identical," while the body bears the greatest similarity to the human, mortal, multifarious, non-conceivable, dissoluble, and never-constant (80b: 1-6).

gral and radical ground-motive come to the conclusion that there is an absolute and unbridgeable antithesis between the Greek conception of the relation between the soul and the body and the scriptural conception of the Christian religion. The former is determined by the apostate ground-motive of form and matter while the latter is determined by the scriptural ground-motive of creation, fall, and redemption through Jesus Christ. The former, at least as long as it consistently follows the Greek ground-motive in its dualistic direction, leads to a dichotomy or split in the temporal existence of a person between a "perishable, material body" and an "immortal, rational soul." The scriptural ground-motive of the Christian religion, however, reveals to us that the soul or spirit of a human being is the *absolute central root-unity* or the *heart* of the whole of that person's existence, because the human being has been *created in God's image*; further, it reveals that humankind has *fallen away from* God in the *spiritual root* of its existence; and, finally, it reveals that in the *heart* or focal point of a person's existence, the life of that person is redirected to God through Christ's *redemptive* work.

In this central spiritual unity a person is not subject to temporal or bodily death. Here too the absolute antithesis obtains. In distinction from the Greek-Orphic belief in immortality that permeated scholastic theology by way of Plato and Aristotle, Scripture teaches us nowhere that a person can rescue a "divine part" of one's temporal being from the grave. It does not teach us that an invisible, substantial form or an abstract complex of functions composed of feeling and thinking can survive bodily death. While it is true that temporal or bodily death cannot touch the soul or spirit of a person, the soul is not an abstraction from temporal existence. It is the full, spiritual root-unity of a person. In this unity the human being transcends temporal life.

Fall, redemption through Jesus Christ, and the revelation of creation are unbreakably connected in the Christian ground-motive. Apostate ground-motives do not acknowledge sin in its radically scriptural sense; for sin can only be understood in true self-knowledge, which is the fruit of God's Word-revelation. To be sure, Greek religious consciousness knew of a conflict in human life, but it interpreted that conflict as a battle in a person between the principles of form and matter. This battle became apparent in the conflict between uncontrolled sensual desires and reason. Sensual desires, which arose from the life stream and ran through one's blood, ought to be controlled by reason. In this view reason was the formative principle of human nature, the principle of harmony and measure. Sensual desires were formless and in constant flux; they [35] were beyond measure and limit. The matter principle, the principle of the ever flowing earthly life stream, became the self-determining principle of evil. The Orphics, for example, believed that the material body was an unclean prison or grave for the rational soul. Those who capitulated to their sensual desires and drives rejected the guidance of reason. They were considered morally guilty in this Greek conception. Nevertheless, reason was often powerless before *Anangkē*, the blind fate that was at work in those boundless drives. Hence the state with its coercive powers needed to help the average citizen grow accustomed to virtue.

Modern humanism recognized a battle in a person only between sensual "nature" (controlled by the natural-scientific law of cause and effect) and the rational freedom of human personality. Humankind's moral duty was to act as an autonomous, free personality. If a person showed a weakness for sensual "nature," that person was considered guilty. Humanism, however, does not show human beings a road towards redemption.

The contrasts between matter and form in Greek ethics and between nature and freedom in humanistic ethics were operative not in the *religious root* of human life but in its *temporal expressions*. However, they were *absolutized* in a religious sense. As a result the Greek and humanistic notions of guilt depend strictly on the dialectical movements between the opposing poles of both ground-motives. Guilt arose from a devaluation of one part of a person's being over against another (deified) part. In reality, of course, one part never functions without the other.

We shall see that Roman Catholic doctrine circumvents the radically scriptural meaning of the fall with the idea that sin does not corrupt the natural life of a person but only causes the loss of the supra-temporal gift of grace. It does acknowledge that "nature" is weakened and wounded by original sin. Nevertheless, the dualism between nature and grace in the Roman Catholic ground-motive stands in the way of fully comprehending the real meaning of sin, even if Roman Catholic doctrine far surpasses Greek thought and humanism with respect to the notion of guilt.

Common Grace

In its revelation of the fall into sin, the Word of God penetrates through to the root and the religious center of human nature. The fall meant apostasy from God in the heart and soul, in the religious center and spiritual root, of humankind. Apostasy from the absolute source of life signified spiritual death. The fall into sin was indeed radical and swept with it the entire temporal world precisely because the latter finds its religious root-unity only in humankind. Every conception that involves a denial of this radical meaning of the fall into sin stands squarely in opposition to the scriptural ground-motive. This is so even if it hangs on to the term "radical," as, for example, the great [36] humanist thinker Kant did in his discourse on the "radical evil" *(Radikal-Böse)* in the human being. Any conception that entails a denial of the biblical meaning of *radical* knows neither the real human being, nor God, nor the depth of sin.

The revelation of the fall, however, does not signify the recognition of an autonomous, self-determining principle of origin in juxtaposition to the Creator. Sin exists only in a *false relation to God* and is therefore never independent of the Creator. If there were no God there could be no sin. The possibility of sin, as the apostle Paul profoundly expressed it, was initially created by God's law. Without the law which commands good there could be no evil. But the same law makes it possible for the creature to exist. Without the law the human being would sink into nothingness; the law determines that person's humanity. Since sin therefore has no self-determining existence of its own over against God the Creator, it is not able to introduce an ultimate dualism into creation. The origin of creation is not twofold. Satan himself is a creature, who, in his created freedom, voluntarily fell away from God.

The divine Word – through which all things were created, as we learn from the prologue to the Gospel of John – became flesh in Jesus Christ. It entered into the root and temporal expressions, into heart and life, into soul and body of human nature; and for this very reason it brought about a *radical redemption:* the rebirth of humankind and, in it, of the entire created temporal world which finds in humankind its *center.*

By his creating Word, through which all things were made and which became flesh as Redeemer, God also upholds the fallen world through his "common grace," that is, the grace given to the community of humankind as a whole, without distinction between regenerate and apostate people. For also those who have been redeemed, continue, in their sinful nature, to be part of fallen humankind. Through common grace the spread of sin is held at bay and the universal demonization of humankind is restrained so that everywhere sparks of God's Light of might, goodness, truth, righteousness, and beauty may shine even in cultures directed by apostasy. Earlier we already pointed to the significance of Roman civil law as an example of the fruit of common grace.

In his common grace God first of all upholds the ordinances of his creation and through them he maintains "human nature." These ordinances are the same for Christians and non-Christians. God's common grace is evident in that even the most antigodly rulers must continually bow and capitulate before God's decrees if they are to see enduring positive results from their labors. But wherever these ordinances in their diversity within time are not grasped and obeyed in the light of their religious root (the religious love commandment of service to God and neighbor), such veritable capitulation or subjection to these ordinances remains incidental and piecemeal. Thus apostate culture always reveals a [37] disharmony arising out of an idolatrous absolutization of certain aspects of God's creation at the cost of other, equally essential, aspects.

God's common grace reveals itself not only in the upholding of his creation ordinances but also in the individual gifts and talents given by God to specific people. Great statesmen, thinkers, artists, inventors, etc., can be of relative blessing to humankind in temporal life, even if the *direction* of their lives is ruled by the spirit of apostasy. In this too one sees how blessing is mixed with curse, light with darkness.

In all of this it is imperative to understand that "common grace" does not weaken or eliminate the antithesis (opposition) between the ground-motive of the Christian religion and the apostate ground-motives. Common grace, in fact, can be understood only on the basis of the antithesis. It began with the promise made in paradise that God would put enmity between the seed of the serpent and the seed of the woman from which the Christ would be born. The religious root of common grace is Christ Jesus himself, who is its King, apart from whom God would not look upon his fallen creation with grace.

There should no longer be any difference of opinion concerning this matter in Reformational-Christian circles. For if one tries to conceive of common grace apart from Christ by attributing it exclusively to God as creator, then one drives a wedge in the Christian ground-motive between *creation* and *redemption*. Then one introduces an internal *split* within the Christian ground-motive, through which it loses its radical and integral character. (*Radical* and *integral* here mean: everything is related to God in its religious root.) Then one forgets that common grace is shown to all humankind – and in humankind to the whole temporal world – as a still undivided whole, solely because humankind is redeemed and reborn in Christ and also because humankind embraced in Christ still shares in fallen human nature until the fulfillment of all things.

But in Christ's battle against the kingdom of darkness, Christ's kingship over the entire domain affected by common grace is integral and complete. For this reason, it is in common grace that the spiritual antithesis assumes its character of embracing the whole of temporal life. That God lets the sun rise over the just and the unjust, that he grants gifts and talents to believers and unbelievers alike – all this is not grace for the apostate individual, but for all of humankind in Christ. It is *gratia communis*, common grace rooted in the Redeemer of the world.

The reign of common grace will not cease until the final judgment at the close of history, when the reborn creation will be liberated from its participation in the sinful root of human nature and will sparkle with the highest perfection through the communion of the Holy Spirit. Then God's righteousness will radiate even in Satan and in the wicked as a confirmation of the absolute sovereignty of the Creator. [38]

Shown to God's fallen creation as a still undivided totality, the revelation of God's common grace guards the truly scriptural Christian community against sectarian "high-mindedness" which leads some Christians to flee from the world and reject without further ado whatever arises in western culture outside of the immediate influence of religion. Sparks of the original glory of God's creation still shine in every phase of culture, to a greater or lesser degree, even if its development has occurred under the guidance of apostate spiritual powers. Humankind cannot deny this without being guilty of gross ingratitude.

It is the will of God that we have been born in western culture, just as Christ appeared in the midst of a Jewish culture in which Greco-Roman influences were evident on all sides. But, as we said earlier, this can never mean that the radical antithesis between Christian and apostate ground-motives loses its force in the "area of common grace." The manner in which scriptural Christianity must be enriched by the fruits of classical and humanistic culture can only be a radical and critical one. Christians must never absorb the ground-motive of an apostate culture into their lives and thoughts. They must never strive to synthesize or bridge the gap between an apostate ground-motive and the ground-motive of the Christian religion. Finally, they must never deny that the antithesis, from out of the religious root, cuts directly through the issues of temporal life. [39]

Chapter 2

Sphere Sovereignty

The scriptural ground-motive of the Christian religion – creation, fall and redemption through Christ Jesus – operates through God's Spirit as a driving force in the religious root of temporal life. As soon as it takes hold of you completely, it brings about a radical conversion of your life-stance and of the whole view of temporal life. The depth of this conversion can be denied only by those who fail to do justice to the integrality and radicality of the Christian ground-motive. Those who weaken the absolute antithesis in a fruitless effort to link this ground-motive with the ground-motives of apostate religions in effect end up taking part in such a denial.

But those who by grace come to true knowledge of God and themselves inevitably experience spiritual liberation from the yoke of sin and from sin's burden upon their view of reality, even though they know that sin will not cease in their lives. They realize nothing in created reality offers the foundations or foothold as a reliable basis for their existence. They grasp how temporal reality and its nuanced multifaceted aspects and structures are concentrated as a whole in the religious root-community of the spiritual dimension of humankind. They see that temporal reality searches restlessly in the human heart for its divine origin, and they understand that the creation cannot rest until it rests in God.

Creation and Sphere Sovereignty

Created reality displays a great variety of aspects or modes of being in the temporal order. These aspects break up the spiritual and religious root-unity of creation into a wealth of colors, just as light refracts into [40] the hues of the rainbow when it passes through a prism. Number, space, motion, organic life, emotional feeling, logical distinction, historical development of culture, symbolic signification, social interaction, economic value, aesthetic harmony, law, moral valuation, and certainty of faith comprise the aspects of reality. They are basically the fields investigated by the various modern special sciences: mathematics, the natural sciences (physics and chemistry), biology (the science of organic life), psychology, logic, history, linguistics, sociology, economics, aesthetics, legal theory, ethics or moral science, and theology which studies divine revelation in Christian and non-Christian faith. Each special science considers reality in only one of its aspects.

Imagine now a science that begins to investigate these distinct aspects of reality without the light of the true knowledge of God and self. The predicament of this science is similar to that of a person who sees the colors of the rainbow but knows nothing of the unbroken light from which they arise. To that person the colors appear to intermingle with each other. If one were to ask such a person where the different colors came from, would that person not be inclined to consider one color the origin of the others? Or would that person be able to discover correctly the mutual relation and coherence between them? If not, then how would one know each color according to its own intrinsic nature? If one were not color blind one would certainly make distinctions but would likely begin with the color perceived to be most striking and argue that the others were merely shades of the absolutized color.

The situation for those who think they can find the basis and starting point for a view of temporal reality in *science* is no different. Time and again they will be inclined to present one aspect of reality (organic life, feeling, historical development of culture, or any of the others) as reality in its completeness. They will then reduce all the others to the point where all of them become different manifestations of the absolutized aspect. Think for instance of Goethe's *Faust*, where Faust says: "Feeling is everything" *[Gefühl ist alles]*.[1] Or think of modern materialism, which reduces all of temporal reality to particles of matter in motion. Consider the modern naturalistic philosophy of life, which sees everything one-sidedly in terms of the development of organic life.

Actually, what drives us to absolutize is not science as such but an idolatrous ground-motive that takes hold of our thinking. Science can only yield knowledge of reality through the theoretical analysis of its many aspects. It teaches us nothing concerning the deeper unity or origin of these aspects. Only religion makes us ask for this unity and origin, because in [41] calling us to know God and ourselves, it drives us to concentrate all that is relative onto the absolute ground and origin of all things. Once an apostate ground-motive takes hold of us, it compels our thinking to absolutize the relative and to deify the creature. In this way false religious prejudices darken our conception of the structure of reality.

Those who absolutize one aspect of created reality cannot comprehend this or any of its other aspects on the basis of their own inner character. They have a false, an untrue view of reality. Although this certainly does not preclude their discovering various important *moments* of truth, they

---

1 Goethe's *Faust*, Walter Kaufmann, line 3456.

integrate these moments into a false view of the *totality* of reality. Precisely in this way they become the most dangerous and poisonous weapons of the spirit of deception.

Historicism

Today we live under the dominion of an idolatrous view of reality that absolutizes the *historical aspect* of creation. It calls itself dynamic, believing that all of reality moves and unfolds historically. It directs its polemic against static views that adhere to fixed truths. It considers reality one-sidedly in the light of historical becoming and development, arguing that everything is purely historical in character. This "historicism," as it is called, knows of no eternal values. All of life is caught up in the stream of historical development. From this viewpoint the truths of the Christian faith are just as relative and transient as the ideals of the French Revolution.

There are many moments of truth in the historicistic view of reality. All temporal things do indeed have a historical aspect. Historical development occurs in scientific endeavor, in society, in art, in human "ideals," and even in the revelation of God's Word. Still, the historical side remains merely one aspect of the full reality given to us in time. The other aspects cannot be reduced to it. It does not reach the root-unity and absolute origin of reality. Because historicism absolutizes the historical aspect, its elements of truth are dangerous weapons of the spirit of deception. Like the tempting words the serpent spoke to Eve in paradise, "You will be like God, knowing the distinction between good and evil" [Genesis 3:5], historicism contains a half-truth.

The scriptural ground-motive of the Christian religion liberates our view of reality from the false prejudices imposed upon us by idolatrous ground-motives. The motive of creation continually drives us to examine the inner nature, mutual relation, and coherence of all the aspects in God's created reality. When we become conscious of this motive, we begin to see the richness of God's creation in the great pluriformity and colorfulness of its temporal aspects. Since we know the true origin and [42] the religious root-unity of these aspects through God's revelation, we do not absolutize one aspect and reduce the others, but we respect each on the basis of its own intrinsic nature and its own law. *For God created everything after its kind.*

The various aspects of reality, therefore, cannot be reduced to each other in their mutual relation. Each possesses a sovereign sphere with regard to the others. Abraham Kuyper called this *sphere sovereignty*.

The creation motive of the Christian religion is engaged in an irreconcilable conflict with the apostate tendency of the human heart to blur, level, and erase the boundaries between the peculiar and intrinsic natures that God established in each of the many aspects of reality. For this reason the principle of sphere sovereignty is of powerful, universal significance for one's view of the relation of temporal life to the Christian religion. This principle does not tolerate a dichotomy (division) of temporal reality into two mutually opposing and mutually separable areas, such as "matter and spirit" which we observed in the Orphic Greek view. A dualistic view of reality is always the result of the operation of a dualistic ground-motive, which knows neither the true religious root-unity nor the true absolute origin of temporal reality.

The principle of sphere sovereignty is a creational principle which is unbreakably connected with the scriptural ground-motive of the Christian religion. It tells us of the *mutual irreducibility*, *inner connection*, and *inseparable coherence* of all the aspects of reality in the order of time. If we consider logical thinking, for example, we find that it is embedded within the logical aspect of temporal reality. While this aspect is irreducible to the others, sovereign in its own sphere, and subject to its own sphere of divine laws (the laws for logical thought), it nevertheless reveals its internal nature and its autonomy only in an unbreakable coherence with all the other aspects of reality. If one attempts to conceive of the logical function as absolute, that is, as independent of and apart from the functions of feeling, organic life, historical development of culture, and so on, then it dissolves into nothingness. It does not exist by itself. It reveals its own true nature only in an inseparable coherence with all the functions which created reality displays within time.

We should, therefore, really see that we can only think in a logical manner as long as we are in our perishable body which functions physico-chemically and which incorporates organic life processes. Our hope of immortality is not rooted in logical thinking but in Christ Jesus. By the light of God's Word we know that our temporal life in all its aspects has a spiritual, religious root-unity that will not decay with our temporal existence. This unity, which transcends our bodily life, is the imperishable soul. [43]

Two Types of Structure
The principle of sphere sovereignty has a concrete meaning for our view of reality. As we saw earlier, the scriptural ground-motive radically transforms one's entire view of temporal reality as soon as this motive begins to penetrate one's life. It then causes us to know again the true *structure* of reality.

There are two types of structure within temporal reality. The first is the structure of the various aspects or modes of being we listed earlier. One is familiar with these aspects only indirectly in everyday life, where we experience them by way of the individual totalities of concrete things, events, societal relationships, etc. In the ordinary experience of our daily life our attention is focused entirely on the latter and we are not interested in focusing on the *distinct aspects themselves* within which these concrete things, events, and societal relationships actually *function*. The latter focus comes about only when we begin to engage in *scientific* thought.

A child, for example, may learn to count by moving the red and white beads of an abacus. Such a child begins to learn numerical relationships by means of these beads, but soon sets the abacus aside in order to focus on the relationships themselves. This process requires a theoretical abstraction foreign to ordinary experience. For the child the numerical aspect and its numerical relations become a problem of logical conceptualization. At first this raises difficulties. Children must learn to set reality aside in their thinking, so to speak, in order to focus on the numerical aspect alone. To carry out such a theoretical analysis, they must subtract something from the full, given reality. The logical function, with which one forms concepts, thus assumes a position over against the nonlogical aspect of number, which resists the attempt to conceptualize it.

In everyday experience reality does not present itself in those aspects that thought chooses to abstract from it, but in the structure of different *individual totalities*, such as things, events, acts, and societal relationships (involving the family, the state, the church, the school, industry, etc.). This is the second, the *concrete* structure of reality (i.e., made up of individual totalities) as it reveals itself to us in time and in which it shows itself in the experience of daily life. This structure is inseparably related to the first. If one views the latter wrongly, it is impossible to gain correct theoretical insight into the former, as we shall see later.

Sphere Universality

If one desires to understand the significance of the creational principle of sphere sovereignty for human society in its full scope, then the meaning of sphere sovereignty for the intrinsic nature, mutual relation, and coherence of the *aspects* of reality (including the aspects of society) must [44] first be understood. Earlier we observed that in their religious root the various aspects are one, just as the colors of the rainbow are unified in light which is not yet refracted. Despite their distinctiveness, the aspects cohere and interconnect in the all-embracing order of time. None exists except in coherence with all the others. This universal coherence and interconnection expresses itself in the structure of each aspect.

Consider, for example, the psychical aspect of reality. In its core or nucleus it is irreducible to any other aspect. Nevertheless, in emotional life one discovers the expression of an internal coherence with all the aspects displayed by reality. Certainly, sensitivity has a distinctive life of its own, namely that of sensory emotional life, which as such is only possible on the basis of organic life. Emotional life is not the same as organic life, although it indissolubly coheres with the latter. In its "life moment," therefore, the aspect of feeling is intrinsically interwoven with the biotic aspect. Likewise, feeling has an emotional moment that binds psychical life to the physico-chemical process of bodily motion. Even though emotion, which itself is nothing more than the movement of feeling, cannot be reduced to the mere motion of particles of matter in the body, it is also true that the movement of feeling cannot occur without chemical movement. Thus there is an intrinsic coherence between the psychical aspect and the aspect of motion. Similarly, the feeling of spaciousness points to the connection between psychical life and the spatial aspect. This moment corresponds to the sensory space of awareness in which one observes colors, sounds, hardness or softness, and other properties which can be perceived by the senses. Sensory space is certainly quite different from mathematical space. Finally, the aspect of feeling also manifests an internal plurality of emotional impressions; this plurality expresses the connection between feeling and the numerical aspect.

But human emotional life is not limited to a coherence with those aspects that *precede* the *psychical* aspect of feeling. It also unfolds itself within its own aspect in the aspects that follow so that we can speak of *logical* feeling, *historical* and *cultural* feeling, *lingual* feeling, feeling for *social* convention, feeling for *economic* value, *aesthetic* feeling, *moral* feeling, and the feeling of *faith* certainty. In other words, the structure of the psychical aspect reflects a coherence with *all* the other aspects.[1]

The universal scope of our psychical life does not let itself be curbed in any way. Within its own sphere psychical life is the integral and complete expression of God's creational work. Together with all the other aspects of one's temporal being, it finds its root-unity in the religious focus of existence: the heart, soul, or spirit, where it is impossible to flee from God. From the religious creation motive of Holy Scripture one discovers the expression of creation's integral (complete) and radical (root penetrating) nature in each of the aspects of God's work of creation. In other words, sphere sovereignty, which guarantees [45] the irreducibility of each different sphere and protects their distinctive laws, finds a correlate in *sphere universality*, through which each aspect expresses the universal coherence of all the aspects in its own particular structure.

---

1 *General Editor's note:* Although Dooyeweerd clearly has the intention of highlighting *anticipations* within the structure of the sensitive aspect, he actually only mentions *retrocipations* (see the glossary for an explanation of these terms) from the various normative aspects to the sensitive aspect. For example, *historical feeling (sensitivity)* represents a *retrocipation* from the historical aspect to the sensitive aspect, whereas *emotional control* illustrates an *anticipation* from the sensitive aspect to the historical aspect. Further on in the text, however, Dooyeweerd correctly speaks about *emotional trust* and *emotional certainty*.

Sphere universality provides the apparent justification for those who seek to absolutize a specific aspect of God's immeasurably rich creation. Let us take an example. Misguided by an apostate ground-motive, someone may seek to find the basic certainty of life in feeling. When it turns out that all the aspects are reflected in psychical life, what will prevent that someone from declaring that feeling is the origin of number, space, motion, logical thinking, historical development, and so forth? Why not ultimately identify *faith* with the *feeling* of trust and certainty?

Our own faith can easily be undermined and impoverished by such false emotional mysticism. In Goethe's *Faust* the naive Gretchen (Margaret) asks the learned Dr. Faust whether or not he believes in God; he, the thinker who has fallen into Satan's power, replies by pointing to the feeling of happiness that flows through us when we contemplate heaven and earth and when we experience love in courtship. He continues with these words:

> Erfüll davon dein Herz, so grosz es ist,
> Und wenn du ganz in dem Gefühle selig bist,
> Nenn es dann, wie du willst,
> Nenn's Glück! Herz! Liebe! Gott!
> Ich habe keinen Namen
> Dafür! *Gefühl ist alles*;
> Name ist Schall und Rauch.
> Umnebelnd Himmelsglut.

> Then let it fill your heart entirely,
> And when your rapture in this feeling is complete,
> Call it then as you will,
> Call it bliss! heart! love! God!
> I do not have a name
> For this. *Feeling is everything*;
> Names are but sound and smoke
> Befogging heaven's blazes.[1]

Besides the idolatry of the psychical aspect there is idolatry of the other aspects of reality. Vitalism, which deifies an eternally flowing stream of life, is no less idolatrously directed than the religion of feeling. Modern historicism, which sets its hope for humanity on unending cultural development, is no less idolatrous than modern materialism, which declares that the aspect of motion investigated by the natural sciences is the beginning and end of reality. [46]

---

1   *Goethte's Faust*. Walter Kaufmann, lines 3451-3458. The emphasis is Dooyeweerd's.

Have we not now begun to see how the religious ground-motive of our life governs and determines our whole view of reality? Is it not obvious that an irreconcilable antithesis is at work between the Christian religion and the service of an idol? In the light of the conflict between the different ground-motives, can we still maintain that the Christian religion is significant only for our life of faith and not for our view of reality? Certainly not! At this point we cannot escape from ourselves. The Christian religion cannot be bartered. It is not a treasure that we can lock away among the relics in an inner chamber. Either it is a leaven that permeates all of our life and thought or it is nothing more than a theory which fails to touch us inwardly.

But what does the Christian ground-motive have to do with the concrete needs of political and social action? This is the key issue today, especially for those who witnessed the liquidation of the various Christian political parties and organizations during the war. After all, one might argue, the Christian *confessions* offer no answers to the political and social questions of the present time. Certainly it is true that the church confessions do not address these problems. Their ecclesiastical character keeps them from venturing into social issues. But if the *ground-motive* of the Christian religion works in our lives, then it radically changes even our view of the inner nature of the state and its relation to the other *societal spheres*. Through the Christian ground-motive we discover the true principles for political life and for societal life as a whole. As we discover these principles, the antithesis between them and those of an apostate orientation will necessarily become evident.

Society and Sphere Sovereignty

As a principle of the creation order, sphere sovereignty thus obtains its second application, since it also holds for the structure of societal forms, such as the family, the state, the church, the school, economic enterprise, and so on. As with the *aspects* of reality, our view of the inner nature, mutual relation, and coherence of the different *societal spheres* is governed by our religious starting point. The Christian ground-motive penetrates to the root-unity of all the societal spheres that are distinct in the temporal order. From that root-unity it gives us insight into the intrinsic nature, mutual relation, and coherence of these spheres.

In terms of the scriptural ground-motive, what is the unity of the different spheres in society? It is the *religious root-community of humankind* which fell in Adam but was restored to communion with God in Jesus Christ. In the revelation of this root-community of humankind, as the foundation for all temporal, societal relationships, the Christian religion is positioned to stand in absolute antithesis to every view of society that absolutizes and deifies any temporal societal form. [47]

We saw earlier that for the Greeks the state was the totalitarian community which having first made human beings truly human by means of its cultural rearing, was therefore justified in demanding from people their entire life in every one of its spheres. The religious motive of *form* and *matter* completely dominated this view. On the one hand human nature was constantly threatened by sensual desires and drives while on the other hand it was granted form and measure by the activity of the *polis*. The city-state was the bearer of the Greek culture religion, which deified such distinct cultural powers as science, art, and commerce in the dazzling array of the Olympian gods. We also saw that initially in Roman culture two societal spheres opposed each other: the *familia* and the Roman state. Each represented an absolute sphere of authority. But during the period of the Byzantine empire the *familia* collapsed and yielded to an unrestrained state absolutism that monopolized every sphere of life, including the Christian church.

In our own time we have witnessed and experienced the demonic tyranny of a totalitarian regime. The Dutch nation, historically developed in a modern constitutional state that circumscribed the liberties of people and citizens with countless guarantees (a state undoubtedly inspired by both Christian and humanistic influences), experienced the burden of totalitarian rule as an intolerable tyranny. And what was the most powerful *principial* basis supporting the resistance? It was that creational principle of sphere sovereignty, rooted in the scriptural ground-motive of the Christian religion. Neither the modern liberal and socialist offshoots of humanism nor communist Marxism could strike this totalitarian state absolutism in its *religious root*. Only when one's eyes have been opened to the religious root-unity of humankind can one gain clear insight into the essential nature, proper mutual relation, and inner coherence of the various societal spheres.

What then is the significance of sphere sovereignty for human society? Sphere sovereignty guarantees each societal sphere an intrinsic nature and law of life. And with this guarantee it provides the basis for an original sphere of authority and competence derived not from the authority of any other sphere but directly from the sovereign authority of God.

Since the time of Abraham Kuyper the term *sphere sovereignty* has become common place as part of this country's everyday language. But the profundity of Kuyper's insight, with respect to the nature of the social order – an insight based on the ground-motive of the Christian religion – was understood by relatively few people at the time or since. The less it was realized that this fundamental principle is rooted directly in the scriptural ground-motive of the Christian religion, the more sphere sovereignty dissolved into an ambiguous political slogan that everyone could interpret in a different way. The [48] increasingly historicistic way of thinking particularly robbed the principle of its religious root, thereby obscuring its true origin and significance. If one views sphere sovereignty merely as a historical occurrence that somehow became rooted in the Dutch nation's character as an expression of its people's love of freedom, then it follows naturally that one might next want to detach the whole concept of sphere sovereignty from that of the constant, intrinsic nature of each of the various societal spheres.

For the new phase of history which we have entered, the principle of sphere sovereignty, as now being articulated, would have the same meaning as the conception of *functional decentralization* [propagated by modern socialism]. This would mean that the different spheres of society, as independent parts, must be incorporated into the state while retaining a certain autonomy. The task of the state would then be decentralized by creating municipalities, provinces, and other parts of the state alongside "new organs" endowed with a public legal regulatory jurisdiction under final supervision of the central government. In this conception the legislative and executive organs of the central government must be "relieved" of a sizable share of their task by a transfer of their authority to "new organs" derived from "society" itself. For members of the Socialist, Roman Catholic, and Anti-revolutionary parties, the principle of functional decentralization is thus left to provide common ground for cooperation. Thus sphere sovereignty, within every new historical-political situation, would then assume a different meaning.

How can one explain why this basic misconception of the principle of sphere sovereignty has become so profound? This we will consider next.

History and Sphere Sovereignty

In our preceding discussion we have begun our explanation of the practical significance of the creational principle of sphere sovereignty for human society. We have pointed out that currently attempts have been made to detach this principle from its religious root by subsuming it entirely under the historical aspect.

With historicism, the principle of sphere sovereignty takes on a purely "dynamic" character, which can be varied according to the needs of the time. In that way sphere sovereignty, in which the antithesis, i.e., the juxtaposition between the scriptural and the anti-Christian starting points in the development of one's view of reality which comes so clearly to the fore, could even be used as a building block in the most recent attempt to find a *synthesis* (reconciliation) between Christianity and humanism.[1]

---

1 *General Editor's note:* At this point the original text contains a section almost fully overlapping with what was just explained. It reads as follows: "In this conception the legislative and executive organs of the central government must be "relieved" of a sizable share of their task by a transfer of their authority to "new organs" derived from

In order to find an answer to the question of why this basic misconception of the principle of sphere sovereignty has become so profound, we must recall that the nineteenth century Historical School in Germany strongly influenced anti-revolutionary political thought, particularly in its view of history. Although the founders of this school were devout Lutherans, their worldview was completely [49] dominated by the historicism that gained ground in humanist circles after the French Revolution.

By "historicism" I mean the philosophical conception that reduces the whole of reality to an absolutized historical aspect. Historicism sees all of reality as a product of ceaseless historical development of culture. It believes that everything is subject to continual change. In contrast to the rationalistic thinkers of the French Revolution, the historicists do not seek to construct a just social order from abstract, rational principles which have no relation to historical development and the individual traits of a specific national character. Rather, the fundamental thesis of the new historical way of thinking is that the entire political and social order is essentially a historical and developmental phenomenon. Its development originates in a nation's individual character, the "national spirit" *[Volksgeist]*, which is the historical germ of an entire culture. The national spirit generates a culture's language, social conventions, art, economic system, and juridical order.

Following the example of the mathematical and natural sciences, earlier humanistic theory had always searched for the universally valid laws that control reality. It constructed an "eternal order of natural law" out of the "rational nature of humankind." This order was totally independent of historical development, and was valid for every nation at all times and in all places. The earlier rationalistic humanism displayed little awareness of the individual traits of peoples and nations. All individual things were regarded as mere instances or examples of a universal rule and were reduced to a universal order. This reduction highlights the rationalistic tendency of this type of humanistic thought.

"society" itself. The different spheres of society must be incorporated into the state by means of public-legal organization. But at the same time these spheres must be left with relative independence, a measure of *autonomy,* as was done with municipalities, provinces, and other parts of the state. These new organs would then take over an important part of the state's task by establishing regulatory jurisdiction under final supervision of the central government. The regulations of these new organs would be maintained with public-legal sanctions. In this way "authority" and "freedom" are to be united in a harmonious manner. For members of the Socialist, Roman Catholic, and Anti-revolutionary parties, the principle of functional decentralization is thus left to provide common ground for cooperation. The sphere sovereignty of the societal structures would then assume a different meaning with each new historical-political situation."

But as a result of the polarity of its religious ground-motive, humanism veered to the other extreme after the French Revolution. Rationalistic humanism (in its view of reality oriented to mathematics and modern natural science), turned into irrationalistic humanism, which rejected all universally valid laws and order. It elevated individual potential to the status of law. Irrationalistic humanism was not inspired by the exact mathematical and natural sciences but by art and the science of history. Art revealed the "genius" and uniqueness of individuality. "Romanticism," which for a time dominated western culture during the Restoration period after Napoleon's fall, was the source of the view of reality defended by the Historical School.

When the Historical School attempted to understand the entire culture, language, art, jurisprudence, and the economic and social orders in terms of the historical development of an individual national spirit, it elevated the national character to the status of the origin of order. It therefore denied the truth that the *individual creature always remains subject to law*. It argued that if the individual potential of a person or nation is the only law for development and action, then this potential [50] cannot be evaluated in terms of a universally valid law. Accordingly, any nation was considered to act rightly and legitimately if it simply followed the historical fate or goal implicit in its individual potential or disposition.[1]

This view of reality was historicistic in the sense explained above. Although the Historical School fundamentally rejected the validity of general laws, it nevertheless tried to compensate for this by seeking to reach a kind of compromise with the Christian belief in "divine providence." It proclaimed divine providence to be a "hidden" law of history, arguing that God's providence rules the history of a nation. As the Christian mask was laid aside, "providence" was replaced by *Schicksal*, the historical destiny or fate of a nation. *Schicksal* played the same role as divine providence; it operated as a norm for the development of a national character.

Careful readers will have noted how closely this view approaches that of the spiritual atmosphere of national socialism and its appeal to providence, to the "Destiny of the German People" *[Schicksal des deutschen Volkes]*. We will do well to keep the affinity between national socialism and the Historical School in mind, for later we shall see that nazism must in essence be considered a degenerate fruit of the historicism propagated by the Historical School.

The Historical School strongly emphasized the bond between past and present. It held that culture, language, art, law, economics, and the social order arise and develop from the national character both unconsciously and apart from any formative influence of the human will. For the Histori-

---

1 *General Editor's note:* The English translation generalized Romanticism's specific reference to the *German people*.

cal School, tradition works as an unconscious power in history. It is the operation of God's providential guidance or, expressed less Christianly, of *Schicksal*, the destiny of a people.

Friedrich Julius Stahl
The founder of the anti-revolutionary political philosophy in Germany, Friedrich Julius Stahl [1802-1861] (who greatly influenced Groen van Prinsterer's second period of intellectual development; that is, after 1850), tried to incorporate this Romantic view of history into a scripturally Christian approach.[1] He failed to see that the historicistic worldview advocated by the Historical School was completely dominated by a humanistic religious ground-motive. According to Stahl, everything in the historical development of a nation that has come about through the silent workings of tradition "independently of human efforts," must be seen as a revelation of God's guidance in [51] history and must be accepted as a norm or directive for further development. Stahl was fully aware of the dangers inherent in such a view of divine providence as a directive for human action. He recognized that within tradition good may be mixed with evil. For this reason he looked for a higher "universally valid" norm for action that could serve as a touchstone for the historical development of a nation. He believed that he had found this norm in the revealed "moral law," *viz.*, the ten commandments. His conclusion was as follows: one ought to accept as a norm for action the tradition of national historical development in the sense of God's guidance in history insofar as this development does not conflict with an expressly revealed commandment of God. Stahl was therefore able to call the norm for historical development a "secondary norm." One could always appeal to the primary norm revealed in the law of the ten commandments. With this reservation, the irrationalistic view of history was incorporated into anti-revolutionary political thought. After Stahl, Groen van Prinsterer followed suit, calling the anti-revolutionary movement the "Christian-historical" movement.

The Historical School contained a so-called Germanistic wing which specialized in the legal history of the Germanic peoples. Its influence upon Stahl and Groen van Prinsterer is unmistakable.

Before the Germanic countries supplemented indigenous law with Roman law in the fifteenth century, society and its legal order were still largely undifferentiated. In general there was no awareness of the idea of the state as a *res publica*, an institution established for the sake of the common good, nor of the *idea of civil law*, which recognizes the individual human being as a legal subject, endowed with legal rights regardless of that

---

1 For a discussion of Stahl's political thought, see Herbert Marcuse, *Reason and Revolution* (Boston: Beacon Press, 1960, 360-374). Cf. also F.J.Stahl, *The Present-Day Parties in the State and the Church* (State College, Pa.: Blenheim Publishing House, 1976).

person's membership in specific communities. With the influence of Roman law these basic ideas were gradually accepted in continental Europe but they were generally put into practice only as a result of the French Revolution.

In the Middle Ages undifferentiated communal spheres were prominent everywhere. They carried out all those tasks for which, at a more highly developed cultural level, differentiated communities come into being. In the countryside, for instance, the undifferentiated community was the manor. The owner of a manor had the legal competence to participate in judicial matters and to issue legal summonses and ordinances which covered nearly every area of society. The owner of large feudal land holdings was endowed with privileges which gave him the legal right to act as lord over every person domiciled on his estate. In the medieval cities the guilds were the undifferentiated units which simultaneously displayed an ecclesiastical, industrial, and at times even a political structure. These guilds were often based on a kind of fraternity which, as an artificial kinship bond, embraced its members with their families in all their activities. At a still higher level it was not at all [52] uncommon that feudal lords exercised governmental authority as if it were private property, which they could indeed acquire and dispose of on the basis of private legal stipulations. All of these undifferentiated legal spheres possessed autonomy; that is, the legal competence and right to act as government within their own sphere without the intervention of a higher authority.

In this feudal setting there was no idea of the state as a *res publica,* organized for the common welfare. When, with an appeal to Roman law, several powerful feudal lords began to try to put into practice the idea of the state with an appeal to Roman law, and to recover those elements of governmental authority which had been relinquished to private power, their efforts were frustrated, for a long time, by the tenacious resistance of the undifferentiated spheres of life which could indeed appeal to their inherited privileges, their ancient origins, etc. As a rule the feudal period also lacked the idea of private civil law with its basic principles of universal freedom and equality of all human beings before the law. On the eve of the French Revolution many remnants of this *ançien régime* had been kept intact in Germany, France, Holland, and elsewhere, even though the historical line of development definitely pointed in the direction of a differentiation process that could end only in a clear distinction between public and private law.

The Germanistic wing of the Historical School wished to continue this process of differentiation. It thus accepted the bountiful fruit of the French Revolution, namely the realization of the idea of the state. At the same time, it sought to harmonize this modern idea with the old idea of the autonomy of the life-spheres. In order to bring this about, it was necessary that autonomy be limited by the requirements of the common good. The autonomous spheres of life, therefore, needed to be *incorporated* into the new state; they had to be accommodated to the requirements of the state as a whole.

Guillaume Groen van Prinsterer

In Germany, the anti-revolutionary thinker Stahl considered such a recognition of the *autonomy* of the societal spheres a vital requirement for a truly "Christian-historical" theory of the state. Similarly, in the Netherlands Groen van Prinsterer fought for an idea of the state along *historical-national* lines which would suit the Dutch national character in its historical development. He was the first person to use the phrase *"souvereiniteit in eigen sfeer"* (sovereignty within its own sphere) with respect to the mutual relation of church and state. But he did not yet view this principle as a *creational principle of universal scope*. He only demanded *autonomy* for the societal "corporations (corporate bodies)," as Stahl had done. For him, trade and industry were only organic members of national life, just like municipalities and provinces. Their autonomy within the state [53] was a merely historical principle rooted in the Dutch national character under God's guidance. At the same time, Stahl and Groen van Prinsterer saw very clearly the basic differences between the state, the church, and the family. Driven by the scriptural groundmotive of the Christian religion, both held that the state should not interfere with the internal life of the other societal spheres. But their compromise with the worldview of the Historical School prevented them from consistently applying this scriptural motive in their political thought.

Abraham Kuyper

Abraham Kuyper was the first to have seen sphere sovereignty as a creational principle and thus to have fundamentally detached it from the historicistic view of human society. In his initial formulation of this idea, however, traces of confusing sphere sovereignty with certain specific forms of autonomy purely founded in Dutch history were still present. When he listed the various sovereign societal spheres, such as the family, the school, science, art, and economic enterprise, he added the municipalities and provinces. Municipalities and provinces, however, are not sovereign spheres themselves but truly "autonomous" parts of the state, and the boundaries of their autonomy are dependent upon the requirements of the whole, the needs of the common good. Autonomy is authority delegated to a part by the whole.

What was the result of this confusion in the political life of the nation? It proved to be impossible in principle to offer a criterion for the limits of autonomy. Increasingly what originally fell under the autonomous jurisdiction of the municipalities and provinces needed regulation by a centralized government. Since this autonomous jurisdiction had been described as "sovereignty within its own sphere," Kuyper's followers began to be embarrassed with the principle itself, particularly because Dutch anti-revolutionary political thought had never severed its links with the Historical School and had remained more or less contaminated with historicism.

Had Kuyper then erred when he asserted that sphere sovereignty was founded in *creation*? Had he not represented something as an immutable principle when it was actually no more than a historically alterable and variable given in the Dutch national character?

Confronted with questions of this sort, many anti-revolutionaries, especially among the more educated, began to adopt a more cautious approach. They advocated a more judicious employment of the word "principle" for political use. "Eternal principles" were considered safe if they were limited to directives "explicitly revealed" in Holy Scripture. The Bible, it was argued, contains no direct texts about sphere sovereignty. In this way the contamination by the historicistic outlook proved to be surreptitiously influencing many people in the ranks of the anti-revolutionaries. [54]

But the foundation laid by Kuyper was so solid that the principle of sphere sovereignty in its true scriptural sense could not be erased from the religious consciousness of those who lived by the Word of God. Granted, certain refinements and further elaboration were still needed. To this end, the important elements of truth in the teachings of the Historical School had to be freed from the framework of the historicistic worldview in order to be incorporated in a truly scriptural view of history.

It was indeed high time that this should come about. For the "new age" knows no mercy for principles that are internally undermined. And never has our spiritually uprooted nation been in greater need of the further evolvement of the creational principle of sphere sovereignty than it is today.

Autonomy and Sphere Sovereignty

Kuyper's great achievement was that he grasped the principle of sphere sovereignty as a creational principle once more. Earlier, however, we saw that the influence of the Historical School was evident in the way in which he sought to apply this principle to society. When in his global summary of the life-spheres he placed municipalities and provinces alongside of the family, the school, art, science, economic enterprise, not to mention the church as temporal institution, he confused genuine sphere sovereignty with a purely historically founded autonomy of parts in the body politic.

Especially today, when the issue of the proper relationship between political, social, and economic structures demands an immediate, principled solution, it is absolutely crucial that we avoid this confusion. For we have already seen that the historicistic worldview has an immense influence in our time. Those who still hold to the constant principles rooted in the creation order are summarily dismissed in today's rapidly proliferating production of "instant" articles in the daily press – that dangerous impulse of journalistic superficiality. These days, proponents of constant creational principles are viewed as fossilized system builders who have not grasped the spirit of our "dynamic age!" But, if ever, this is true today:

> Was ihr den Geist der Zeiten heisst,
> Das ist der Herren eigner Geist
> In dem die Zeiten sich bespiegeln.
>
> What spirit of the time you call,
> Is but the scholar's spirit, after all,
> In which times past are now reflected.[1] [55]

Historicism nourishes itself on the absolutization of the historical aspect of reality. To counter it there is only one antidote: exposing the hidden religious ground-motive which operates behind a seemingly neutral mask of supposedly profound scientific insight. All the masks of essentially apostate ground-motives become transparent under the searching light of divine truth through which humankind discovers itself and its Creator.

Autonomy of the parts of a whole and sphere sovereignty of various societal relationships that fundamentally differ from one another due to their restrictive intrinsic nature, are two quite different matters. In a differentiated society the degree of autonomy depends upon the requirements of the particular whole of which the autonomous community remains a part. Sphere sovereignty, however, is rooted in the constant, inherent character of the life-sphere itself. Because of their intrinsic natures, differentiated spheres like the family, the school, economic enterprise, science, and art can never be parts of the state.

Earlier we briefly discussed the undifferentiated state of society during the Middle Ages. Some remnants of that undifferentiated situation managed to survive until the French Revolution. In that type of undifferentiated state of affairs, genuine sphere sovereignty cannot yet express itself in the social order. For when the boroughs, guilds, towns, and regions alike each display within their own respective purviews the traits of some of the most divergent social structures, it is impossible to differentiate between them according to their own respective "inner nature" criteria. For this very reason, their autonomy could only be delimited by virtue of a specially crafted formal criterion that did not exclude anything from that internal authority regardless of the actual legitimacy, or lack thereof for the claim to such authority. Thus the basis for autonomy was not the intrinsic nature of these communities, for these communities did not as yet have a differentiated nature of their own. Their autonomy rested entirely on the ancient customs and privileges granted by feudal lords.

---
1 *Goethe's Faust,* Walter Kaufmann, lines 577-579.

As we noted earlier, what was lacking was the *authentic idea of the state*. By this we mean the idea that the state's governmental authority is not private property but a public office which must be exercised exclusively for the common good or the public interest. Precisely because of this, the autonomy under the *ançien régime* before the French Revolution was not limited by the public interest of the state but was exclusively defined in a purely formal manner by existing legal customs and privileges. When a powerful lord attempted to subject this autonomy to the requirements of the public interest, the autonomous corporate entities would invariably appeal to their special rights and freedoms guaranteed by these customs and privileges.

In the end, when the true idea of the state was actually implemented in its full scope by the French [56] Revolution, the undifferentiated life-spheres had to be eliminated. As a result, modern municipalities and provinces are therefore not comparable to the old boroughs, shires, towns, estates, and manors. They are parts of the modern state, and they display the differentiated, intrinsic nature of parts of the body politic. Thus, when it comes to the relation between the state and its parts, one can speak of neither sphere sovereignty nor autonomy in the sense of the old regime. In principle, both municipal and provincial autonomy depend upon the demands of the common good of the state as a whole.

Granted, Thorbecke and some of his followers held that the municipal, provincial, and national economy formed three independent spheres which could be mutually delimited according to their nature.[1] However, reality proved stronger than doctrine. It was simply impossible to offer an intrinsic criterion for the delimitation of these three "spheres." The extent to which the common good of the body politic could permit municipalities and provinces an autonomous sphere of self-government depended entirely upon historical development and its coherence with juridical life. By contrast, sphere sovereignty is rooted in creation, not in history.

But this does not in any way imply that the whole question of municipal and provincial autonomy can be removed from the list of fundamental political problems. A truly *Christian*-historical idea of the state, in which the Christian religion also determines the *way in which history is viewed*, demands that the national character as it became shaped historically be indeed taken seriously into account. This is essential, not because this national character, in and of itself, would provide a norm for the political theory of the state, but because its historical development does demand a norm of differentiation. This norm requires undifferentiated forms to

---

1   Johan Rudolf Thorbecke (1798-1872), leading liberal Dutch statesman of the nineteenth century was the main opponent of Groen van Prinsterer. One need only glance at the title of his dissertation to understand how strongly he was influenced by the Historical School: *On the Essence, and on the Organic Character of History [Ueber das Wesen und den organischen Charakter der Geschichte]*.

break open and unfold. At the same time, the *process* of differentiation carries with it historical individualization that must also work its way through on the national level, i.e., in the development of individual *nations*.

What does *historical individualization* mean? We must pursue this further, for it is here that the scriptural view of history immediately comes to the fore.

It cannot be said often enough that historicism, which today is much more influential than the scriptural view of history, arises out of the [57] absolutization of the historical aspect of reality which is investigated by the science of history. But the integral, complete, and radical (penetrating to the root of created reality) character of the scriptural motive of creation makes us see this aspect in its irreducible nature and in its unbreakable coherence with all the other aspects of reality. In its core it is irreducible to the others, but at the same time in its inner structure it displays a complete expression of this aspect's universal coherence with the other aspects. This expression is the work of God's creation, which is integral and complete.

Earlier I discussed the universal coherence of the aspects in connection with the psychical aspect, by calling this coherence the sphere universality of each aspect. It is the correlate of sphere sovereignty. In order to perceive God's ordinances for historical development, it is necessary that we search for them in the historical aspect and in its unbreakable coherence with the structures of the other aspects. If this search is not to go astray, then the scriptural ground-motive of creation, fall, and redemption through Jesus Christ must be our only point of departure and our only religious motivation.

Biblicism

Some may object by posing the following questions: Is such an intricate investigation really necessary to gain insight into God's ordinances for historical development? Is it not true that God revealed his whole law in the ten commandments? Is this revelation not enough for the simple Christian? I answer with counter questions: Is it not true that God placed all the spheres of temporal life under his laws and ordinances – the laws that govern numerical and spatial relationships, physical and chemical phenomena, organic life, emotional feeling, logical thinking, language, economic life, and beauty? Are not all these laws, without exception, grounded in God's creation order? Can we find explicit scriptural texts for all of them? If not, should we not acknowledge that God put the painstaking task to humankind to discover them? And admitting this, can we still hold that it makes no difference whether in this search we start from the ground-motive of the Word of God or are guided by unscriptural ground-motives?

Those who think they can derive truly scriptural *principles* for political policy formation solely from explicit Bible texts, have a very mistaken notion of the nature of Scripture. They see only the letter, forgetting that the Word of God is spirit and power which must penetrate our whole attitude of life and thought. God's Word-revelation puts people to work. It claims the whole of our being; where death and spiritual complacency once held sway in us, it wants to conceive new life. Spiritually lethargic people would [58] rather have the ripe fruits of God's revelation fall into their laps, but Jesus Christ tells us that wherever the seed of God's Word falls on good soil, we ourselves must bear fruit.

Today Christians face a fundamental question, namely, what historical yardstick do we possess in this new age for distinguishing between the reactionary and the substantially progressive directions in history? We cannot derive this criterion from the ten commandments, for they were not meant to save us from investigating God's creational ordinances. To answer this basic question, one needs insight into the specific ordinances that God established for historical development. It requires in-depth investigation. Our search will be protected against derailment if the creation motive of God's Word obtains complete control in our thinking.

Barthianism

But I already hear another objection, coming this time from the followers of Karl Barth. The objection is this: what do we know of the original ordinances of creation? How can we speak so confidently of creation ordinances, as if the fall had never happened? Did not sin change them in such a way that they are now ordinances for *sinful* life? My reply is as follows.

The ground-motive of the divine Word-revelation is an indivisible unity. Creation, fall, and redemption cannot be separated. But Barthians virtually make such a separation when they confess that God created all things but refuse to let this creation motive completely permeate their thinking. Did God reveal himself as the Creator so that we could brush this revelation aside? I venture to say that whoever ignores the revelation of creation understands neither the depth of the fall nor the scope of redemption. Relegating creation to the background is not scriptural. Just read the Psalms, where the devout poet rejoices in the ordinances that God decreed for creation. Read the book of Job, where God himself speaks to his intensely suffering servant of the richness and depth of the laws which he established for his creatures. Read the gospels, where Christ appeals to the creational ordinance for marriage in order to counter those who aimed at trapping him. Finally, read Romans 1:19-20, where the creational ordinances are explicitly included in the general revelation to the human race. Whoever holds that the original creational ordinances are unrecognizable for fallen humankind because they were supposedly fundamentally altered by the advent of sin, essentially ends up denying the true significance of God's *common grace* which maintains these ordinances. Sin did not change the creational decrees but the direction of the human heart, which turned away from its Creator.

Undoubtedly, this radical fall impacts the way in which humankind [59] discloses the powers that God enclosed in creation. The fall affects natural phenomena, which humankind can no longer control. It impacts itself in theoretical thought led by an idolatrous ground-motive. It appears in the subjective way in which humankind gives form to the principles established by God in his creation as norms for human action. The fall made special institutions necessary, such as the state and the church in its institutional form. But even these special institutions of general and special grace are based upon the ordinances that God established in his creation order. Neither the structures of the various aspects of reality, nor the structures that determine the nature of concrete creatures, nor the principles which serve as norms for human action, were altered by the fall. A denial of this leads to the unscriptural conclusion that the fall is as broad as creation, i.e., that the fall destroyed the very nature of creation. This would mean that sin plays a self-determining, autonomous role over against God, the creator of all. Whoever maintains such a position denies the absolute sovereignty of God and grants Satan a power equal to that of the Origin of all things.

Certainly, then, this objection from the Barthian camp may not keep us from searching for the divine order for historical development as revealed in the light of the creation motive. [60]

Chapter 3

History, Historicism, and Norms

Historicism, sacrificing reality to its historical aspect, is the fatal illness of our "dynamic" times. There is no cure for this unwholesome view of reality as long as the scriptural creation motive does not regain its complete claim on our life and thought. Historicism robs us of our belief in abiding standards; it undermines our faith in the eternal truth of God's Word. Historicism claims that everything is relative and historically determined, including one's belief in lasting values.

Bid it halt before the gates of your faith, if you wish. The demon of historicism will not be shut out so easily. It has bribed your gatekeepers without your knowing it. Suddenly it stands in your inner sanctum and has you in its power. It asks: do you claim that Holy Scripture discloses *eternal* truth? Do you, imprisoned in your dogmas, not understand that the Bible, which you accept as God's revelation, itself underwent the process of historical development? Is it not true that the road from the Old to the New Testament is the great highway of history? If the Old Testament is the revelation of God, do you not understand that this revelation apparently developed historically into that of the New Testament? Or do you still believe that the book of Joshua contains the divine rule of life for today's Christian? Can you still sing the Jewish psalms of revenge without experiencing a clash with your modern Christian consciousness? Do you really mean to say that the content of your Christian faith is [61] identical with that of the first Christian community or with that of the Bible believing Christian of the Middle Ages? If so, solid historical research will quickly end your illusion. Even your use of archaic terms cannot prevent you from coloring them with new meaning. The meaning of words changes with historical development, which no power on earth can halt. You speak of political principles and appeal to sphere sovereignty, forgetting that we live in "dynamic" times. Change is everything, constancy of principle is nothing! You live in an age that finally has overcome the dogmatic prejudice regarding the existence of abiding standards that are not subject to historical development. To feel at home in today's society you must place yourself midstream in the movement of history. To be listened to today you must be open to the spirit of the age. Above all you must be progressive, for then the future is yours.

These are the surreptitious ways through which historicism manages to enter the heart of modern humankind. Some unsuspecting theologians accepted its claims insofar as temporal reality was concerned but tried to preserve the eternal value of Christian truths. This, however, was a colossal mistake, because if one accepts historicism's view of temporal reality, it does not stop short of the shelter of one's faith, since faith itself belongs to temporal reality. Furthermore, historicism is driven by a religious ground-motive that takes its stance in radical opposition to the ground-motive of the Christian religion.

The Historical Aspect
Earlier we saw that at an early stage historicism partially infiltrated anti-revolutionary political thinking in its view of history. It is not an overstatement to say that the dangerous spirit of historicism permeates all of modern reflection on human society. In view of its vast influence, it is extremely important to observe once again that even though one may try to limit historicism to a view of temporal reality, historicism takes root only when the creation motive of divine revelation loses its hold upon one's worldview. Academic training or the lack of it are irrelevant here. Historicism is more than a philosophical theory. It belongs to the "spiritual hosts of wickedness" [Ephesians 6:12] which claim not only our thinking but our whole way of life.

When historicism abandoned the creation motive it made a serious error: it identified the historical *aspect* of reality with *history* in the concrete sense of *what has happened*. Even Groen van Prinsterer appealed to "it is written" and "it has come to pass" as the two key pieces of evidence condemning the idolatrous philosophy of the French Revolution. [62] But "it has happened" may not be equated with the historical *aspect* under which scholarly research concerning what has happened takes place. I can scarcely warn enough against this fundamental error that leads directly into the embrace of historicism. It is a blunder made continually, even by believing thinkers. Moreover, this first concession to historicism has filtered down from scientific theory into the worldview of the average person.

Concrete events like wars, famines, revolts, the rise of new political forms, important discoveries, inventions, and so forth, all belong to concrete reality which in principle functions in *every* aspect, without exception. Indeed, the things of our everyday experience and the various spheres of society – such as the family, the school, and the church – function in every aspect as well. If, however, one identifies the historical aspect with "what has occurred," then one forgets that concrete events display a great many other aspects not historical in character. The result is that reality is equated with just one of its aspects (the aspect abstracted by the science of history). One then abandons the Christian motive of creation and becomes a historicist. What are the consequences of this stance?

Ask people what they understand by "history." Their prompt answer will be: whatever has happened in the past. This answer is correct. In the ordinary experience of daily life one does not direct one's attention to the abstract aspects of reality that are distinguished in a theoretical approach. In ordinary experience, attention is focused on reality's second, concrete structure: the structure of things, events, and so on. But it is futile to delimit the field of investigation for the science of history in terms of the criterion "what has happened."

Consider, for example, the following event: yesterday a person smoked a cigar. Today this event belongs to the past. But is it therefore a *historical* event, fit for entry into the annals of history? Of course not. And yet, closer reflection reveals that this event does have a historical aspect. In the Middle Ages people did not smoke. The introduction and popularization of tobacco in western culture was certainly an event of historical significance. One's own activity of smoking takes place in a historical context of culture, and one cannot ignore the introduction and establishment of this means of enjoyment in our culture. Although the event of smoking displays a historical aspect when contrasted with medieval means of pleasure, yet the event itself is not characterized *typically* by its historical aspect. Other events, by contrast, are typically historical, such as the French Revolution and the capitulation of Japan and Germany in the last world war. Typically historical events act *formatively* in world history.

Surely, the contrast between different kinds of events is known [63] implicitly in ordinary (non-theoretical) experience. No one will say that smoking a cigar is a typically historical event. Nor will one consider a natural event like a rockslide or a flood a historical event as such. Such occurrences become historically significant only in connection with their effects on human culture.

It is imperative, therefore, that we do not identify the historical aspect of reality with the concrete events which function in it and which display all the other aspects that God gave reality in his creation order. The historical aspect must be distinguished from the aspects of organic life, emotional feeling, logical distinction, and so forth. The basis for this distinction is not *what* occurs within the historical aspect but *how* something occurs in it. The primary concern of the historian, therefore, is to grasp the core of the historical *mode* of concrete events. The historian needs a criterion for distinguishing the historical aspect of reality from the other aspects. Historicism lacks such a criterion, since in its view the historical aspect and the whole of reality are one and the same.

The current criteria for carrying through this distinction are completely useless. If, for instance, one argues that the science of history is the science of becoming or development, then one forgets that the natural sciences also deal with becoming and development. When one acknowledges both organic development and historical development, then the cardinal question is this: what is the specifically *historical* character of a developmental process? Certainly, the organic development from the seed to the full grown plant or from the embryo to the mature animal is not the kind of development that concerns the science of history.

What then is the core or nucleus of the historical aspect of reality? Whoever grasps it correctly cannot fall prey to the view of historicism any longer. But it is understood only when the creation motive of Word-revelation intrinsically governs one's view of reality, for then historicism has lost its hold upon one's thought. The nucleus of the historical aspect, that which guarantees its proper nature and irreducibility, is the *cultural* way of being. Cultural activity always consists in giving form to material in free control over the material. It consists in giving form according to a free design.

Culturally formative activity is different from the activity by which lasting forms arise in nature. The marvelous rock crystals, the honeycomb, the spider's web, and so on, are not cultural forms because they do not originate through the free design and free control of a material. They arise through the natural processes and instincts that move according to fixed, unchangeable schemes and laws.

The story of creation itself indicates that the cultural mode of formative activity is grounded in God's creation order. God immediately gave humankind the great cultural mandate: subdue the earth and have dominion [64] over it. God placed this great cultural command in the midst of the other creational ordinances. It touches only the historical aspect of creation that is subject to cultural development.

The cultural way of being is the way reality reveals itself in its historical aspect. Usually the term *culture* refers to whatever owes its existence to human formation in contrast to whatever develops in "nature." It is then forgotten that the cultural way of being is no more than an aspect of concrete things and events, and that a so-called cultural object such as a chair also functions in the aspects of reality that are not themselves cultural in character.[1]

The Greek culture religion deified the cultural, the nuclear moment of the historical aspect. Its form motive stood in religious antithesis to the matter motive, which deified an eternal flux of life. Still, in the Greek form motive one did not find the typically relativistic and dynamic mo-

---

1 *General Editor's note:* Here Dooyeweerd once again mentions the various aspects of reality.

ments that confront us in modern historicism. Their absence was due to the fact that in the Greek form motive the cultural way of being was completely detached from the moment of development, which binds the historical aspect to the organic aspect. Since in the religious ground-motive of Greek antiquity the culture religion was absolutely antithetical to the old religions of the flux of life, the cultural form motive had to sever all ties with the motive of the older religions. Thus, for instance, the form motive led Greek thought to the belief in an eternal, immutable world of forms, a world completely separate from the earthly stream of life. In the religion of the Olympian gods this belief assumed a form that appealed to the imagination of the people; the Olympian gods were invisible, immortal, brilliant gods of form. They were personifications of the various cultural powers who lived far beyond the fate of mortals.

Modern historicism, by contrast, is dominated by the religious ground-motive of humanism (nature and freedom). It views culture in terms of unending historical development, rejecting all the constant, creational structures that make this development possible. Historicism rejects the constant structure of the historical aspect which contains the divine decrees for historical development. As a result it has no reliable standard for distinguishing reactionary and progressive tendencies in historical development. It faces the problems of the "new age" without principles, without criteria. Because of its historicistic and relativistic view of life, the slogans with which it battled national socialism and fascism had no reliable value. The same holds with equal force for the slogans "democracy," "the rights of individuals," "law and order," and "freedom."

At the same time we must acknowledge that anti-revolutionary thought also revealed its weak spot in its conception of history in particular. Certainly, the scriptural basis of its position – It is written! – provided a powerful [65] weapon against historicism. Nevertheless, as we saw before, anti-revolutionary thought allied itself with humanistic historicism in its view of history. It was inevitable that this alignment would be avenged precisely in the present phase of world history: today the historicistic spirit of the "new age" can be combated effectively only if confronted in the arena of historical development itself. This encounter requires the complete spiritual armor of the Christian religion.

In my critique I do not mean to denounce the great work of Stahl and Groen van Prinsterer. My critique has a constructive aim. It is offered in a spirit of deep gratitude for the labors of these Christian leaders and thinkers. But their work can be continued in their spirit only if the scriptural ground-motive of the *Reformation* continues to operate in it. If weaknesses in their spiritual heritage become apparent, they must be cut away without hesitation. Today's primary need is a deeper scriptural insight into the relation between the creational principle of sphere sovereignty and historical development. Today our culture needs clarity with respect to the ordinances that God established for historical development in creation. Therefore those who become impatient may grant us the opportunity to dedicate more space to these fundamental issues.

Cultural Power

The core or nucleus of the historical aspect of reality is the *cultural* way of being. The cultural mode of an activity consists in control over material by formation according to a free design. This free control applies to both persons and things, although the former is primary. Free control reveals itself in the historical formation of *power*. Without personal power a discovery or invention that aims at controlling "nature" cannot be historically *formative*. For example, the great Italian artist of the early Renaissance, Leonardo da Vinci, was also a great scientist. It was said he already knew how to construct an airplane. But this knowledge went with him to the grave. It remained his private property. If he had gained support for his invention, it could have had a formative effect on world history. For that, Leonardo needed historical power formation and historical influence, which he had as an artist but not as an inventor.

What then is the nature of the personal power that equips the genuine molder of history? The most distorted notions present themselves with respect to this question, also in Christian circles. Many equate power with brute force. Today many Christians, misled by this identification, consider it un-Christian to strive for the consolidation of power in organizations that aim at applying Christian principles to society. They believe that power may play no part among Christians. Especially theologians in Barth's circle – I am thinking of Emil [66] Brunner's book *Das Gebot und die Ordnungen* – view the state as a half-demonic being because of its organization of power.[1] Christians may speak of love and justice with an unburdened conscience, but as soon as power comes into their purview they have probably lent their ears to the devil.

Such opinions indicate that the creation motive of the Christian religion has retreated from the worldview of these Christians. As a result, these Christians can no longer understand humankind's fall and redemption through Jesus Christ in its full scriptural significance. The unbiblical impact of their view becomes apparent when we recall that God reveals himself as the Creator in the original fullness of power. God is almighty. At creation God charged humankind with the cultural mandate: subdue the earth and have dominion over it. Throughout history God reveals himself as the Almighty.

Because of the fall, the position of power to which God called humankind in the development of culture became directed toward apostasy. But

---

[1] Emil Brunner. *The Divine Imperative*, trans. Olive Wyon (Philadelphia: The Westminster Press, 1947).

Christ Jesus, the Redeemer, revealed himself as the possessor of power in the full sense of the word: "All authority in heaven and on earth has been given to me," says the risen Lord [Matthew 28:18]. He charged his apostles to proclaim the power of the gospel among all nations.

The spiritual power of the gospel is of course quite different from the sword power of the government. In turn, both of these powers are essentially different from the power of science, art, capital, a labor union, or an organization of employers. But regardless of the concrete structure in which the historical formation of power reveals itself, power is not brute force. It is rooted in creation and contains nothing demonic. Jesus Christ explicitly called himself the ruler of the kings of the earth. He even summoned the sword power of governments to his service, for all power in heaven and on earth was given to him. Only sin can place power in the service of the demonic. But this holds for every good gift of God: for life, feeling, thinking, justice, beauty, and so forth.

Insofar as power has been entrusted to human beings as creatures, it is always cultural. It implies a historical calling and task of formation for which the bearer of power is responsible and of which she must give account. Power may never be used for personal advantage, as if it were a private possession. Power is the great motor of cultural development. The decisive question concerns the *direction* in which power is applied.

Finally, contrary to a frequently held opinion, the formation and exercise of power are not subject to natural laws. They are subject to *norms*, to the rules of what *ought* to be. The norms for the exercise of [67] power are intrinsically historical norms. Nations and bearers of power are subject to them. It is not true, for example, that the individual national character is itself the norm for cultural development, as the Historical School taught. This irrationalistic view of history must be rejected emphatically, for the creation motive compels us to acknowledge that in every area of life the law of God stands above the creature subject to it. The creature is the subject *(sujet)* of divine order. But the ordinances placed by God over the process of historical development can be transgressed by nations and bearers of power. This possibility of transgression confirms the truth that these ordinances are norms. One cannot disobey a natural law, such as the law of gravity.

Actually, whenever one speaks of the contrast between "historical" and "unhistorical" and calls unhistorical action "reactionary," one accepts the existence of truly historical norms. When one characterizes a certain political trend as "reactionary," one makes a historical value judgment that presupposes the application of a norm for historical development.

An example of reactionary policy in the Netherlands was the attempt of William I in 1814 to restore at least partially the outmoded land rights of the nobility and the old estates *[Stände]* of the realm. Manorial rights, which brought governmental authority into the domain of private ownership, were remnants of the undifferentiated state of society in the Middle Ages. The old system of estates, too, was a relic of medieval society. Neither the manorial nor the estate system could adapt themselves to the result of the French Revolution; namely, to the modern idea of the state and its clear demarcation of public and private law. The so-called counter-revolutionary movement in the Restoration period did not simply attempt to resist the *principles* of the French Revolution; it sought to eliminate whatever was associated with the French Revolution including the modern idea of the state. It tried to turn the political clock back to the old regime with its feudal relationships. From the outset, the Anti-revolutionary Party[1] opposed the counter-revolution, recognizing that it was a reactionary and unhistorical movement. It realized that the political efforts of the counter-revolutionaries conflicted with the norm for historical development.

But how do we know that God placed historical development under norms and not, for instance, under the natural laws that hold for electrical and chemical phenomena or for the organic development of life? The normative character of historical development is apparent from [68] the place God assigned the historical aspect in the creation order. The contrast between historical and unhistorical action refers back to the opposition found in the logical aspect of reality between what agrees with the norm for thought and what conflicts with this norm. If one contradicts oneself in a logical argument, we accuse the person of arguing *illogically*. The logical/illogical contrast presupposes that our thought function is placed under logical norms that can be transgressed. Among the various aspects of reality the aspect of logical distinction is the first that displays a contrast between what ought to be and what ought not to be. The divine ordinances or laws for all subsequent aspects are normative in character. Norms are standards of evaluation, and as such they can be employed only by creatures who, endowed with a logical function, are capable of rational distinction.

Some maintain that norms appear already in the organic aspect. After all, we call an organism healthy or unhealthy depending upon whether or not it functions according to the "norm" for health. But this judgment rests upon a misunderstanding. A norm exists only for creatures who are *responsible* for their own behavior and who are *accountable* for conduct that transgresses norms. Our ability to give account in this way is possible only on the basis of the faculty of logical discernment. Surely, no one would hold a sick plant or animal responsible for the abnormal function-

---

1 The anti-revolutionary movement had been in existence in Holland for several decades under the leadership of Groen van Prinsterer, before Abraham Kuyper founded the Anti-revolutionary Party in 1879.

ing of its organism. No one would blame it for its sickness. Yet, we do hold someone accountable for arguing illogically. Accountability is also at stake when we blame a political movement for its reactionary attitude toward historical development, or when we say that a person behaves in violation of social norms, speaks ungrammatically, does business uneconomically, writes poor poetry, acts unjustly, engages in immoral conduct, or lives in unbelief.

Norms are given in the creation order as *principles* for human behavior. Within the historical aspect, as well as in all subsequent aspects of reality, these principles require *formation* by competent human authorities. The process of giving form to normative principles must always take into consideration the level of development of a people, for in form-giving all subsequent aspects of human life are interwoven with the cultural-historical aspect. Giving form of any kind always refers back to cultural formation in historical development. Accordingly, the principles of decency, courtesy, respect, civility, etc. require formation in social intercourse, in our concrete social manners. Likewise, lingual principles require the forms of language; the principles of economic value require economic forms; the principles of harmony require the forms of style; legal principles require the juridical forms of laws, decrees, statutes, and regulations. All the later aspects thus display an inseparable coherence with the historical aspect. [69]

If the creation motive does not govern one's thinking, it may seem that social intercourse, language, economics, art, justice, morality, and faith are in essence historical phenomena, as if they are of purely *historical origin*. But the creation motive of God's Word, which continually reminds us that God created all things according to their own nature, keeps us from this historicistic error and sharpens our ability to distinguish the aspects of reality. For example, positive *law*, in its human formation, is not *historical* in nature. In contrast to historical formation which presupposes the power of those who give form to cultural principles, the legislator's formation of positive law requires legal power and juridical competence. Legal power cannot be reduced to power in the historical sense. Such a reduction results in an identification of justice with power, which is tantamount to an abolition and negation of justice.

The persistent claim of national socialism that a nation establishes its right to exist through a historical power struggle was a typical outcome of historicism. "Might is right" was the political slogan of the totalitarian state. The slogan was all the more dangerous because it contained a moment of truth. It is indeed true, as we shall see later, that in world history a world judgment is brought down over the various nations, though never in the sense that right dissolves into might. The figure of "legal power" does indeed point to the inseparable coherence between the jural and the historical aspects of reality. Without power in the historical sense juridical power cannot exist. Nevertheless, the nature of each power is intrinsically different.

Tradition

All historical formation requires power. Formation thus never takes place without a struggle. The progressive will of the molder of history invariably clashes with the power of tradition, which, as the power of conservation, opposes every attempt to break with the past. In tradition one finds the embodiment of a cultural, communal heritage acquired in the passing of generations. Tradition shapes us, as members of a cultural area, in large measure quite unconsciously, because we have been nurtured within it from our childhood and thus begin to accept it as a matter of course without taking stock of its intrinsic worth. The wealth of tradition is immeasurably richer than the shares which individuals can appropriate for themselves. Anyone who dares to oppose it is never confronted merely with a few conservatively prone souls but with a communal power binding the past to the future and stretching across entire generations. The innovator almost always underestimates the conserving power of tradition, for such a person sees only the surface of the present [70] where tradition appears mainly as inertia, as a retarding force. But tradition has deep dimensions that reveal themselves only gradually in careful historical research. Only in that light does the investigator begin to understand how great the power confronting the shaper of history actually is.

It is childish to complain about tradition as if it were a grouchy old person who simply swears by what is and who fails to appreciate anything new. Culture cannot exist without tradition. Historical development is impossible in its absence. Imagine that every new generation would try to erase the past in an earnest effort to start afresh. Nothing would come of it. The world would be a desert, a chaos.

Cultural development, then, is not possible without tradition. The power of tradition is grounded in the creation order, since the cultural mandate itself is one of the creational ordinances. However, truly historical development also demands that a culture not vegetate upon the past but unfold itself.

Progress and renewal have a rightful place in history alongside tradition and the power of conservation. In the power struggle between both forces the progressive will of the shaper of history must bow before the *norm of historical continuity*. The revolutionary spirit of reconstruction, which seeks to dismiss the past entirely, must accommodate itself to the vitality of forms of tradition insofar as they conform to the *norm of historical development*. Surely, this norm of historical continuity is not a "law of nature" working itself out in history apart from human involvement. In every revolution guided by false principles an attempt is made to reverse the existing order completely. The French Revolution, for example, tried to begin with the year "one." But quickly it had to moderate its revolutionary intentions under the pressure of tradition. If any revolutionary spirit is able to overcome the power of tradition, culture itself will be annihilated. Though this may be possible, humankind *cannot* overturn the creation order, which binds historical development to abiding norms. The creature cannot *create* in the true sense of the word. Humankind cannot create a genuine culture while completely destroying the past.

A typical mark of the historicistic spirit of the age is the belief that the distinction between conservative and progressive directions in history can replace the religious antithesis as the line of demarcation for political parties. This suggestion, first made in this context by the historian Johan Huizinga,[1] has gained wide support, particularly in the Dutch National [71] Movement. It is symptomatic of the spirit of our time that this distinction originates in the historical aspect of reality itself, for the viewpoint that the demarcation between political principles and goals can be made on the basis of this historical criterion is plausible only when one absolutizes the historical aspect. It will become clear, however, that this criterion is insufficient, even from a historical point of view, for a proper assessment of the main direction of political aspirations.

In examining the structure of the historical aspect, we uncovered the normative principle of historical continuity. Although the Historical School also arrived at this principle, it gave this norm an irrationalistic twist that led toward an acceptance of a *fait accompli* and raised the individual national character as the "destiny of the nation" to the status of law. Appealing to "God's guidance in history" only masked these unscriptural conceptions which conflict with the motive of creation. The norm of historical continuity does not arise from the national character. Rather, nations and rulers are subject to it. Good and evil may be mixed in the national spirit and in tradition, which, for this reason alone, demonstrates that these latter two cannot function as norms themselves.

But if neither tradition nor the national character are norms, then is the norm of continuity an adequate standard for judging the pressing question as to what is progressive and what is reactionary in historical development? Evidently not. Not every movement that announces itself as progressive contributes to true cultural progress. In retrospect it may become apparent that it is basically reactionary.

National socialism undoubtedly claimed that it was an extremely progressive movement. Was that claim justified? Let no one answer too hastily, for I fear that many would be embarrassed if they were asked for the

---

1 The reference here is to Huizinga's book *In the Shadow of To-Morrow: A Diagnosis of the Spiritual Distemper of our Time* (London: William Heineman Ltd., 1936).

criterion of their historical value judgment. It is precisely the *historicist* who lacks such a criterion. What do we gain if on the historicistic basis one claims that nazism trampled the "rights of individuals" and the "foundations of democracy?" If everything is in historical flux and if the stability of principles is a figment of the imagination, then why prefer an ideology of human rights to the ideals of a strong race and its bond to the German soil? Is the modern conception concerning the "rights of individuals" still the same as in the days of the Enlightenment or the French Revolution? Are the modern views of democracy identical with those of Rousseau? If not, then from where does modern historicism derive the right to describe its own internally undermined ideology as progressive and call the vital ideals of nazism terribly reactionary?

Surely, the quest for the norms of historical development must continue. We have pointed out that the norm of historical continuity itself is not decisive with regard to the search for a creationally based criterion which will enable us to distinguish between genuine progress in historical development and a disintegrated reactionary historical trend. The norm of continuity needs further clarification. This can be arrived at only on the basis of the ground-motive of God's Word. [72]

Disclosure and Differentiation

Historical formation occurs in the battle between conservative and progressive cultural powers.

Tradition and Culture

Conservative power guards tradition, which binds the present to the past. In the power struggle the progressive will of the historical shaper ought to accommodate itself to the vital elements in tradition. The revolutionary trait of a progressive trend to establish a complete break with the past must therefore be molded by the norm of historical continuity if indeed a culture is not broken apart but rather unfolded through further historical development. We have pointed out that the norm of historical continuity itself is not decisive with regard to the search for a creationally based criterion which will enable us to distinguish between genuine progress in historical development and a disintegrated reactionary historical trend. Tradition itself, however, is not a norm or standard for determining what one's attitude should be toward a power that calls itself "progressive." Tradition contains good and bad, and thus it is itself subject to the historical norm. Even the criterion that a progressive direction ought to take its point of departure from the vital cultural elements in tradition is not yet sufficient.

By the "vital" elements in tradition we refer to the inseparable coherence of historical development with the development of organic life. I have repeatedly stated that the historical aspect of reality cannot exist without this link. In the divine creation order, all aspects of reality are placed in an unbreakable coherence with each other. If any were left out of this coherence, the others would lose their meaning and the possibility for their existence. It is a consequence of the integral character of God's creational work that every aspect of his work coheres inseparably with the others. Only in this coherence is it possible for each aspect to reveal its irreducible, unique nature.

The historical aspect maintains its coherence with the organic aspect through *cultural life*. Cultural life should follow its own development. As such, it cannot be reduced to organic life, even though cultural life cannot exist without organic life. Historical development cannot be seen simply as an extension of the organic development of plants, animals, or human beings. Organic development takes place in accordance with the specific natural laws prescribed by God in the creation order. Creatures are not responsible for the process of the birth, growth, and death of their organisms. But, as we saw earlier, the historical development that takes place in cultural life is subject not to natural laws but to norms, to the rules of what ought to be. These norms presuppose the human ability to make rational distinctions, and they are given by God as principles requiring concrete formation by those who possess historical power.

Because historical development is subject to norms instead of natural laws, it is improper to view the "vital forces" in tradition, to which we have to attach ourselves in the continued formation of history, as *natural* [73] givens not subject to standards of historical evaluation. In particular one should not go along with the Historical School, which argued that "unconscious, historically vital forces" and the "individual national character" operate in the process of history under "God's providential guidance" just like the "vital force" in a bodily organism. Such an appeal to "God's guidance in history" can only serve as an escape from one's own responsibility for the course of cultural development. In this way of thinking "God's guidance" became identical with *Schicksal*, the destiny or fate of a nation. In practice "God's guidance" was reduced to the point where the national character itself became the norm. In other words, responsibility for cultural development was relegated to a mysterious "national spirit" *[Volksgeist]* that could not be altered and that swept the members of a national community along like an irresistible fate.

A view of history led by the scriptural motive of creation comes to an entirely different conclusion. In cultural tradition "vitality" is not rooted merely in the national character, nor does it signify only that large parts of tradition are still supported by enough historical power to prevent their eradication. Both are indeed necessary for historical development but, by themselves, they are not sufficient. True "vitality" in a historical sense only points to that part of tradition which is capable of further development in conformity with the *norm for the opening or disclosure of culture.* This norm requires the differentiation of culture into spheres that possess their own unique nature. Cultural differentiation is necessary so that the creational ordinance, which calls for the disclosure or unfolding of everything in accordance with its inner nature, may be realized also in historical development.

This point is eminently important for the pressing issues of the "new age." Indeed, we may not rest until we have gained clear insight into the meaning of the historical norm of differentiation and into this norm's foundation in the divine creation order.

Undifferentiated Societies
Earlier I have repeatedly discussed the condition of undifferentiated societies. In such societies there was as yet no room for the formation of life-spheres characterized by their own inner nature. The entire life of the members of such a society was enclosed by the primitive, undifferentiated bonds of kinship *(familia or gens)*, tribe or folk *(Volk)*, which possessed an exclusive and absolute religious sphere of power. These bonds were distinguished only by their size and scope. They fulfilled all of the tasks for which at a higher level of culture societal structures are developed which display an intrinsic nature peculiar to themselves, like the state, the church, the business enterprise, the school, etc. At an [74] undifferentiated level, the community absorbed the individual person. There was as yet little concern for the lives of individual persons as such. Their entire status was dependent upon their membership in the primitive community. If they were ostracized from that community, they had no rights or peace. They were outlaws. The same held for the stranger or foreigner who did not belong to the kinship, tribe, or folk community.

If one considers a primitive community in terms of its historical aspect, one discovers that it consisted of a completely undifferentiated cultural sphere. Differentiated spheres of civilization that unfold themselves according to their own nature, such as science, art, trade, the church, the state, the school, sports organization, and so forth, did not exist. Culture was bound rigidly to the needs of the organic development of communal life. It had a predominantly vital, organic character. The idolatrous religions that stamped these cultures were basically religions that focused on organic life.

Tradition was all-powerful in a primitive, undifferentiated culture. Its guardians were the culture's priestly leaders. They immediately rejected any attempt at renewal, believing that the gods would not approve. They also guarded fearfully against the infiltration of foreign influences in the lives of the people. If such a culture remained in this undifferentiated state, it isolated itself from cultural intercourse with other peoples. Bound to the organic development of communal life, it stood outside of world history. When the tribe became extinct, the community disappeared from the scene without a trace.

These, for instance, were the characteristics of the Papuan tribe of the Marindamin in New Guinea. Only a few of its members still exist. This extinct culture had little to offer to the historical development of the human race. By contrast, we saw with the Greeks and Romans that their culture developed into a real world culture after an originally primitive phase. Its influence continued into the Christian-Germanic world, and it became one of the foundations of our modern western civilization.

Medieval Society

Medieval society was also largely undifferentiated. But in terms of its historical aspect, it is evident that medieval culture was vastly different from the culture of the pagan Germanic tribes of the pre-Christian era. Largely through the intermediary of the Christian church, medieval Germanic culture was tremendously enriched by Greco-Roman culture. It also underwent the deeply formative influence of Christendom. The Roman Catholic Church, which became the leading power in medieval cultural development, was a highly differentiated societal bond. Under its leadership science and art flourished. It established universities. Because a real body politic was still lacking, the church functioned as the organization [75] of all Christendom. It transcended the boundaries of tribe and nation and with its canon law, strongly influenced by Roman law, it produced a global ecclesiastical law. The church was catholic, that is, it embraced all Christians regardless of their origin.

But in medieval culture, which itself went through a number of developmental phases, the institutional church was largely the differentiated superstructure of a substructure which was to a large extent still undifferentiated. Both structures, according to the Roman Catholic view, related to each other in the way that "grace" related to "nature." This religious ground-motive of nature and grace operated as the central dynamic force in western cultural development during the Middle Ages. We will discuss this more fully later. In the present context we shall note only that the "natural" substructure underneath the ecclesiastical institute of grace displayed much that was primitive and undifferentiated. In the dominant medieval conception there was one great community of Christendom, the *corpus Christianum*. The pope was its spiritual head while the emperor was its worldly head. Their relation was not analogous to the modern relation between church and state, for a differentiated body politic did not exist. The emperor was only the head of the "natural substructure" of the church. This substructure was constituted by church members. The church, in fact, was the all-embracing bond of Christendom, which was differentiated in its superstructure, but undifferentiated in its substructure.

For this reason medieval culture was essentially ecclesiastical. National differentiation was largely unknown. The fact that the substructure was undifferentiated enabled the church of that time period to control the whole of cultural life.

Let us examine this natural substructure more closely. When the old Germanic sib or clan (a patrilineal familial community comparable to the Roman *gens*) disintegrated, the Germanic guilds preserved the totalitarian principle lying at the foundation of this undifferentiated societal sphere. Originally a guild was an artificial clan, a fraternity based not on natural lineage but on voluntary membership under oath. Voluntary membership did not indicate, as the famous legal historian Otto Gierke held, that the limits of primitive society had been transcended.[1] Investigations [76] by anthropologists and ethnologists have shown that secret "lodges" (communities requiring an oath) were a common feature among primitive peoples. The medieval guild revealed its primitive character in its totalitarian and undifferentiated structure. It embraced its members in all the spheres of their lives, and it could be seen as a model for any undifferentiated community built upon the basis of voluntary membership. When the medieval town arose, the *burghers* or *porters* (those who guarded the gates) united in a so-called burgh guild. When outside the walls the merchants established merchant districts, they joined together in merchant guilds. The later trade guilds originated in the same way. The trade guilds were not like modern business corporations; originally they were primitive fraternities that clearly betrayed the pagan heritage of the old religious communities of the Frankish era in their rituals. The guild also served as a model for the country boroughs, which sometimes are explicitly called "guilds" in the historical documents.

A second model for the undifferentiated substructure of medieval society was the Germanic home or household community, the counterpart to the Roman *familia*. Like the *familia*, this household defined the religious sphere of authority of the gods of home and hearth who represented the continuity of life between the household's ancestors and its living members. The head of the household exercised absolute and totalitarian power, just like a Roman *pater familias*. He had the power of life and death over

---

1 Dooyeweerd is referring to the third volume of Otto von Gierke's work *Das deutsche Genossenschaftsrecht*, 4 vols. (1868-1918; Graz: Akademische Druk U. Verlagsanstalt, 1954). Only sections of this book have been translated into English. The latest that has appeared is called *Associations and Law: The Classical and Early Christian Stages*, trans. and intro. George Heiman (Toronto: University of Toronto Press, 1977). For the questions discussed by Dooyeweerd, one can consult an earlier translation of part of the third volume: Otto Gierke, *Political Theories of the Middle Ages*, translated, with an introduction by F.W. Maitland, in 1900 (Boston: Beacon Press, 1958), especially the section on "Unity in Church and State," 9-21.

all who belonged to the household. He possessed an absolute right to them and to the household properties.

Power in the Germanic household community was called *Mund*. One became independent *[mundig]* if one were released from the *Mund* of one's lord and established a household community of one's own. In contrast to the guild principle, the *Mund* principle expressed the personal dominion of the chief over those who belonged to him. The first Merovingian kings built the entire organization of the great Frankish realm on this *Mund* principle.

The Frankish kingdom, established by Clovis in the fifth century, gradually subjugated many of the Germanic tribes on the European continent. It expanded its religiously rooted household power far beyond its original limits by subjecting all its subordinates to a general *Mund* and by bringing the governors and military leaders into a narrower, special *Mund* sphere. The Frankish church and other groups who depended upon royal protection because of their helpless station fell under this special *Mund*. The old Germanic tribal kings already had extended their original household power or *Mund* through the formation of a so-called *trustis*, a royal retinue *(Gefolgschaft)*. Prominent German youths belonged to it who under oath accepted the royal service of [77] knighthood and subjected themselves unconditionally to the *Mund* of their royal *Führer*, who had the power of life and death over them. The first Frankish kings made a special effort at extending their royal company *(Gefolgschaft)*, from which they recruited their palace aides and central administrative officials. The later feudal system, under which the vassal personally subjected himself to his lord, incorporated this basic idea of *trustis*, even though the feudal system itself had a different origin.

Hitler's Retrogression
Hitler – consciously reaching back to this ancient Germanic example – built his *Führerstaat* on the primitive and essentially pagan principle of the *Gefolgschaft*. He used this principle in a totalitarian fashion as a guide for organizing all of life into a deified "Greater Germanic Empire." Every sphere of life, including the economic sector, was incorporated into the totalitarian national community in the light of the principles of *Führer* and *Gefolgschaft*. Each sphere was delivered over to the exclusive power of a "divine leader." The idea of a differentiated state was explicitly pushed into the background in favor of the ancient Germanic idea of the *nation [Volk]*. But members of the German *Volk* were not encouraged to recall that the principle of the sib or clan had constantly asserted itself over against the *Führer* principle in ancient Germanic society. Even though national socialism made the "study" of these "national beginnings" an integral part of cultural education, it carefully avoided the historical truth that the Frankish kings vehemently

opposed the principle of the clan whenever the clan asserted itself in society. The clan's demand for recognition was a threat to the *Führer* principle.

The ancient Germanic sibs did not know of lords and subjects. They were associations that granted their members equal rights. The relation of authority and subjection was foreign to them. Not until the Frankish realm collapsed in the ninth century could the guilds, based on the sib principle, develop freely and act as a counterbalance to the authoritarian principles of *Mund* and *Gefolgschaft*. These principles were now being incorporated – in a fragmented manner, to be sure – in the feudal system, with its radical structure of authority and subjection in the relationship between lords and vassals.

The fundamental difference between the cultural development of classical Rome and the medieval Germanic world was this: when the Roman city-state arose, the ancient bonds of lineage lost their significance for good while the undifferentiated sphere of authority of the Roman household *(familia)* remained limited to its original boundaries. Independently of the Roman household, a process of differentiation brought forth both a true body politic *(res publica)* and a global civil law *(ius gentium)*. Yet in Germanic countries the undifferentiated sib and the [78] equally undifferentiated household community became the mutually opposed models for organizing the worldly "substructure" of medieval society. Above this structure only the Roman Catholic Church could form a differentiated cultural community of global impact.

Did national socialism then follow a truly progressive line when it imposed its totalitarian ideas upon western culture in accordance with the model of the old Germanic *Führer* principle? I hope that by now it has become apparent that a truly scripturally based answer is possible, and that this answer will also incoporate a historical judgment upon the totalitarian tendencies which still threaten our cultural development even after the fall of national socialism.

Differentiation

Let us examine more closely the second norm for historical development that we have explored thus far. This norm requires the differentiation of culture into spheres that possess a proper nature of their own. This norm can be understood in its scriptural sense only when seen in immediate relation to the creation order. Viewed in the light of the creation motive, historical development ought to bring the wealth of creational structures, in the cutural aspect as well, to full, differentiated disclosure. Only in the differentiation of culture can the unique nature of each creational structure reveal itself fully.

Historical development is nothing more than the cultural aspect of the great process of becoming which has to continue in all the aspects of temporal reality in order that the wealth of the creational structures can fully come to fruition in time. The process of becoming presupposes creation; it is the working out of creation in time. Time itself is encompassed by the creation. The process of becoming, therefore, is not an independent, autonomous process that stands over against God's creation.

In all its aspects, the process of becoming develops, in conformity to law, from an undifferentiated phase to a differentiated phase. The organic development of life begins from the still undifferentiated germ cell, out of which the separate organs gradually differentiate. The emotional life of a newborn child is completely undifferentiated, but gradually it unfolds into a differentiation of sensuous feeling, logical feeling, lingual feeling, artistic feeling, juridical feeling, and so forth. The course of human societal development is no different. Here too, undifferentiated forms gradually differentiate into the various societal structures through a lengthy process of historical development. This differentiation occurs in accordance with its *historical* aspect by means of a "branching out" of culture into the intrinsically different power spheres of science, art, the state, the church, industry, trade, the school, voluntary organizations, etc.

Cultural differentiation necessarily terminates the absolute and exclusive [79] power of the undifferentiated life-spheres. No differentiated life-sphere – in accordance with its true nature – can embrace a person in all cultural relationships. Science is no more capable of this than art; the state is no more suitable to do this than the institutional church, the world of business, the school, or a labor organization. Why is this so? Because each of these spheres, *in accordance with its inner nature*, is limited *in its cultural sphere of power*. The power sphere of the state, for instance, is characterized typically as the power of the sword. This power is undoubtedly awesome, but it cannot embrace the power of either the church, the arts, or the sciences. The cultural power exercised by any sphere of life is limited by that sphere's nature. As a temporal institution the church cannot claim the whole of cultural power. God did not give the church the historical calling that he gave to science, to art, to the state, or to economic enterprise. The church's spiritual power cannot incorporate the other power spheres.

Certainly, ecclesiastical power was very extensive in the Middle Ages when the Roman Catholic Church embraced all of Christendom. The papal ban could suspend even one's duty to obey a worldly government. But even at that time the church had to recognize the inherent limitation of its power. It was careful never to gird itself with the swordpower of temporal government. It allowed "profane" science its own cultural sphere of power, pressing its ecclesiastical power only in matters that affected the "souls of the faithful." Yet, according to its conception of its special task, the church demanded the *leadership* of all of cultural life. For this reason one can indeed speak of an overextension of ecclesiastical cultural power. The church overreached itself not because of the nature of the church's spiritual power but because of the religious ground-motive that ruled all of medieval culture: the motive of nature and grace in its typically Roman Catholic understanding. As the leading cultural power, the Roman Catholic Church was the bearer of this ground-motive, which hampered the differentiation of the "natural substructure" of medieval culture. The Roman Catholic ground-motive had a totalitarian propensity to conceive of temporal society in terms of the scheme of the whole and its parts. This inclination was related to the fact that in the ground-motive of nature and grace the scriptural motive of creation had become largely overtaken by the Greek form-matter motive.

Still, one can speak of an overextension of the cultural power sphere of the church only if other differentiated cultural spheres, such as art and science, already exist alongside the church. When culture remains in a primitive and undifferentiated stage, it has only one undifferentiated sphere of power. Although households, clans, and tribes may exist alongside each other, they are not distinct according to their nature. A process of over-extension in culture, therefore, presupposes a [80] process of differentiation. It thus conflicts with the norms that God established for differentiation in his creation order. Every extreme expansion of the historical power sphere of a specific life-sphere occurs at the expense of the other life-spheres, for it retards their unfolding in an unhealthy way.

Cultural Economy

We have now arrived at a more precise determination of the norm for historical development. I shall call it the *principle of cultural economy*. If we observe carefully, we notice that this principle is nothing other than the principle of sphere sovereignty applied to the process of historical development. "Cultural economy" requires that the historical power sphere of each differentiated cultural sphere should remain limited to the boundaries set by the true nature specific to each life-sphere.

The principle of cultural economy is a guarantee that the view of history developed so far is indeed on the course charted by the scriptural motive of creation. The line of true historical progression is clearly marked out by the creational ordinances themselves. Wherever a totalitarian image of culture is held up as the ideal that results in erasing the hard won recognition of sphere sovereignty – whether this is done by appealing to ancient Germanic customs or to the medieval church – one can be certain that we are faced with a reactionary direction in history. We should not be deceived by the adjective "progressive," a label that any new spiritual movement gladly claims for itself. A tree will be known by its fruits!

Individualization and National Identity

We will now observe how, as the historical norm of differentiation begins to take effect, the aspect of culture begins to *disclose* its meaning. This *disclosure* occurs when the aspect of culture concretely expresses its inner coherence with the subsequent aspects of reality and thus reveals its "sphere universality." We have discerned these as the aspects of language, social intercourse, the economic aspect, the aesthetic aspect of beautiful harmony, the jural aspect, the moral aspect and the faith aspect.

We have seen that a culture which has not yet begun to differentiate isolates itself from cultural intercourse among peoples and nations which play a role in world history. Such a culture is bound rigidly to the organic aspect of the community and to a nature religion of the stream of life. In these cultures neither science, independent arts, a body politic, nor an independent industrial life can arise. For every differentiated life-sphere depends, for its historical development, upon *cultural intercourse* [81] in world history. With the cultural exchange the historical aspect discloses its coherence with the aspect of social intercourse.

In this connection we should note that differentiation of the distinct cultural spheres goes hand in hand with *individualization*. Individualization here refers to the development of genuinely individual *national* characteristics. Because of it, one can speak, for instance, of French, British, and Dutch cultures. A primitive, enclosed culture is never *national*. "National" is characterized by the individuality of a people as an expression of its common historical experiences and of its disclosure as a cultural community. This historical individuality is first developed in the cultural interaction of civilized peoples. This individuality is thus entirely different from the individual traits of tribal and racial communities which are based on "vital" or organic factors.

The national differentiation of culture is thus consistent with the *disclosure* of culture. In the idea of the "Greater Germanic Empire" propagated by national socialism, the *national* element was purposely suppressed. Here too one can ascertain the reactionary character of national socialism as a historical and cultural movement. It nourished itself on the myth of "blood and soil," which had no room for the national individuality of culture. National individuality was replaced by the primitive idea of a *people [Volk]* based upon the "vital" or organic community of race and tribe.

The *national* character of a people is not a product of nature but the result of culturally formative activity. Cultural formation is subject to the norm that God established for the historical disclosure of culture. Thus a specific instance of national individualization, developed in real terms, in a particular time and place, can never be elevated to the status of a norm. For such a specific instance may well display anti-normative traits such as a lack of initiative, sectarianism, untrustworthiness, bourgeois provincialism, an illusion of national grandeur, or an apostate glorification of national culture.

The norm for the formation of a nation consists in a *type* of cultural individuality which *ought* to be realized with increasing purity as the *special calling* of a people. We will illustrate this with reference to the Dutch nation.

The Dutch national character can be viewed as a "normative type." In accordance with this "type," the character of the Dutch nation is marked by its Calvinistic bent, its humaneness, its down-to-earthness and sober lifestyle, its religious and political sense of liberty, its enterprising spirit stimulated by its constant struggle against the sea, its pronounced international orientation, its special aptitude for the art of painting and natural-scientific research, etc. The spiritual earnestness of the Dutch [82] national character, nourished by Calvinism, carries with it an orientation towards fundamental principles that places its mark upon political parties, education, and social organizations.

One can undoubtedly claim, therefore, that it is in keeping with the national character of the Dutch that attempted syntheses between contradictory worldviews lose their effect especially in times of spiritual revitalization. At the same time, one may certainly not reduce the antithesis between Christianity and humanism to a typically Dutch cultural phenomenon. Religion is not determined by national culture, but vice versa; it is religion that brings its formative power to bear on national culture. Since the religious antithesis, posited by the scriptural ground-motive, has been a major influence on the nationality of the Netherlands by means of the cultural power of Calvinism, the continued impact of this antithesis, also in political party formation and societal organization, is certainly not to be considered as antinational.

The Dutch National Movement does not do justice to the Dutch national character when it expects the abolition of the antithesis in political and social life to reinforce the Dutch national consciousness. If indeed the scriptural ground-motive were no longer to have an impact on political and social principles, then the national character would be subject to a fundamental *degeneration*. This would prove that the Dutch people had erased the impact of its scriptural-calvinistic formation in history.

At this point the Dutch National Movement may posit the question: is it not true that humanism has also worked formatively on the Dutch national character? Undoubtedly it has, to a very great extent. From a purely historical point of view it has done more for the recognition of public freedom for religious convictions than did seventeenth century Calvinism. It has worked formatively on scientific and artistic talents and on political institutions.

In these respects humanism has indeed fulfilled its own cultural calling. But before it succumbed to a period of inner decay, humanism was always very conscious of its antithesis with scriptural Calvinism. Particularly in the Netherlands it never hesitated to acknowledge the close connection between its political principles and its worldview whenever confronted with scriptural Christianity. A truly Dutch humanism is a principled humanism that in its own way expresses the spiritual earnestness of the Dutch national character. If Dutch humanism no longer sees the necessary connection between its religious conviction and its political and social principles, then it has degenerated internally both in its worldview and in its historical role as a national power in Dutch culture. The entire national identity degenerates if it becomes unfaithful to its normative historical type. [83]

God's Judgment in History
Cultural differentiation leads to the rise of national individuality. It also opens the way for *personal and individual potential* to make itself felt in history. Individual personality is no longer absorbed in the undifferentiated community, which earlier determined the whole of cultural activity, but receives an opportunity for the free unfolding of its talent and genius. It is in this context that the individual shapers of history enter the stage. Their formative activity takes on worldwide historical significance.

Individual traits are of course not absent in primitive, closed cultural spheres. But this cultural individuality displays a relative uniformity throughout the successive generations maintained by the power of fixed tradition. To be sure, exceptionally talented individuals do appear in primitive cultures, as anthropologists have observed repeatedly. Their influence, however, is limited to the narrow boundaries of a closed community. A disclosed culture, on the other hand, has individual forms of world-historical character upon which individual leaders place their personal stamp.

Genuine *historical consciousness* arises first in an opened up, disclosed culture. This consciousness begins to distinguish what is historically significant from the historically insignificant. It also contributes to the urge to record what is historically memorable in symbols, such as historical accounts, monuments, inscriptions, etc. In the relatively uniform life of a closed, primitive culture, the muse of history does not have materials for her chronicle. The lack of historical consciousness in such a culture results in the lack of historical writing. Although in any undeveloped society one finds certain curious-sounding myths concerning the origin of its people and the origin of the world, one searches in vain for truly historical information concerning the development of its culture. Such a culture lacks a critical awareness of distance with respect to the past. Only an opened culture reveals the remarkable connection between the cultural aspect and the lingual aspect whose nucleus is symbolic designation or signification by means of either words or other signs. Thus the presence of monuments, historical inscriptions, or chronicles is a reliable criterion for determining that a culture has passed beyond the undifferentiated stage.

Without doubt many remnants of primitive cultural formation exist even in very highly developed and opened up cultures. Reminders of old pagan customs are still with us today: Easter bonfires, Father Christmas, the "celebration" of an eclipse, and so on. But such remnants are not *alive* in [84] our culture. They are the petrified, fossilized relics of tradition. Today we classify them as "folklore." National socialism tried to restore new life into the petrified remains of a primitive and pagan Germanic culture. These relics were accorded a place of honor in the culture of the "race" in accordance with the demands of the national-socialistic myth of "blood and soil." A more pronounced retrogression or a bleaker spirit of reaction is not known in the history of the world. National socialism can be explained only as the poisonous leaven of a directionless historicism that lost all consciousness of historical distance in the face of the dead remains of tradition.

Once the process of differentiation in culture begins, the connections between the historical aspect and the later aspects of reality disclose themselves. We have already mentioned the connection with the aspects of language, social intercourse, and economy.[1] The relation between the historical aspect and the aesthetic aspect may serve as an additional illustration. Only when a culture observes the principle of cultural economy does it guarantee *harmonious* cultural development. Every transgression of the historical norm expressed in this principle leads to *disharmonious* cultural development.

Examples of such disharmony are many. In the days of the Enlightenment the influence of the humanistic ideal of science granted virtually unlimited power to the natural sciences. All progress in the history of humankind was expected to come from the further development of science. Due to its penetration into the church, the first victim of the humanistic deification of science was the life of faith. "Modernism," preached from the pulpit by enlightened preachers, spread a spirit of arid and homespun provincial rationalism which strangled biblical faith. For the "enlightened," the miracles and the mysteries of faith in God's revelation were outdated. Science, after all, had a natural explanation for everything.

At the same time, economic, legal, and moral life were infected with a spirit of superficial utilitarianism and individualism. The state was seen as

---

[1] *General Editor's note:* At this point Dooyeweerd summarizes once more his analysis of the disclosure of the cultural-historical aspect accomplished through the opening up of the historical aspect in its anticipatory coherence with the aspects mentioned.

an artificial product constructed from "elements," just like a compound in a laboratory. Even art fell under the influence of the rationalistic spirit of the age. It was subject to rigid, rational formulas and to inflexible artistic patterns.

In the long run culture cannot survive under an overextension of the power sphere of natural science. A *judgment* then begins to take place in history, which opens up the relation of the historical to the jural aspect of reality. Under God's guidance, the French Revolution executed this judgment. And after its liquidation, the French Revolution was in turn [85] followed by a period of reaction, the Restoration, in the great struggle for the freedom of nations against the conqueror Napoleon. In a similar way the medieval overextension of ecclesiastical power, which subordinated every cultural expression to its authoritarian leadership, was followed by an individualistic counter-force which rejected every belief in authority and attempted to liberate itself from every societal bond. What a great historical judgment has been executed over the excessive expansion of the cultural power of historical science in our most recent historicistic and relativistic period! The first phase of this judgment is already behind us: we have witnessed the unspeakably bloody and reactionary regime of nazism, the degenerate spiritual offspring of modern historicism. Totalitarian "racial" *[volkse]* ideals, inspired by the myth of "blood and soil," reverted western culture to the dark night of the pagan nature religions. Moreover, these totalitarian ideals were backed by the military power of a mighty modern state. The total Germanic *Volk* community – incorporated in a totalitarian state! The military power of the German nazi state expanded without bounds, attempting to break all opposition from the other cultural spheres. Science and art, child rearing and education, industry and technology, labor organizations and philanthropy – all were made subservient to the pan-Germanic ideal of the *Volk*. Each became a segment of the all-embracing state. The totalitarian state led to a totalitarian war among the nations that made no distinction between soldier and civilian. Great cities and great cultural treasures were transformed into smoking ruins. Certainly this was God's judgment in world history!

The Second World War has ended. But has the political and military defeat of the totalitarian states also delivered us from the spirit of modern historicism with its overestimation of the folk community and its flight into an all-encompassing whole? Do we not detect totalitarian ideas of either an ecclesiastical or political nature all around us? Surely today, no one desires centralized state power. Today people prefer "functional decentralization," which seeks to unburden the central organs of government by creating "new societal organs" and by recognizing their autonomy and self-government, albeit still under control of the authorities. What is not recognized, however, is the great creational principle of sphere sovereignty, the principle that sovereignty is rooted in the intrinsic nature of the life-spheres according to their creational structures. Neither is the divine norm for historical development recognized which is rooted in the principle of sphere sovereignty. This is the norm of differentiation, which demands that the structures of creation be brought to disclosure also in the cultural aspect of human society. Nor do people today discern the norm of cultural economy, which restricts each sphere [86] of life from expanding its cultural power beyond what is in keeping with its own nature.

Many still live in the relativistic, leveling world of historicistic thought. There is much talk of *industrial democracy*, but there is little evidence of careful thought as to whether democracy, as a typical *political* form of organization, can be transplanted to the life of industry, whose structure is so very different. There is much talk of the *autonomy* and *self-government* of the spheres of life within the state in terms of a universal planning scheme, as if the relation between the nonpolitical spheres and the state is quite similar to the relation between the state and its autonomous parts. Especially today, when considering the whole international situation, it is hardly conceivable that the pendulum of world history will swing back from an absolutization of the community to an overestimation of individual freedom, the danger of totalitarian ideas, no matter what their guise, is greater than ever.

In view of this, the scriptural conception of the spiritual antithesis *must* continue to assert itself in today's political and social life. It has perhaps never been needed as urgently as in these times of spiritual uprootedness and disruption. The continued permeation of the spiritual antithesis is today the only way, not to divide the nation but, to the contrary, to save the best features of our national identity.

To this point we have explored the scriptural view of history in terms of the biblical motive of creation. But the indivisible unity of the Christian ground-motive demands that we now place this history under the full light of humankind's radical fall and its redemption through Jesus Christ. Ultimately, disharmony in the historical process of cultural development can be understood only in terms of the fall, and the antithesis can be grasped only in terms of redemption. [87]

Chapter 4

Faith and Culture

The Structure of Faith

Thus far we have seen that the relations between the historical aspect and the later aspects of reality become transparent in the process of cultural disclosure. We have traced these relations through the jural aspect, finding that with the "judgment of God in world history" historical development points forward to the jural aspect of the divine creation order. Beginning again with the juridical relation, we shall now examine these relations in more detail.

Might and Right in History

The connection between law and history reveals itself in a typical way in political life. In war, for example, the government's neglect of national defense avenges itself. According to its typically inner nature and order, the state is historically founded on a monopolistic organization of the power of the sword within its territorial area. Only on the basis of this power can the state fulfill its typical destination as the public-legal community of government and people. Before all else the state ought to obey the historico-political norm to actualize and maintain the typical foundation of its legal existence as an independent power. If the state fails to protect this foundation, it does not deserve independence. Thus Hegel's claims that a nation proves its right to exist in war and that history reveals a "higher justice" contained a moment of truth. But unfortunately these claims rested on a dangerous confusion of might [88] and right, a typical consequence of the historicistic view of reality. Hegel denied the validity of international law, arguing that international relations were governed simply by the "law of the strongest." National socialism later elevated this Hegelian position to the status of unquestioned dogma.

As such, historical might can never be identified with legal right. Nevertheless, the norm God established in historical development for the formation of power by a state, cannot be understood outside of its connection with the jural norm. Everywhere the ordinances of God which obtain for the various aspects of created reality display an indissoluble, mutual coherence, for their root-unity lies in the single religious commandment that we love God with all our heart. Here the creation order reveals its integral character.

Only by recognizing the demands of law [the jural = *recht*] as a unique aspect of society can one speak of the execution of a divine judgment in history revealed in the historical power struggle. Indeed, this struggle would never exhibit the features of a historical judgment without a connection with law *[recht]*.

Earlier we found that the violation of the norm of cultural economy based on excessive expansion of power belonging to a specific cultural sphere necessarily avenges itself in history. This led us to the conclusion that the differentiated life-spheres of disclosed culture do indeed possess an original right of their own. Juridically too, then, the life-spheres are sovereign in their own sphere. In other words, the life-spheres do not derive their right to develop according to their own inner nature from the state. A state law which fundamentally violates the juridical sphere sovereignty of nonstate spheres cannot be viewed as valid law, for God did not give the state an absolute and unlimited juridical power. Rather than absolute sovereignty over other life-spheres, the state alone possesses sovereignty within its own sphere, limited by its specific nature and order *[levenswet]* granted to it by God. Only in conjunction with this true juridical sphere sovereignty, established for each of the life-spheres by God's legal ordinance, can one properly speak, also within the aspect of cultural development, of the differentiated spheres of life as having a world historical right to the recognition of their own unique spheres of competence.

Love of Culture

Only a recognition of this historical right of culture can lead to the unfolding of a love of culture which in turn is the first condition for a harmonious development of civilization. Only when science, art, commerce, and technology are free to follow their own law of life does cultural love flourish, while without a moral zeal for fulfilling a historical task, a culture shrivels up and withers away. If science and art are bound to a totalitarian state [89] or church, they soon lose their inner authenticity. No longer inspired by love for their cultural task, scientists and artists become instruments in the hands of a tyrannical regime which denies them their own right to cultural life.

The love of culture opens up the bond between the historical and moral aspects of reality. The core of the moral aspect is the principle of love insofar as love reveals itself in the temporal relationships of life. In accordance with the various life-spheres, the principle of moral love differentiates itself into neighborly love, love for parents and children, patriotic love, love of scientific truth, love of artistic beauty, and so forth.

Faith as the Boundary Aspect

The last and all-controlling relation which discloses itself in the process of historical development is the link between history and faith. Ultimately, the faith of the leading cultural powers determines the entire direction of the opening process of culture. The religious ground-motive behind all cultural development in a phase of history manifests itself within time first in the faith of those who are called to form history. The connection between faith and history requires special attention because of the exceptional place the aspect of faith occupies in the temporal world order; lying at the boundary of time and eternity, this aspect is the last in temporal reality.

Although faith is the ultimate boundary function of our life as human beings, it should not be confused with the religious root-unity of the heart, soul, or spirit of human existence. For it is from the heart that the departure points of our temporal life emanate, including those of our temporal faith life. For all human beings faith is a subjective function of their inner consciousness, whether one is a believer in Christ or whether one's faith lies in the direction of apostasy. In terms of direction and content, faith is either an apostate faith or the faith that is active in a person through the Holy Spirit. Both faiths operate within the same structure of the temporal function of consciousness which God gave human nature at creation. Both are enclosed within the boundary aspect of temporal reality.

All temporal creatures other than human beings function objectively in the aspect of faith. All temporal things are objects of a person's subjective faith function, just as their color and taste are objects of sensory perception and their logical characteristics are objects of conceptualization. The majestic words that open the book of Genesis, "In the beginning God created the heavens and the earth," ought to determine the content of our faith with reference to creation; for heaven and earth, together with all that has unfolded in them, are, within time, objects of either this faith or an apostate faith that turns away from the revelation of God's Word. [90]

By relating the origin of all things to an eternal flux of life, the pagan nature religions made all creatures the objects of their primitive faith. The same holds for the modern evolutionist, who believes that whatever lives has come forth from one original source. Similarly, for anyone who believes the Scriptures, all things are the objects of faith in creation.

More pointedly, there are many concrete things which are characterized by an objective faith function; that is, their distinctive purpose or quality is intrinsically related to subjective human faith life. For example, the entire structure of a church building is characterized by its objective liturgical destination. Or consider the bread and wine of holy communion. In the faith life of the partakers, bread and wine are objects of faith as symbols of our Savior's crucified body and the blood he shed. As faith symbols they are a means of strengthening the believers' faith.

All of this would be without meaning if the reality of the bread and wine were closed off in the physico-chemical aspect of these entities. This is not the case. These entities display an object function in all post-physico-chemical aspects, including the aspect of faith.

We must thus make clear distinctions between the following:

1. The faith aspect of reality.
2. The subjective function of belief which human beings possess in this aspect.
3. The objective function which all temporal things possess in this aspect.
4. The content of our subjective faith.

Our subjective faith function is subject to God's revelation, as the norm for faith. Moreover, it issues from the religious root of our temporal life, namely, the heart, soul, or spirit of a person. Because of the fall into sin, the hearts of human beings turned away from God and the religious ground-motive of apostasy took hold of their faith and of their whole temporal life. Only the Spirit of God causes the rebirth of our hearts in Christ and radically reverses the direction of our temporal function of faith.

Abraham Kuyper was probably the first to regain for theology the scriptural insight that faith is a unique function of our inner life implanted in human nature at creation. Scholasticism had forsaken this insight completely under the influence of the unscriptural ground-motive of nature and grace. Roman Catholic scholastic thought identified faith with belief in Roman Catholic doctrine, arguing that faith was the supranatural gift of grace to the intellect, by means of which the intellect accepted the supranatural truths of salvation. Thus the faith function became a supranatural extension of the logical function found in human nature. Faith consisted in a purely intellectual acceptance, but by means of a higher light that transcended the limits of natural reason. The insight into the unique nature of the function of faith within the boundary [91] aspect of temporal reality had completely disappeared from this scholastic conception.

The Greek conception of human nature, which was shaped by the religious form-matter motive and which the scholastic thinkers had accepted, was the reason for this disappearance. In the light of this Greek conception, the scholastic thinkers viewed "human nature" as a composition of a "material body" and a "rational soul" (characterized by the logical function of thought). The soul was considered the immortal form of the material body. From the outset Greek philosophy depreciated faith, relegating it to the lower realm of sense perceptions. In the Greek view theoretical thought was the only road to truth; "belief" was merely subjective opinion [doxa] which did not rest on any reliable ground. When scholasticism accepted the Greek view of human nature, its only alternative was to transfer faith to a supranatural realm since in the Greek conception the faith function did not deserve a place in the "rational soul." The scholastics thus put faith completely outside of "human nature" by placing it in the "realm of grace."

Today's dialectical theologians (Barth, Brunner, and others) have not escaped from the unscriptural ground-motive of nature and grace despite the fact that their view of "natural life" is not Greek but more in line with humanism. They identify "nature" with "sin." As a result they can indeed acknowledge that the humanistic view of nature is radically sinful in its pride, while at the same time not replacing the humanistic view with a scriptural approach. Barth explicitly maintains that an absolute gap divides "nature" from "grace." For him the Christian faith, a divine gift of grace, does not have a single point of contact with "sinful human nature." He understands faith as the exclusive activity of God which occurs entirely without human input.

Kuyper's scriptural view of the faith function must be firmly upheld against all such departures from the revelation of the Word. The status of the faith function has a decisive effect on our view of the scope of the antithesis in temporal life and on our view of history. Consequently, we must investigate the nature and place of the function of faith in temporal life further.

Faith and Revelation

The connection between faith and history led us to examine more closely the place of the faith aspect in the entire order of all the aspects of reality. The exceptional place of faith in temporal life is misunderstood completely if its position as the boundary between time and eternity is not grasped. Faith is both the boundary aspect of temporal reality and the window facing eternity.

Faith cannot exist without God's revelation. By nature faith is [92] oriented to this revelation. In unspiritual and ambiguous use of language the term belief often has the meaning of "opinion" and "uncertain knowledge." (In a sentence like this, for instance: I believe that I have met you before.) This was the preferred usage in Greek philosophy, as we have already seen. True faith, however, is the exact opposite of uncertain opinion; for in the core of its meaning it is ultimate certainty in time with respect to the sure ground of one's existence, a certainty acquired when one is grasped in the heart of one's being by a revelation from God, the origin of all things. No matter how deeply it has fallen away from the truth, faith is always oriented to divine revelation. Therefore terms like "intuitive certainty" and "evidence" do not sufficiently describe the nucleus or core of faith.

Divine revelation connects the temporal with the eternal. God is the eternal one who is revealed to humankind in time. Christ Jesus, the Word become flesh, is the fullness of divine revelation. It is precisely this revelation that represents the great stumbling block for the arrogant thought of the apostate; humankind does not desire God's revelation because it threatens its pretended self-sufficiency. Humankind wants to hold God at an infinite theoretical distance in order to speculate about God in peace as the "most perfect Being," a "Being" who stands far removed from whatever touches temporal life. But God does not respect the theoretical, humanly contrived division of time and eternity. God is revealed in the midst of time. Sinners redeemed by Christ who hear this revelation pray: "Lord have mercy upon us. We have covered your world with hatred, anger, blood, and tears. And look, you are there and you see it all!" This is the revelation of God in his Word and in all the works of his hands! Revelation throws the fire of the antithesis upon the earth. It divides parents and children; it sets friend against friend; it drives rifts within the nation; it turns humankind against itself. "Do not think that I came to bring peace on earth." says the Savior; "I have not come to bring peace, but a sword" [Matthew 10:34].

The Analogies of Faith

It is the unbreakable connection between the revelation of God and the function of faith (along with the faith aspect in which this function works) that accords faith its position as the boundary between time and eternity. As such, the faith function is encompassed within the temporal world order. It belongs to temporal life just as the organic, psychical, logical, and lingual functions do. The structure of the faith aspect itself demonstrates that faith stands in time; like the structures of all the other aspects, its structure expresses a coherence with every other aspect of temporal reality. The aspect of faith is the last in the temporal order. The [93] others precede it. Nevertheless, it is related to what transcends time; namely, to the absolute ground and origin of all temporal life.

Thus the nuclear moment of the structure of the aspect of faith points beyond time to the religious root and origin of our temporal existence. At the same time, this nuclear moment is bound up inseparably with a whole series of moments that point back to the nuclear moments of all the earlier aspects. Consider, for example, faith's relation to the moral aspect. Faith in the real sense of the word is not possible without adoration or worship. Faith has a moral analogy in adoration which refers to love, to the core of the moral aspect. But adoration is naturally directed to God. If it is directed to a creature it becomes idolatrous. This orientation of faith also implies that magic – found among pagan nations as well as in medieval

Christendom and at the time of the Renaissance – is not really an authentic religious phenomenon. Certainly magic is impossible without some kind of faith. But as such it is directed at "controlling" natural forces with improper means. In essence therefore it is not a religious act directed to the adoration of a deity.

The structure of faith also exhibits a juridical analogy that points to the connection between the faith aspect and the jural aspect. The God who reveals himself to humankind has the right to adoration of faith. Certainly, this right is not a "right" in the original jural sense. It is not comparable with the right of buyers to their goods or the right of owners to their property. Rather, it is a juridical analogy within the meaning of faith which, like a moral analogy, points beyond time to the religious relation of dependence that characterizes the bond between God and humankind.

The scriptural reference to justification by faith is also a juridical analogy. This justification should never be understood in a technically legal sense but, like the other juridical analogies, its faith meaning can be grasped only through its coherence with the jural aspect of reality, which is one of the aspects that binds the aspect of faith to the temporal order. Divine revelation first of all directs itself to the heart, to the religious center of existence, and from there it moves to one's whole temporal life in the total coherence of its aspects. Thus God's righteousness, the meaning of which is given in faith, cannot be understood without reference to the jural aspect.

The structure of faith displays a further analogy with the aesthetic aspect whose nuclear kernel is beautiful harmony. In faith we find a moment of harmony through which humankind is brought into true communion with God. This is not aesthetic harmony. Indeed every attempt to conceive of faith aesthetically leads to its denaturing. But precisely because faith orients all the aspects of reality toward God, the aspect of faith is interwoven with the aesthetic aspect as well. [94]

Faith also reveals a structural, inner coherence with the economic aspect of reality. True faith is always accompanied by a readiness to sacrifice. Even among pagans sacrifice is an essential expression of faith life. True sacrificial readiness of the Christian faith rests upon humankind's evaluation of either temporal or eternal treasures. Christ's answer to the rich young man who asked, "Teacher, what good deed must I do, to have eternal life?" was this: "Go, sell what you possess and give to the poor, and you will have treasure in heaven; and come, follow me" [Matthew 19:16f]. Here the economic analogy within faith comes clearly into focus. All temporal possessions without Christ cannot be compared with the treasure guaranteed to us in the Kingdom of God. They must be sacrificed for the "pearl of great value," as Christ proclaimed in the parable [Matthew 13:45,46]. Again, the valuation that occurs in faith is not economic, but it is inseparably interwoven with economic valuation.

Also essential to the structure of faith is an analogy with the aspect of social intercourse. Inherent in faith is the believer's communion with God and with fellow believers. Fellowship in faith is of a spiritual nature. It cannot be reduced to intercourse in the social sense, which is subject to the uniquely social norms of politeness, tact, good manners, courtesy, respect, and so forth. But fellowship in faith does refer back to the nuclear moment of the social aspect.

A lingual analogy too is inherent in the structure of faith. In the core of its meaning the lingual aspect is symbolic signification accomplished through the use of signs (words, gestures, signals, and so on). Inherent in faith is a symbolism in which the revelation of God is "signified," made plain to us. The lingual analogy within the meaning of faith is not reducible to the original function of language. Holy Scripture signifies for us the true revelation of God's Word. This revelation can be understood only through faith guided by the Holy Spirit who operates in the religious ground-motive of God's Word-revelation. If we read Scripture with an unbelieving heart we may indeed grasp the lingual meaning of its words and sentences, but their true faith meaning *[geloofsbetekenis]* escapes us. Thus the exegesis of Scripture is not simply a linguistic matter that is the concern of expert philologists. It is not even a purely theological affair, which only presupposes solid scientific, theological knowledge. A Jewish rabbi reads Isaiah 53 differently than a believing Christian, and a modernistic theologian does not discern its prophecy of the atoning suffering and death of the Mediator. Whoever does not understand the religious ground-motive of Scripture lacks the key to faith knowledge. This biblical ground-motive is not a theoretical truth which one can understand scientifically. Rather, it is the all-controlling, dynamic power of God's Spirit which must open our hearts to what God [95] has to say to us, and which, with our hearts thus opened, must unveil the faith meaning of Holy Writ. But again, even though the lingual analogy lying within the structure of faith cannot be reduced to the original meaning of language, faith cannot exist without it. Exegeting Scripture may not be a merely linguistic matter, but it is not possible without linguistic analysis.

It is hardly necessary to explain the dangers of the "allegorical" exegesis of Scripture practiced by Gnostics and Greek church fathers in the first centuries of the Christian era. Allegorical exegetes are fond of quoting Paul: "the letter kills, the Spirit makes alive" [2 Corinthians 3:6]. But God bound his Word-revelation to Scripture, thereby linking faith meaning to lingual meaning. Those who sever this bond do not follow the guidance of God's Spirit but merely their own arbitrary views. As a result they cannot understand the faith meaning of Scripture.

Earlier we discussed the unbreakable bond between faith and history which we approached from the structure of the historical aspect. We established that faith, driven by a religious ground-motive, necessarily leads the opening process in historical development.

Viewed from the side of faith, we find that the structure of the faith aspect expresses a coherence with the historical aspect by means of a historical analogy. This analogy consists in the formation of faith in keeping with the line of development of divine revelation as the norm of faith. This formation occurs in the doctrines of faith. As living possessions of the church, these doctrines may not be confused with dogmatic theology, the scientific theory concerning doctrine. Only ecclesiastical authority based on the Word of God can establish and maintain the teachings of the Christian faith. Theological theories concerning these doctrines can never be equated with ecclesiastical authority, because science lacks authority with respect to doctrine, while the church lacks authority in the sphere of science.

The confusion of ecclesiastical dogma (articles of faith) with theological dogmatics (scientific theory about dogma) is a continual source of division and schism within the church. Ecclesiastical dogma has its own historical development that is closely linked to the historical power struggle between Christ's church and heresy – a struggle of life and death for maintenance of the scriptural ground-motive of the Christian religion. Heresy constantly arose in theological and philosophical circles that were susceptible to unscriptural ground-motives. As a result the church was forced to seek theological advice in formulating its dogma. But in such matters the key issue was always the upholding of the disputed articles of faith, not the binding imposition of a theological theory concerning them. [96]

Since the fundamental task of church doctrine is to give positive expression to the religious ground-motive of the Word of God, it is always accountable to that Word. But with respect to its faith aspect, divine Word-revelation itself maintains an inner coherence with history. Revelation displays a progression from the Old to the New Testament, and the New Testament itself is historically founded in the appearance of Christ. This progression, however, does not mean that in its function as the norm for faith God's revelation is a historical phenomenon. Such a misconception is the fundamental error of historicism, which denies every solid ground of truth by absolutizing the historical aspect of reality. Only when the inherent nature of faith and its inner coherence with the aspect of historical development are seen, does this error become fully transparent. The structure of the faith aspect displays an analogy with history, but this analogy – this "link" – maintains its faith character. God's Word-revelation maintains its eternal truth for faith, which in its core points beyond time. With respect to its temporal aspect as norm for faith, the divine Word-revelation displays a progressive disclosure – from Old to New Testament – of divine truth. This disclosure is historically founded. But also in this progressive character the divine norm for faith maintains its own nature in distinction from that of historical development.

Faith also exhibits a logical analogy in its structure, which guarantees faith's unbreakable connection with the aspect of logical thought. By nature faith is the sure knowledge that rests on spiritual discernment. It is not blind suggestion, for it is able to give account of its grounds. Thus faith cannot exist without a foundation in logical distinction, and yet faith's discernment of the truth in principle is different from logical conceptualization. It is oriented to the eternal matters that transcend human concepts, matters that, according to Paul, can only be "spiritually discerned" [1 Corinthians 2:14]. Spiritual discernment is possible only when one's heart is given in full religious surrender to the guidance of the Holy Spirit.

By nature the spiritually discerned, sure knowledge of faith is linked with firm trust. This moment expresses an analogy with the aspect of feeling within the faith aspect. The trust of faith is never without a feeling of security, but this trust is not itself an emotion, for emotions undergo changes and depend on moods. The trust of faith seeks its reliable ground not in feeling and in mood but in the Word of God alone.

All these traits assure the peculiar nature of a true life of faith, which expresses the link between faith and the organic aspect of human existence. The life of faith, which has a maturation of its own from childhood to adulthood, is inseparably joined with the organic development [97] of life. Nevertheless, it retains its own irreducible character and obeys its own law. It is spiritually nourished by prayer, by the preaching of the Word, and by the use of sacraments. "Spiritual nourishment" must be related to the developmental stages of faith life, as the apostle Paul indicated when he spoke of "feeding with milk" the children of faith who cannot yet bear "solid food" [1 Corinthians 3:2]. The relation, explicitly mentioned by Paul, between the faith function and the organic function also includes the intimate relation between faith and the senses: "faith comes from what is heard" [Romans 10:17]. Greek thinkers, who held that philosophic theory was the only true way of knowing God, would have considered this statement sufficient proof for their judgment on the worthlessness of faith for knowing the truth. For them the "rational soul" had to disengage itself from the deceptive appearance of reality produced by the senses.

In conclusion, the relation between faith and history, viewed from either side, places before us very difficult questions. We have shown that the life of faith is susceptible to disclosure and deepening, just as the historical life of culture is subject to a process of disclosure. In every aspect of reality prior to faith we can distinguish a closed and an open condition. An aspect is closed when it only displays relations which point back to earlier aspects of reality. An aspect is opened when those moments which point ahead to the later aspects of reality are also unfolded.

For example, the emotional life of an animal exists in a closed condition. Bound rigidly to the senses of the living organism, it cannot rise above the sensory level. In the case of human beings, on the other hand, one can speak of an opened emotional life, since logical feeling, historical feeling, lingual feeling, aesthetic feeling, juridical feeling, etc. manifest a relation between the aspect of feeling and subsequent aspects.

At this point in our inquiry two problems immediately present themselves. In the first place, how are we to conceive of an opening process with respect to the life of faith? How are we to think of faith in a closed condition, when the aspect of faith, the last aspect, stands at the border of temporal reality? No later aspects follow it. And related to this problem is the second question: how is it possible that genuine cultural disclosure takes place under the direction of an apostate faith that is governed by an idolatrous ground-motive? What influence does apostate faith have on the manner of cultural disclosure in historical development? Not until these two extremely important questions have been answered will we understand the significance of the antithesis between the Christian religion and apostate ground-motives for historical development. [98]

Faith in a Closed Culture

Let us briefly set the context for the first problem. Cultural disclosure in history is led by faith. Like any other aspect, the historical aspect of reality is either closed or opened. In a closed state an aspect reveals itself only in its inner coherence with earlier aspects; it is therefore rigidly bound to them. The inner connections with the later aspects of reality unfold by means of an opening process which deepens the entire meaning of the earlier aspect.

It is beyond doubt that primitive cultures, in their strictly closed condition of undifferentiation, are wholly in the grip of a particular faith. Whoever studies the life of primitive pagan peoples is always struck by the close connection between their entire society and its religion and conceptions of faith. How is it possible that also in this situation faith gives guidance to life while this guidance does not lead to real disclosure in the cultural and later aspects of society? Can we speak of a closed and open state also with respect to the aspect of faith?

Christian theology has always distinguished between the general revelation of God found in "nature" (meaning the whole of God's work of creation) and the general and special Word-revelation. While it may seem reasonable to look to the revelation in "nature" for our reference point in discussing the specific sense of the "closed" structure of the faith function, we must be attentive to the original relation between God's "natural revelation" in all the works of his hands and the general Word-revelation.

By creating the world, God revealed himself in creation both in its religious root (the heart of a person) and in its temporal order and coherence. But from the very beginning the revelation of God in all the works of his hands was upheld and explained by the Word-revelation which, even after the fall, directed itself not to a few persons in particular but to the whole of humankind. An independent line of development in Word-revelation which was no longer directed to the whole of humankind began first with Abraham. Of this "special revelation" the people of Israel became the provisional separate bearer until the appearance of the Word itself in the flesh.

In this Word-revelation God speaks to humankind, and humankind is called to listen in faith. For only by faithfully listening to this Word of God can the true meaning of God's revelation in the "nature of creation" and in "all the works of his hands" disclose itself. The fall from God began at the point where humankind no longer listened to the Word, for in turning its heart away from the Word it closed off the human faith function to the voice of God.

As a result of the fall, God's revelation in creation, but especially his [99] revelation in the heart of humankind, took on the character of a judgment. Where the heart shut itself in and turned from God there also the function of faith closed itself off from the light of God's Word. Nevertheless, the faith function still remained in the boundary position between time and eternity. According to its very nature it remained oriented to the firm Foundation of truth and life who revealed himself in creation. After the fall, however, humankind sought this firm foundation within creation itself by idolatrously absolutizing what is, in fact, relative and nonself-sufficient. Humankind's direction became apostate, and natural faith became unbelief before the Word of God.

By the "closed structure of faith," then, I mean the ultimate extent of faith's capacity for apostasy: faith fallen to its lowest point. In the light of the revelation of God's Word this low point can be detected in the order of creation itself. It is to be found at that point where apostate faith prevents the disclosure of both the historical aspect and the later normative aspects. If this is indeed the maximum extent or low point in the apostate direction of faith, then we have arrived at the answer to our first question, whether we can speak of a closed and an open condition of faith. It is important for one's view of history to gain insight into the low point in the apostasy of faith, for only in terms of that point can one understand primitive cultures. In its closed structure, faith can never be the starting point for a positive development and opening of the faith function implanted in humankind at creation. Rather, the closed condition of faith is the ultimate extent of its decline, degeneration, and deterioration. Yet it is possible that such a closed structure may function as the starting point for disclosure in the process of apostasy. This issue we will discuss later.

The starting point for positively opening and deepening the life of faith to the fullness of the Christian faith must be sought in the structure of the faith function as it was originally created in humankind. It must be uncovered in its original openness before the divine revelation of the Word. Because of the fall, this positive disclosure is possible only through God's Spirit, who in grace opens a person's heart. The Spirit does not create a new faith function in a person but opens the fallen function of faith by radically transforming faith's direction. This is a conversion dependent upon the rebirth of the heart, a conversion that fallen humankind itself can never bring about.

If even at the fullest extent of apostasy the faith function always operates within the structure of the aspect of faith as such, and if in apostasy faith still remains bound by its law – namely, divine revelation – then the question arises as to what principle of divine revelation continues to normatively control even the most apostate faith, free of all human invention and arbitrariness. As I mentioned above, this revelational principle may be found in the temporal creation order itself under the light of God's Word, for the closed structure of an aspect [100] is always characterized by its rigid and inert dependence upon the earlier aspects of reality. On a closed level of historical development all cultural life is bound statically to the emotional and organic aspects of reality. Accordingly, the apostate faith that grips a primitive culture deifies the mysterious and closed "forces of nature" that control not only life and death but fertility, sterility, and in general the entire biological and sensual aspects of primitive society. Because of its rigid ties to emotional drives, its belief in gods is frequently founded on fear, though one must certainly not attempt to explain the origin of primitive religion in terms of fear. A similar impossibility is the attempt of the French sociologist Emile Durkheim to explain the origin of primitive religion from the standpoint of social organization.[1] It is the uncomprehended revelation of God that fills humankind with fear and trembling.

Deifying the closed forces of nature chains the normative functions of human existence to "irrational nature." The "night of nature" blankets a primitive community. Through the deification of an endless stream of life, the Greek matter motive of the old nature religions filled primitive Greeks with a fear of the blind fate of death *(Anangke)*. Inevitably and unpredictably fate struck them and cut off every hope for a better future. In that situation, the function of faith did not have a revelational principle for a norm other than the deity which revealed itself immanently within the "closed forces of nature."

A closed revelational principle becomes a curse and a judgment for humankind in the degeneration of its faith. Nevertheless, this principle is still

---

[1] The reference is to Emile Durkheim, *The Elementary Forms of Religious Life,* trans. Joseph Swain (New York: Free Press, 1965).

grounded in the divine creation order and thus stands above human invention and arbitrariness. Therefore the revelation of the Word, which finds its fulfillment in Christ Jesus, does not eliminate a closed revelational principle (God indeed reveals himself also in the forces of nature). Rather, the Word-revelation uncovers the true meaning of the closed revelational principle by relating it to the ground-motive and the root-unity of divine self-revelation: creation, fall, and redemption through Jesus Christ.

Primitive faith often gives positive shape to the closed revelational principle – the revelation of God in the forces of nature – in the most fantastic ways. When people's hearts and faith are closed to revelation, they begin to interpret the divine revelational principle, the norm for faith autonomously. Deifying uncomprehended forces of nature stimulates their imagination in many ways; people such as these spin wild and barbaric myths around their primitive nature gods. These myths often strike the "enlightened" Westerner as strongly pathological. To add to their "sense of superiority," Westerners [101] prefer to "explain" primitive mythologies in a rational, natural-scientific way. But such attempts at rational explanation are utterly unsound. Goethe already ridiculed them in his *Faust* when he let the "enlightened" thinker, filled with powerless indignation over someone's faith in demons and ghosts, say these priceless words:

> Ihr seid noch immer da? Nein, das ist unerhört.
> Verschwindet doch! Wir haben ja aufgeklärt!
> You still are there! Oh no! That's without precedent.
> Please go! Have we not brought enlightenment?[1]

Over against the enlightened Westerner we hear the word of our Lord: "But this kind never comes out except by prayer and fasting" [Matthew 17:21]. Indeed, whoever holds that modern science has radically eliminated the belief in natural demons has forgotten that a whole array of "modern" demons stands ready to occupy the vacant places in today's apostate faith. Superstition is stronger than natural science; its origin lies not in the mind but in the religious root of human existence alienated from the divine revelation of God's Word.

Faith, as we saw, is in a "closed condition" when it is at the uttermost limits of its apostasy from the revelation of the Word. At that point it has fallen to a primitive deification of the uncomprehended forces of nature that control the sensual and biotical aspects of society. In a closed condition of faith humans lack any awareness that they transcend the inorganic, plant, and animal kingdoms.

Example: Mana Belief

The disintegration and dispersion of a sense of human personality, present among many primitive, pagan peoples expresses itself in a particular way in the so-called mana beliefs. The well-known ethnologist Robert

---
1 Goethe's *Faust,* Walter Kaufmann, lines 4158-4159.

Codrington first called this belief to the attention of the scientific world in his book on the Melanesians (1891).[1] Since then it has been shown that the mana belief exists under different names among various primitive peoples across the face of the earth (also in "Neo-Guinea"). From the lively debate that ensued after its discovery one can distill these tentative results: the mana faith is characterized by a peculiar fluidity, by a strange interflux of the "natural" and the "supernatural," and of the "personal" and the "impersonal." Mana is a mysterious life force. It rises above the familiar, [102] everyday face of life and embodies itself fragmentarily in mythical figures which can be either plants, animals, spirits, a whole clan or tribe, or unusually shaped inorganic things (such as rocks, stones, and so on).

Totemism is markedly influenced by mana belief. In it an animal or plant is worshiped as the male or female ancestor of a clan or family. The clan members identify themselves with the totem; they are eagles, or kangaroos, or date palms, and so forth. This identification clearly shows how diffuse and dispersed the awareness of personality is in a closed structure of faith. Here again the truth of the unbreakable relation between self-knowledge and knowledge of God comes to the fore.

Apparently many primitive peoples entertained a vague notion of a highest deity alongside a belief that bewilderingly revolved around a mysterious life force. This deity had no direct dealings with human beings and it was not worshiped in an organized fashion. Should we nevertheless understand it as a remnant of the general revelation of the Word among these peoples? One should be cautious at this point, for information is often too vague and too contradictory to warrant such a conclusion. In any case, the primitive conception of a "highest god" had no discernible influence upon primitive society. The truly operative beliefs were indeed in a closed state.

Disclosure of an Apostate Faith

Now we turn to our second main problem: the disclosure of faith in an apostate direction. How are we to understand this kind of disclosure? How is it possible? A discussion of this problem is of eminent importance for our idea of historical development, since the latter always takes place under the guidance of faith.

It cannot be denied that an apostate faith of pagan peoples who eventually became leaders in world history underwent an opening process after an initial period of primitive and diffuse "nature belief." This process was directly related to the fact that such peoples went beyond their more or less primitive cultural conditions. Among the Greeks, for instance, we observe a clear transition from originally primitive nature religions, which

---

[1] See Robert Codrington, *The Melanesians: Studies in their Anthropology and Folklore* (New Haven: HRAF Press, 1957).

worshiped the impersonal and formless stream of life, to a culture religion, in which the gods became idealized cultural powers of personal, superhuman form and shape. In this process of development and opening, apostate religion transcended the primitive belief in nature and oriented itself to God's revelation in the normative aspects of temporal reality. Giving cultural form to its idolatrous faith, fallen humankind conceived of its gods in the shape of idealized, personal deities. Led by this unfolding of faith, the norm of historical [103] differentiation began to work itself out in Greek cultural development. This in turn was accompanied by an individualization of culture, which took place in a more encompassing and truly national cultural community.

The famous German scholar Ernst Cassirer called attention to this state of affairs from a quite different point of view.[1] He observed that in primitive societies the whole completely swallows up the individuality of its members. But as soon as the belief in personal gods arises, individuals begin to free themselves from this absorption into society. At last the individual receives a certain independence and "personal face" with respect to the life of the clan and the tribe. Moreover, along with the trend toward the individual arises a new tendency toward the universal, for more embracing and differentiated societal entities rise above the narrower unities of the tribe and the group. Personal culture gods were indeed the first national gods of the Greeks, and as such they created a common Hellenic consciousness. As the universal gods of the Greek tribes they were bound neither to a single place or region nor to a specific place of worship. Thus the liberation of personal consciousness and the elevation of national consciousness took place here in a single disclosure of apostate faith. Indeed, an opening of faith in apostasy from divine revelation of the Word can be understood only as a process whereby human beings become conscious of themselves in their apostasy. The structure of the faith function has no moments that are related to later aspects of reality for, as we have seen, the faith aspect is the last one in the temporal order of aspects. As a result, the sole option for apostate faith, in order to achieve disclosure, is to reach to the apostate religious root of human existence – namely, human self-consciousness.

When humankind becomes conscious of the supremacy of its "rational" functions over the "irrational" forces of nature, faith in its apostate direction rises above the rigid confines of primitive faith in nature. Seeing itself and its gods in the light of the "rational" or normative aspects of temporal reality, humankind takes science, culture, art, and morality as its objects of deification. It is only in this process of acquiring a self-awareness in

---

1   Cassirer's discussion of this point is in volume two of *The Philosophy of Symbolic Forms,* intro. Charles Hendel, trans. Ralph Manheim (New Haven: Yale University Press, 1955).

faith that fallen humanity discovers the freedom it has to be engaged in designing the form of its historical future in a constant struggle with the power of tradition. When faith prevails in a closed state, tradition within a society remains omnipotent.

Example: Egypt
Inscriptions in Egyptian pyramids are probably the oldest existing records that document the gradual development of apostate faith from a [104] closed condition to a deification of the jural and moral functions of the human personality. These inscriptions show how belief in immortality increasingly accentuates the ethical conception of the human ego. For example, in the older texts, Osiris, god of the dead, was still a half animal who, by magical formulas, was implored to accept the souls of the dead. But gradually this god was conceived of as the judge of good and evil. Increasingly, the power of magic was replaced by a plea, made before the divine judge, in which the soul defends its right for immortality.

The outcome of this development is as follows: guided by an apostate disclosure of faith, a process of historical opening takes place which also moves in an apostate direction. As a result we must ask: how does historical opening in the direction of apostasy reveal itself? This will be treated in more detail in the next subsection.

Thus far we have seen how it is possible for the life of faith to open itself in a direction away from revelation. Our task now is to investigate how the process of an opening of culture takes place in historical development under the guidance of apostate faith.

Disclosure of an Apostate Culture
The apostate direction of faith always reveals itself in deification and absolutization of certain aspects of creation. If apostate faith leads the opening of culture, then it breaks the norm of cultural economy, which results in a sharp disharmony in cultural life.

Let us briefly summarize our earlier discussions dealing with the norm of cultural economy. Searching for a criterion to distinguish a healthy progressive direction from a reactionary direction in historical development, I pointed out that God subjected historical development to genuine norms. These norms or measures of assessment must be discovered from the complete coherence of the divine world-order; that is, they must be found by investigating the way in which the cultural-historical aspect is connected with all other aspects of temporal reality. We noted that in a closed and primitive condition culture displays an undifferentiated character. It is utterly closed off from fruitful cultural intercourse with nations that are included in the process of world history. Tradition is all-powerful in such closed cultures, and the entire communal life of primitive peoples is in the grasp of a pagan belief in nature which in its closed state makes a true opening of culture impossible.

We also found that the first criterion for detecting a genuine opening of culture lies in the norm of differentiation. It appeared that this norm entails nothing else but the principle of sphere sovereignty, as it finds its foundation in the divine order of creation, because God created everything after its kind. Specifically, we found that the principle of sphere sovereignty reveals itself in its historical aspect [105] through the norm of cultural differentiation which holds that a true opening of culture is possible only when it unfolds itself into the differentiated spheres of the state, the church, science, art, industry, commerce, and so forth. This process of differentiation enables each societal sphere to reveal its own inner nature and it allows each to have its own sphere of power in history. Yet, we have also noticed that this process of differentiation, in accordance with the order established by God, can only unfold when the norm of cultural economy is observed. This norm brings to expression the inner coherence between the historical aspect and the economical aspect of reality.

This implies that every excessive expansion of the power of a given differentiated sphere (such as that of science of the power of the state) conflicts with harmonious cultural development and occurs at the expense of the healthy growth of other spheres. Because it incites a reaction from the threatened spheres, cultural disharmony avenges itself in the world judgment of history. At this point we can pull our argument together: the excessive expansion of power within a given cultural sphere always occurs under the guidance of an apostate faith which absolutizes and deifies such a cultural sphere.

Example: The Enlightenment

Consider, for instance, the Enlightenment of the eighteenth century, when a humanistic faith in the omnipotence of the modern science of nature dominated western culture. The Enlightenment ideal was to control reality by discovering those laws of nature which determine the course of phenomena in a strictly closed chain of cause and effect. The method of the new science of nature was foisted on the other sciences. It consisted in analyzing complex phenomena into their "simplest elements" whose relations could be determined by mathematical equations.

One can hardly deny that the natural sciences developed immensely under the influence of Enlightenment humanism. But behind the investigations stood a religiously dynamic force: the humanistic science ideal. It influenced even Christian scientists, although some – think of Pascal – strongly protested against the overextension of natural-scientific methods.

The historical influence of the science ideal, however, was not limited to the cultural sphere of science. Driven by faith, the ideal reached out to every other cultural area. "Enlightenment" through advance in science was the slogan of the day. All "progress" of humanity was expected from a rational explanation by science. Similarly, every aspect of human society was viewed in terms of the "natural-scientific method." Society itself required dissection into its "simplest elements": individuals. The new method led to an individualistic view of human society that no longer had an eye for the inner nature of different societal collectivities, such as the church, the state, and the family. Moreover, morality became [106] thoroughly individualistic, built on the superficial ethical principle of utility. Enlightenment faith entered the churches in the form of "modernism," devastating Christian faith wherever it managed to gain influence. In economic life it enthroned the *homo eonomicus*, the fictitious person motivated exclusively by its economic self-interest. Even art did not escape the influence of this new faith; it was strait-jacketed into the rigid, rationalistic forms of "classicism." In short, healthy, harmonious development of culture was prevented by the impact of natural science which went far beyond its limits at the expense of other spheres of western civilization.

There is indeed another side to our assessment of the Enlightenment faith. We would be entirely remiss if we failed to recognize its great significance for the unfolding of western civilization. The Enlightenment was formative in history and active in opening culture beyond the scope of natural science and technology based on that science. With respect to economics it opened the way for developing individual initiative which, in spite of its originally individualistic emphasis, greatly advanced industrial life. With respect to the legal order it pleaded untiringly not only for the establishment of the rights of individual persons, which form the foundation of today's civil law, but also for the elimination of undifferentiated juridical relations that treated parts of governmental authority as "commercial objects." The Enlightenment also laid many cornerstones for the modern constitutional state under the rule of law *(Rechtsstaat)*. In the area of criminal law it contributed to the introduction of more humane treatment, to the abolishment of the torture rack, and to the elimination of witch trials. Without ceasing it pleaded for freedom of speech and freedom of religion. In all these areas the Enlightenment could contribute to authentic historical formation only because it followed the path of genuine cultural disclosure. Its revolutionary ideas, in their actualization, had to be adjusted to the divine ordinances. In its power struggle against tradition, these ideas were bent under the pressure of the norm of historical continuity, with the result that they lost their moments of subjective arbitrariness. The Enlightenment also had to adapt itself to the influence of the Reformation which, even though it played only a secondary role, still asserted itself in historical development.

But the dark side of the Enlightenment contribution to the disclosure of western culture consists in the dissolving impact of its individualism and rationalism which resulted in a severe disharmony of western society. The "judgment" in world history was executed over the Enlightenment. It elicited the reaction of historicism with its overestimation of human communal life. However, a truly biblical view of history must not, in its battle against Enlightenment ideas, seek [107] accommodation with historicism which opposed the Enlightenment in a reactionary manner. A truly scriptural view of history cannot deny the fruitful and beneficial elements of the historical influence of the Enlightenment. Like the sound elements of the historicistic view of reality, they must be valued as the fruits of common grace.

Every cultural movement, however inimical to God in its apostasy, must be properly acknowledged for its historical merits to the extent that it has indeed contributed to cultural disclosure – a matter that must be assessed in the light of the divinely posited norms for the development of culture. For a truly scriptural view of history cannot be bigoted and narrowminded. It shares neither the optimistic faith in a rectilinear progress of humankind nor the pessimistic belief in the imminent decline of the West. Behind the great process of cultural development it recognizes the battle in the root of creation between the civitas Dei and the civitas terrena, the Kingdom of God in Christ Jesus and the kingdom of darkness. It knows that this battle was decided at Golgotha and that the victory of the Kingdom of God is sure. It knows that the great antithesis between the ground-motive of the divine revelation of the Word and the ground-motive of the apostate spirit operates in the power struggle for the future of western civilization. It knows too that God uses the apostate powers in culture to further unfold the potentials which he laid in the creation.

Through blood and tears, through revolution and reaction, the process of historical development moves on to the day of judgment. Christians are called, in the name of him to whom all authority in heaven and on earth was given, to take part in the great power struggle of history with the commitment of their entire personalities and all their powers. The outcome is sure, and this gives the Christian, no matter what turn particular events may take, a peace and rest that befit a conqueror.

The Radical Challenge of the Word of God

We have seen that the ground-motive of the Christian religion – creation, fall, and redemption through Jesus Christ – is a spiritual dynamic which transforms one's entire view of reality at its root as soon as it lays full claim on one's attitude to life and thought. We have also seen that the Christian ground-motive molds our view of history, for it offers us a firm criterion to distinguish truly progressive and disguised reactionary trends. We have recognized the all-embracing significance of the Christian ground-motive for the burning issues of the "new age." We have understood how this ground-motive unmasks today's dangerous community [108] ideology and its totalitarian tendencies. We have noted that the Christian ground-motive posits the unshakable firmness of God's creation order in opposition to the so-called dynamic spirit of our times which refuses to recognize the existence of firm foundations for life and thus sees everything "in terms of being in motion." We have come to know the divine radicality of this ground-motive that touches the religious root of our lives. We have, I hope, come to realize that the Christian ground-motive permits no dualistic ambiguity in our lives, no "limping with two different opinions" [1 Kings 18:21].

Consider the cost of taking this radically scriptural Christianity seriously. Ask yourself which side you must join in the tense spiritual battle of our times. Compromise is not an option. A middle-of-the-road stance is not possible. Either the ground-motive of the Christian religion works radically in our lives or we serve other gods. If the antithesis is too radical for you, ask yourself whether a less radical Christianity is not like salt that has lost its savor. I state the antithesis as radically as I do so that we may again experience the full double-edged sharpness and power of God's Word. You must experience the antithesis as a spiritual storm that strikes lightning into your life and that clears the sultry air. If you do not experience it as a spiritual power requiring the surrender of your whole heart, then it will bear no fruit in your life. Then you will stand apart from the great battle the antithesis always instigates. You yourself cannot wage this battle. Rather, the spiritual dynamic of the Word of God wages the struggle in us and pulls us along despite our "flesh and blood."

My effort to deepen our awareness of the scope of the antithesis is directed even at fully committed Christians. I believe that if Christianity had held fast to the ground-motive of God's Word, and to it alone, we never would have witnessed the divisions and schisms that have plagued the church of Christ. The source of all fundamental schisms and dissensions is the sinful inclination of the human heart to weaken the integral and radical meaning of the divine Word. The truth is so intolerable for fallen humanity that when it does take hold of people, they still seek to escape its total claim in every possible way.

The creation motive alone already strikes this fallen world so awesomely that humankind ought to see itself in utter desolation before God, from whom it can never escape. Think of the powerful words of Psalm 139:

> Whither can I go from thy Spirit?
> Or whither can I flee from thy presence?
> If I ascend to heaven, thou art there;
> If I make my bed in Sheol, behold, thou art there. [109]

Human beings cannot sustain one atom of their existence before the Creator as their own property. Nowhere in all of creation can they find a certainty or refuge which might provide a hiding place for their sinful existence independent of God. They simply cannot bear this.

The threefold ground-motive of the Word is an indivisible unity. When one takes away from the integral character of the creation motive, the radical sense of fall and redemption is no longer understood. Likewise, whoever tampers with the radical meaning of fall and redemption cannot experience the full power and scope of the creation motive. [110]

Chapter 5

The Great Synthesis

Early Setting
When the Christian ground-motive entered the Hellenistic, late-Greek world of thought, its indivisible unity was threatened on every side. Already in the first centuries of its history, the Christian church fought a battle of life and death in order to keep its ground-motive free from the influences of the Greek ground-motive and the ones that later intermingled with Greek religion in its contact with the different near-eastern religions, notably Persian Zoroastrianism.

All of these nonbiblical ground-motives were of a dualistic nature, divided against themselves. Torn by an inner conflict, they knew neither God the Creator, the absolute origin of all things, nor humankind in the root of its being. This is the case because they opted for an apostate direction.

We have discussed the Greek form-matter motive at some length in previous chapters. It originated in an unreconciled conflict within Greek religious consciousness between the older nature religion and the newer culture religion of the Olympian gods.

We have demonstrated in an earlier context how the *matter motive* served as the spiritual motive power in the older religions of nature. The religions deified the eternal flux of life as it originated from "mother earth." This stream of life was impersonal and without any form. Whatever was born from it in an individual form and shape was doomed to decline, in order to allow the cyclic movement of birth, maturation, passing away, and rebirth to continue in the whole of "nature" without interruption. In this process of the "machine-work of births" no rational calculable order governs since it is controlled by *blind fate*, by the dreadful *Anangkē*.

As we have seen, the *form motive*, by contrast, finds it origin in the younger culture religion of the Greeks, which deified the cultural powers of Greek society. Since this motive oriented itself to the cultural aspect of temporal reality (which is characterized by the shaping of a given material according to a free rational design), these deities became the gods of form, measure, and harmony. They left "mother earth" from whose womb the eternally flowing stream of life originates. They acquired their seat on the mountain of Olympus where they were raised to become radiant form gods with a super-sensory (invisible) form and shape, elevated above the fate of mortals, free from all influences of the earthly matter principle. But then, as mere culture gods, they did not have any power over the fate of mortals. The matter motive of the older religion of life remains the opposing power directed against the form motive.

The ground-motive which governed the entire Greek world of ideas thus exhibited two faces which, as it were, looked at each other with hostility. The *matter motive* had its foundation in the deification and absolutization of organic development (the biotic aspect of life of created reality); the *form motive*, by contrast, had its foundation in a deification of the *cultural aspect* of created reality, in a deification of human culture.

The spiritual momentum of this internally divided ground-motive led mature Greek thought to accept a twofold origin of the world. Even when Greek thinkers acknowledged the existence of a cosmic order originating through a divine design and plan, they still categorically denied a divine *creation*. Greeks believed that whatever came into existence arose merely through a divine activity of giving form to an already present and formless matter. They conceived of divine formation only in terms of human cultural activity. The [111] "rational deity" was merely a "heavenly architect" who formed a given material according to a free design. This deity was not able to forestall the blind, autonomous activity of the matter principle.

A dualistic conception of human nature was directly related to this dualistic idea of divine nature. Yet, as we have already seen, a person's self-knowledge depends upon knowledge of God. Just as the rational deity found the autonomy of the matter principle over against itself, human nature found within itself the basic duality of a "rational soul" and an earthly "material body." According to the Greek understanding the actual center of the rational soul was theoretical thought, which was divine in character. The soul was the invisible "form" of human existence, and in its theoretical thought capacity it was immortal. By contrast, the material body, the "matter" of a person's being, was subject to the stream of life and blind fate.

In the Hellenistic period it was not difficult to combine the Greek ground-motive with the dualistic ground-motives of the near-eastern religions with which the Greeks had already made acquaintance. The ground-motive of the Persian Zoroastrian religion consisted of a battle between a divine principle of light and an evil principle of darkness. Thus one could easily identify the Greek form motive with the Zoroastrian motive of light and the Greek matter motive with the evil principle of darkness.

The Great Synthesis

The Temptation of Dualism

The Christian church realized the enormous danger which the Greek-Zoroastrian ground-motive posed for the pure ground-motive of divine revelation. In its life-and-death struggle against this motive the church formulated the doctrine of the divine essential unity of the Father and the Son (the Word or *Logos*) and soon afterwards the doctrine of the trinity of Father, Son, and Holy Spirit. This determination of the basic doctrinal position of the Christian church was not intended as a scientific-theological theory but as a necessarily imperfect formulation of the living confession of the Body of Christ, in which the pure ground-motive sought expression. Specifically, these creedal formulations broke the dangerous influence of Gnosticism during the early centuries of the Christian church, so that a purely scriptural point of departure for theology was restored.

Under the influence of the Greek and near-eastern dualism the unbreakable unity of the ground-motive of the Divine Word-revelation, that of creation, fall, and redemption through Christ Jesus and the communion of the Holy Spirit, was broken apart. A schism was introduced between creation and redemption, between the God of the Old Testament and the God of the New Testament. In the spirit of Greek philosophy the speculative theoretical knowledge of God, the *gnosis*, [112] was elevated above the faith of the Christian congregation.

Particularly through maintaing the unbreakable unity of the Old and the New Testament the Christian church during this period managed under God's guidance to conquer the religious dualism accompanying this gnosticism in its attempt to create a split between *creation* and *redemption*. Yet, we shall see how the Greek ground-motive in a hidden way continued to exert its influence within Christian thinking.[1]

We have seen how the Christian church, as soon as the gospel entered into the the Greek world of thought, got involved in a battle of life and death against the ground-motive of Greek culture, which threatened to overpower the biblical ground-motive.

Under the influence of the Greek and Eastern dualism the unbreakable unity of the ground-motive of the Divine Word-revelation, that of creation, fall and redemption through Christ Jesus and the communion of the Holy Spirit, was broken apart. A schism was introduced between creation and redemption, between the God of the Old Testament and the God of the New Testament. In the spirit of Greek philosophy the speculative theoretical knowledge of God, the *gnosis*, was elevated above the faith of the christian congregation. This was the dangerous effect of the so-called Christian

---

1 *General Editor's note*: The subsequent five paragraphs, owing to the nature of the original series of articles, partially overlap with the preceding three.

Gnosticism. The apostle John had already been forced to warn against one of the forerunners of "Christian Gnosticism," the sect of the Nicolaitans.

But also outside this cricle, amongst the so-called apostolic church fathers, who had set out to defend the Christian religion against Greek thought, the influence of the Greek ground-motive was evident.

The Greek church fathers in particular conceived of creation as being the result of the divine activity of giving form to matter. Therefore, since they could not consider matter itself to be divine, they did not want to fully acknowledge that the Word, through which all things were created and which became flesh in Jesus Christ, is synonymous with God. Accordingly, they degraded the Word (the *Logos*) to a "semigod" who, as "mediator" of creation, stood between God and creature. And also in this context the speculative theoretical knowledge of God, elaborated in a philosophical theology, was positioned above the faith of the church community.

Accordingly the Christian religion, in a precarious fashion, was seen as a higher moral theory. Christ's atoning sacrifice on the cross was pushed to the background in favor of the idea of a "divine teacher" who advocated a higher moral walk of life.

In this way the Christian religion, through the operation of the Greek ground-motive, was robbed of its indivisible and radical character.

Under the mask of a higher theoretical knowledge of God a view was introduced which superficialized the Word-revelation into a "higher ethical doctrine."

Neither creation, nor the fall, nor redemption were understood in their scriptural meaning. Even after the Christian church established the doctrine of the Trinity the influence of the Greek religious ground-motive continued in the thought of the church fathers.

Augustine
The orthodox direction of Christian thought reached a high point in Augustine. Augustine placed his stamp on Christian reflection until well into the thirteenth century and even afterwards he maintained a considerable influence. The ground-motive of his thought was undoubtedly scriptural. After his conversion his powerful, talented intellect increasingly drew from this source. However, the Christian theology of his day was confronted with philosophical problems which cried out for solutions. Insofar as the church fathers had been philosophically educated – Augustine very much so – they had come to absorb the Greek way of thought. They had appropriated its views of cosmic order, [113] human nature, and human society. The church fathers attempted to rid these conceptions of their pagan elements and to adapt them to the Christian religion. However, they failed to see that these elements were rooted in

The Great Synthesis

a pagan ground-motive. They failed to understand that this ground-motive controlled not merely a few components but its entire foundation and elaboration. In other words, they failed to see that because of its radical character the ground-motive of the Christian religion demands an *inner reformation* of one's scientific view of the world order and of temporal life. Instead of *reformation* they sought *accommodation*; they sought to adapt pagan thought to divine revelation of the Word.

This adaptation laid the basis for *scholasticism*, which even up to the present has continued to impede the development of a truly reformational direction in Christian life and thought. Scholasticism seeks a *synthesis* between Greek thought and the Christian religion. It was thought that such a synthesis could be successfully achieved if philosophy, with its Greek basis, were to be made subservient to Christian theology.

Here again Augustine played a key role. He denied the autonomy of philosophy, that is, its independence with respect to the Christian faith. For he saw clearly that the Christian faith must give guidance also to philosophic thought, for without this guidance it would be dominated by an apostate faith. As such this idea was utterly scriptural. However, Augustine's search for accommodation and synthesis led him to work this out in an unacceptable way. Philosophy, not intrinsically reformed, was not allowed to develop itself independently but had to be subjected to the control of dogmatic theology. Philosophical questions could be treated only within a theological frame of reference. Augustine attempted to christianize philosophy along these lines, as if theological theory and the Christian religion were identical.

One cannot deny that Augustine was influenced by the Greek conception of contemplative theory, which presented itself as the path toward the true knowledge of God. Earlier, Aristotle had elevated metaphysics (philosophical theory of first principles, which culminated in "theology" or the philosophical knowledge of God) to the "queen of the sciences." She was to "enslave" all other sciences, who would never be allowed to contradict her. Augustine merely replaced this Greek notion of "philosophical theology" with Christian theology, as the scientific theory concerning Christian doctrines.

Augustine did accept the ground-motive of revelation in its purity. But he could not develop it radically because the Greek ground-motive, transmitted by Greek philosophy, placed a firm hold upon his entire worldview. For example, he read the creation account with Greek eyes. According to him "the earth without form or void" signified still unformed [114] "matter," although in opposition to the Greek notion he believed that this matter was created by God. Likewise, he conceived of the relation between the "soul" and the "body" within the framework of the Greek ground-motive. For him the soul was an immortal substance characterized by the faculty of theoretical thought. The body was merely a "material vehicle" of the rational soul. The divine revelation of the religious root-unity of human existence was thus again undermined by Greek dualism.

Especially in his doctrine of "original sin" the Greek matter motive exerted a dangerous practical impact on Augustine's entire view of life. For Augustine "original sin" was sexual desire. Marriage was merely a therapeutic device to control unbounded lust after the flesh. Unfortunately, this view has crippled Christian marital ethics for centuries. As a rule, Christians did not see that original sin is seated in the heart and not in a temporal, natural drive. The sexual drive was viewed as sinful, and sexual abstinence was applauded as a higher Christian virtue. But this asceticism is not scriptural; its lineage reaches back to Plato, who explained sensual drives in terms of the ominous principle of matter. At the same time, Augustine did defend the scriptural teaching of the radical fall. He understood the depravity that lies at the root of human nature.

The example of Augustine clearly demonstrates how even in a great father of the church the spiritual power of the Greek ground-motive worked as a dangerous counterforce to the ground-motive of revelation. It is not right to conceal this out of love and respect for Augustine. Insight into matters where Augustine should not be followed need not detract from our love and respect for him. It is an urgent matter that we, openly and regardless of who is involved, choose sides in the issue: *reformation* or *accommodation*. This question dominates Christian life today. Only the ground-motive of God's revelation can furnish us with the appropriate answer.

The Roman Catholic Ground-Motive

The effort to bridge the foundations of the Christian religion and Greek thought had to lead over time to the further attempt to find a deeper reconciliation between their respective religious ground-motives. During the Middle Ages, when the church of Rome gradually gained control over all of temporal society, this attempted religious synthesis produced a new dialectical ground-motive in the development of western culture: the well-known motive of "nature and grace" (nature and supernature). Its inherent ambiguity and disharmony dominated even the thought of [115] the Reformation to a great extent, although the Reformation had overcome its dialectical tension in principle by returning to the scriptural teaching of the radical significance of the fall for human nature and to the confession of justification by faith alone.

The Impact of Greek Thought

How did Roman Catholicism conceive of "nature?" It derived its concept of nature from Greek philosophy. As we saw earlier, the Greek view of "nature" *(physis)* was entirely determined by the religious motive of matter and form. The matter motive lay at the foundation of the older nature religions which deified a formless, eternally flowing stream of earthly life. Whatever possessed individual form arose from this stream and then passed away. By contrast, the form motive controlled the more recent Greek culture religion, which granted the gods an invisible, imperishable, and rational form that was supranatural in character.

Aristotle listed the various meanings of the word *physis* in Greek thought in chapter four of the fifth book of his famous *Metaphysics*. In his account, the ancient concept of "nature" alternated between a formless stream of becoming and decay (the matter principle) to an imperishable and invisible form, which was understood as the enduring essence of perishable things. For Aristotle, who gave religious priority to the form principle, the second meaning was the most authentic. He defined "nature" as the "substantial form of things which in themselves possess a principle of movement (becoming, growth, and maturation)." In this way he sought to reconcile the principles of form and matter.

Aristotle's Greek view of nature was pagan. Nevertheless, the Roman Catholic ground-motive of nature and grace sought to accommodate the Greek ground-motive to that of divine revelation. The scholastics argued that whatever was subject to birth and death, including human beings, was constituted of matter and form. God created all things according to this arrangement. As a *natural* being, for example, they held that a person consists of a "rational soul" and a "material body." Characterized by its capacity for thought, the rational soul was both the "invisible, essential form" of the body and an imperishable "substance" that could exist apart from the body.

Moreover, scholasticism maintained that when God created humankind he furnished it with a "supranatural" gift of grace, a suprahuman faculty of thought and will by which a person could remain in a correct relationship with God. Humankind lost this gift at the fall, and as a result it was reduced to mere "human nature" with its inherent weaknesses. But this human "nature," which is guided by the natural light of reason, was not [116] corrupted by sin and thus also does not need to be restored by Christ. Human nature is only "weakened" by the fall. It continues to remain true to its innate "natural law" and possesses an autonomy, a relative independence and self-determination in opposition to the realm of grace of the Christian religion. Nature is only brought to a higher form of perfection by grace, which comes from Christ and reaches nature through the mediation of the institutional church. This grace must be earned and prepared by good works in the realm of nature.

Clearly, this new religious ground-motive conflicts with the motive of creation, fall, and redemption at every point. It introduces an internal split into the creation motive by setting up a distinction between the natural and the supranatural and by restricting the scope of fall and redemption to the supranatural. This restriction robs the scriptural ground-motive of its integral and radical character. Broken by the counterforce that "accommodated" the Greek nature motive to the creation motive, the scriptural motive could no longer grip a person with all its power and absoluteness.

One consequence of this dualistic tendency was that the scholastic teaching on the relation between the soul and the body left no room for insight into the radical meaning of either the fall or redemption in Jesus Christ. If the human soul is not the spiritual root-unity of a person's *whole* temporal existence but consists of "the rational form of a material body," then how could one speak of the corruption of a person in the very root of that person's nature? Sin arises not from the function of thought but from the heart, from the religious root of our being.

Like the Greek form-matter motive, the ground-motive of nature and grace contained a *religious dialectic* which drove life and thought from the natural pole to the supranatural pole. The naturalistic attitude summoned the ecclesiastical truths of grace before the court of natural reason, and supranatural mysticism attempted to escape "nature" in the mystical experience of "grace." Ultimately this dialectic led to a consistent proclamation of an unbridgeable rift between nature and grace; nature became independent, losing every point of contact with grace. Only the official authority of the Roman Catholic Church was sufficiently powerful to uphold the religious pseudo-synthesis by formally denouncing the heresies that openly tried to make this entry using this very ground-motive. Its defence drew heavily on the philosophy of Thomas Aquinas [1225-1274], the prince of scholasticism.

Thomas Aquinas
For Thomas "nature" was the independent "stepping-stone to grace," the substructure of a Christian superstructure. He construed the mutual [117] relation between these antithetical motives in Greek fashion, understanding it as a relation between "matter" and "form." He believed that nature is matter for a higher form of perfection bestowed upon it by grace. In other words, the Redeemer works in the manner of a sculptor who shapes his material into a new form.

But it is evident that this construction, derived from Aristotle, could not truly reconcile the inherently antinomic motives of nature and grace. Real reconciliation would have been possible only if a higher standpoint had been found that could have transcended and encompassed both motives. However, such a higher motive was and is not available. To the Church of Rome today "grace" is not "everything," for otherwise grace would "swallow up" nature. But does this state of affairs not testify that the Roman Catholic ground-motive was not that of God's Word? Is it not clear that the nature motive diverged significantly from the creation motive of scriptural revelation?

Surely, the Roman Catholic Church did not incorporate the Greek ground-motive into its own view of nature without revision. Since the church could not accept a dual origin of the cosmos, it tried to harmonize the Greek motive with the scriptural motive of creation. For Roman Catholicism it no longer meant the acceptance of a twofold origin of the world, as it did for the Greeks, for in that case *creation* would have been lost.

One of the first consequences of this accommodation was that the form-matter motive lost its original religious meaning. But because of its pretended reconciliation with the Greek nature motive, Roman Catholicism robbed the biblical creation motive of its scope.

To the Greek mind neither the matter of the world nor the invisible pure form could have been created. At best one could admit that the *union* of form and matter was made possible by divine reason, the divine architect who formed the available material. According to Thomas, though, the medieval doctor of the church, the concrete matter of perishable beings was created simultaneously with their concrete form. However, neither the *matter principle* (the principle of endless becoming and decay) nor the *pure principle of form* (the principle of perfection) were created. He held that they are the two metaphysical principles of all perishable existence. As to their origin, Thomas was silent.

Thomas also maintained that the principle of matter was the principle of imperfection, arguing that what "comes into being" is still imperfect. But how it possible that a principle of imperfection finds its origin in God? Conversely, he continually called the "thinking soul," the "rational form" of human nature, "divine." He never referred to matter as divine. Clearly, the Greek form-matter motive led to a dualism in Thomas's conception of the creation, a dualism reinforced by the contrast between nature and supernature. Unintentionally, Thomas allowed the Greek form-matter motive to overpower the creation motive of the Christian [118] religion. Although he did acknowledge God as the "first cause" and the "ultimate goal" of nature, he divided the creation order into a natural and supranatural realm. And his view of the "natural order" stemmed from Aristotle.

The Pretended Biblical Basis

Roman Catholic thinkers believe that the contrast between nature and grace is biblically based. They appeal in particular to Romans 1:19-20 and 2:14-15. We are obliged to consider these texts in detail, beginning with Romans 1:19-20, where we read:

> For what can be known about God is plain to them, because God has shown it to them. Ever since the creation of the world his invisible na-

ture, namely, his eternal power and deity, has been clearly perceived in the things that have been made.

Did not Paul himself therefore affirm that one can attain a degree of knowledge concerning the true God by means of the *natural light of reason*? We need only refer to the very text itself. Nowhere does Paul say that a person arrives at this knowledge through the natural light of reason. On the contrary, he writes: "what can be known about God is plain to them, because *God has shown it to them*." In this very context Paul refers to God's general revelation to fallen human beings who, because of their apostate inclination, "by their wickedness suppress the truth" [Romans 1:18]. Revelation is heard and understood only in *faith*. A person's *faith* function is active also in concrete human thinking. It is through sin that faith developed in an apostate direction, according to Paul. Because a person's heart turned away from God, Paul lashes out against the idolatrous tendencies of both the Greeks and the the "barbarians": "Claiming to be wise, they became fools" [Romans 1:22].

Thomas employed the Aristotelian idea of God in his "natural theology." This idea was the product not of purely intellectual reasoning but of the religious ground-motive of Greek thought. The various "proofs" for the existence of God, which Thomas developed in Aristotle's footsteps, stand or fall with one's acceptance of both the form-matter ground-motive and the religious priority Aristotle attached to the form motive of Greek culture religion. For Aristotle God was pure form that stood completely apart from matter. This divine form was "pure thought" itself. Aristotle did not grant matter, the principle of the eternal stream of life, a divine status, for matter represented the principle of imperfection. On the premise of this idea of God, Aristotle's first proof of the existence of such a deity is a tight logical argument. It [119] proceeds as follows: everywhere in our experience we perceive movement and change. Every motion is caused by something else. If this too is in motion it again presupposes a cause for its motion. But this causal chain cannot possibly be infinite, since an infinite chain of causes can never be complete. Hence there must be a first cause that is itself not moved. There must be an "unmoved mover" causing the entire process of motion. The "unmoved mover" is God, pure "form," who is therefore perfect.

This proof seems *logically* sound. For the thinker who proceeds from a belief in the autonomy of theoretical thought in the Thomistic sense, it seems that not a single presupposition of faith plays any part. After all, the proof starts from undeniable data of experience (the continuous change and motion of temporal things) and restricts itself to a consistent reflection on the concept of the cause of motion.

So it may *seem*. But suppose that I agree with the early Greek philosophers of nature. Suppose that I see the truly divine as an eternal flux of life and not as an absolute form. My faith would then reverse the direction of the entire "proof." The proof would proceed as follows: in our experience we always perceive completed forms – the forms of plants, animals, human beings, and so forth. However, we also see that all these forms arise and pass away. If this process of becoming and perishing were halted, the great stream of life itself would cease. This in turn would signify the end of whatever comes to exist in individual form and shape. The great stream of life, which stands above all form and which is itself formless, cannot itself become or pass away. It is therefore the first cause of all that receives concrete form. This first cause is God.

I trust that the reader will agree that this proof of the existence of God is as logically sound as that of Thomas's "natural theology" and that it too begins from undeniable data of experience. But the *belief*, the *presupposition* that lies at the basis of this second proof, is different; the truly divine is found not in pure form, as Thomas taught, but in the matter principle of the eternally flowing life stream.

Clearly, our logical thinking is not "autonomous" with respect to faith. It is always guided and directed by a faith commitment which in turn is controlled by the religious ground-motive that grips one's thinking either implicitly or consciously. The ground-motive of Thomas's thought, the Roman Catholic motive of nature and grace, was a motive that allotted a place to the Greek motive. It is foreign to Scripture and to its message of creation, fall, and redemption through Jesus Christ in communion with the Holy Spirit.

The Roman Catholic thinker will appeal further to Paul's statement in Romans 2:14-15, which reads: [120]

> When Gentiles who have not the law do by nature what the law requires, they are a law to themselves, even though they do not have the law. They show that what the law requires is written on their hearts, while their conscience also bears witness and their conflicting thoughts accuse or perhaps excuse them. . . .

This text has stimulated much speculation. It has been hailed as proof of the influence of the Greek view of nature in Paul's thought. Certainly it is true that Paul, an educated person, was familiar with this Greek view. But Paul's statement cannot possibly mean that he advocated the self-sufficiency or independence of natural understanding over against divine revelation. The text must be read against the background of the passage just considered, where we saw that God engraved the law into the heart of a person's existence already in his "general revelation." The scholastics interpreted this law as a rational, natural law that one could know by "the natural light of reason" apart from faith. Accordingly, they translated the word *heart* with the word *mind*, a reading that eliminated the profound meaning of Paul's words. Paul makes his statement in the context of a hard-hitting sketch of the deep apostasy of both Jew and Greek, on account of which both were lost. This statement is therefore governed by the motive of the fall, which affects the spiritual root of existence. What is the sin of heathens if they know the law for creation only "rationally" and if this law is not engraved into their hearts, into the root of their being?

The Church of Rome of course does not teach that sin arises in the mind. To the Roman Catholic mere rational knowledge of the law is not sufficient to justify Paul's judgment that whoever sins perishes. Rather, the law as the law of general revelation is written into a person's heart, and therefore one is without excuse. Serious damage to the brain may cause the temporal loss of moral conscience and may force a person to lie, steal, or deceive. A mentally deficient person may lack an intellectual understanding of what is good or bad. But the law that is inscribed within our hearts touches the hidden root of life, where judgment is reserved for God alone.

The Roman Catholic View of Natural Society

The philosophical system of Thomas Aquinas stands behind the official Roman Catholic view of the state and of the other societal spheres. It is undoubtedly true that in Roman Catholic circles some adhere to conceptions other than those of Aquinas. Augustinian orientations, for instance, are certainly not [121] overlooked. But Thomistic philosophy, supported by official commendation in a series of papal encyclicals, has a special status among Roman Catholics. The two famous social and socio-economic encyclicals *Rerum novarum* (1891, from Leo XIII) and *Quadragesimo anno* (1931, from Pius XI) are based on a Thomistic foundation. They present guidelines for a solution to social questions and to the problems of economic order from a Roman Catholic vantage point.

The Social Nature of Rational Human Beings

Thomas's view of human society was completely dominated by the religious ground-motive of nature and grace in its Roman Catholic sense. The main lines of his view of *natural* society were derived from Aristotle. We have already noted that in conformity with Aristotle he conceived of human nature as a composition of form and matter.[1] The rational soul was the "form" and the material body was the "matter" of a human being, which owed its real being to the soul. Every creature composed of form and matter arose and came into being; and the principle of form gave this becoming the direction toward a goal. By nature, every creature strove to reach its perfection through a process whereby its "essential form" realized itself in the matter of its body. Thus a plant

---

1 *Translator's note:* This conception of human nature is the basis for Thomas's view of society.

naturally strove to develop its seed into the mature form of a plant, and an animal developed itself toward its mature form. The natural perfection of human beings consisted in the complete development of their rational nature which distinguished them from plants and animals. Their rational nature was equipped with an innate, rational, natural law that urged them to do good and to refrain from evil. Thus, according to Thomas, humankind *naturally* strove toward the *good*. This conception radically conflicts with the scriptural confession of the total depravity of "human nature."

Thomas also believed that one could not attain one's natural perfection as an isolated individual. Human beings came into the world naked and helpless, and therefore they depended on society, which had to aid them by providing for their material and moral needs. Thus for Thomas a social inclination or a predisposition toward society is also innate in rational human nature. This social propensity develops in stages, through the formation of smaller and larger communities that are mutually related in terms of *lower* to *higher*, *means* to *end*, *part* to *whole*.

The lowest community is the family, which provides the opportunity for satisfying a person's lower needs, such as food and sex. The highest community is the state, which brings a person's social tendency to perfection. All the lower communities relate to the state as their completion; for, unlike the other natural societal forms, the state is the overarching and perfect community. It possesses autarchy and self-sufficiency, since [122] in the natural realm it is the highest and most embracing community. The state is based on the rational disposition of human nature. Its essence is *characterized* by its *goal*, the common good. This natural goal is also the immediate basis of governmental authority, without which the body politic cannot exist. Thus, if the state is grounded in "nature," so is the authority of government. Thomas certainly recognized that *ultimately* the government's authority is rooted in the sovereignty of the Creator but, in typically Roman Catholic fashion, *he inserted the motive of rational nature between humankind and the Creator*. In this nature motive the Greek form-matter motive came to expression.

Insofar as it fully influences one's view of human society, the scriptural creation motive always points to the intrinsic nature of the life-spheres of our temporal existence. The scriptural conception that God created everything after its own nature does not have room for the idea that in the natural realm the state is the perfect community embracing both individuals and other societal structures as its *parts*. What is essentially *part* of a *whole* is determined exclusively by the *inner nature* of the *whole*. It is undoubtedly correct to maintain that provinces and municipalities are parts of the state; governed by the same intrinsic law of life, they are of the same intrinsic nature. Similarly, it is correct to say that hands, feet, and head are essential parts of the human body. They are only members of the body, and as such their nature is determined by the intrinsic nature and law of the whole.

A whole-part relationship does not exclude the possibility that the parts possess *autonomy* within the whole. Municipalities, counties, and provinces[1] are indeed constitutionally autonomous. That is to say, they are relatively independent within the whole. They institute bylaws and regulations that govern their internal affairs even though the ultimate control rests with a central authority. But in the modern state the limit of this autonomy always depends upon the interest of the whole, the so-called common good.

From a scriptural point of view the relation between the state and the life-spheres of different internal structures is radically distinct from the whole-part relationship within the state. For example, marriage, the nuclear family, the church, the firm, the sphere of scholarship, and that of art, according to their intrinsic character and peculiar law of life, should never be described as parts of the state. In principle they are of a nature different from the institutionalized body politic. They are sovereign in their own sphere, and their boundaries are determined not by the common good of the state but by their own intrinsic nature and law. This does not exclude an interconnection with the state. Yet this relation does not concern the jurisdiction of any non-political sphere, since it only involves matters falling within the sphere of competence of the state.

In other words, each sphere must leave the principle of sphere [123] sovereignty intact. For its practical application, sphere sovereignty demands a closer investigation of the internal structure of the various life-spheres. Kuyper was correct in his view that this principle finds its foundation in creation. In the present context it is of vital importantce to emphasize that this principle is rooted in the ground-motive of the Divine Word-revelation. When the integral character of the creation motive is operative in one's life and thought, sooner or later it leads to a recognition of sphere sovereignty.

The Principle of Subsidiarity

The Greek nature motive, with its dualism between the form principle and the matter principle, permeated Thomas Aquinas's view of human society. In his opinion the state, based on the rational nature of human beings, was necessary so that the rational form of human nature could arrive at perfect development and so that the matter principle – expressed in sensuous desires – could be held in check.

In conformity with Greek thought, Thomas held that the state was the total, all-inclusive community in the realm of nature. All the other life-

---

1 *General Editor's note:* Dooyeweerd here also refers to parts of the Dutch state which are not found in most other states, such as *"waterschappen," "veenschappen"* and *"veenpolders."*

spheres were merely its subservient parts. Thomas therefore conceived of the relationship between the state and the other natural spheres of life in terms of the whole-part relation. Certainly he would not have defended a state absolutism that would govern all of life from "above." The modern totalitarian regimes of national socialism and fascism would have met an unwavering opponent in Thomas, as they did among the modern Thomists. Thomas immediately added a restriction after declaring that individuals and "lower" communities were parts of the state; he maintained that they were parts only insofar as they were of the *same order*. To begin with, this limitation excluded the supranatural order from the jurisdiction of the state. Both the individual and marriage (in its sacramental superstructure) participated in the supranatural order, and the jurisdiction of the state did not extend beyond the natural. Secondly, this limitation signified that Thomas's view of the state was anticentralist in principle. Thomas argued that the state is constructed *from below* in a hierarchy of lower and higher communities. Whatever could be adequately taken care of by a lower community should not be subsumed by a higher community.

The famous principle of *subsidiarity* is rooted in this train of thought. The encyclical *Quadragesimo anno* (1931, from Pius XI) defended "subsidiarity" as a guide for delimiting the state's task in the organization of labor and industry. The principle of subsidiarity holds that the state should contribute to the common good only those elements which individuals cannot provide, either by themselves or by means of the lower communities. At first glance this principle seems to be another name for "sphere sovereignty." Those who agree with Groen van [124] Prinsterer's views concerning the structure of the state are likely to be attracted to the idea that the state should be organized not from above but from below. Yet a decisive difference exists between the principles of subsidiarity and sphere sovereignty.

Roman Catholic social theory developed the principle of subsidiarity on the basis of the Thomistic view of a person's "rational nature," which itself was derived from the Greek concept of nature. This Greek "concept of nature," which flows, as we have sufficiently substantiated, from the form-matter motive as religious ground-motive of Greek culture, is here operative.

Humankind's natural perfection, which consisted in realizing the "rational essential form" of its nature, could not be attained in isolation. Everyone came into the world naked and helpless, with the result that one depended upon the community for providing one with one's "material" and "rational-moral" needs. Hence a social propensity lay implanted in one's rational nature, a propensity that developed step by step in the societal forms which began with the lowest (the family) and ended with the state, the perfect and highest community in natural society.

Meanwhile, the human being as an *individual* always remained the Thomistic point of departure, for that person alone was truly a *substance*. In the context of Greek thought this meant that the individual possessed an *independent* existence while the community was regarded as merely a *unity of order* borne by the individual. In this pattern of thought a community like the state does not possess *the same reality* as the individual, just as one cannot ascribe the same reality to the *color* red as to a red *rose*. The color red is only a property of the rose and presupposes the rose as its bearer.

For analogous reasons the official Roman Catholic view maintains that the state and the lower societal communities cannot exhaust the reality of the individual as a "natural being." The rational law of nature holds that individuals depend on the community only for those needs which they cannot fill themselves as individual human beings. The same natural law also holds that a lower community like the family or the school depends on the higher communities (ultimately on the state) only for those interests that it itself cannot handle. Basically, this hierarchical structure describes the substance of the principle of subsidiarity.

But Thomism still conceived of both the individual and the lower societal communities in the natural realm as parts of the whole, as parts of the state. It is against this (essentially Greek) view of human society that the scriptural principle of sphere sovereignty directs itself. Rooted in the creation motive of revelation, sphere sovereignty compels us to give a precise account of the intrinsic nature of the life-spheres. God created everything according to its own nature. Two parts that completely differ in kind, can never become parts of the same whole.

This insight into the inner structure and nature of the differentiated [125] spheres was alien to Thomistic social theory. Thomism distinguished communities only in terms of the immediate *purpose* they served in their cooperation toward the natural perfection of human beings. For example, marriage (apart from its ecclesiastical, sacramental dimension) was understood as a juridical institution grounded in human nature for the sake of the procreation of the human race. Does this definition focus at all on the intrinsic nature and structure of the community of marriage? If so, what should we say of a marriage in which children are no longer expected? What is the inner norm of the marriage bond in its internal character? Does one really identify the *inner* nature of married life by describing it as a *juridical* institution? Would not marriage be sheer hell if the juridical point of view would guide all of its affairs?

Following Aristotle, Thomas looked upon the family as a natural community serving the lower economic and sexual needs of life. The family consisted of three relations: husband and wife, parents and children, and master and servants. Does this in any way approach the internal character of the family? Does the family really include the servants? Is it true that the family serves only the "lower needs?"

Lastly, Thomistic social theory considered the state to be the perfect human community. Its goal was the "common good" of its members. I ask: *how can this teleological goal orientation help us define the internal nature and structure of the state?* The concept of "common good" in Thomistic political theory was so vague that it applied also to the "lower" societal structures. For example, the modern Thomist does not hesitate to speak of the "public interest" of an industrial corporation in distinction from the "specific interest" of the persons who work within it. For the Thomist the "common good" in the body politic can only refer to the interest of the "whole" that embraces all the "lower" communities and the individuals as "parts." From this perspective, however, it is impossible to indicate an inner criterion for the "common good," since a Thomist does not see the state according to its own intrinsic nature and structure. We know how even the most revolting state absolutism seeks to justify itself with appeals to the common good. As we mentioned earlier, Thomism certainly does not desire an absolute state, but it has no defence against state absolutism other than the principle of subsidiarity, a principle derived not from the intrinsic nature of the life-spheres but from the Aristotelian conception of the "social nature" of humankind and of the "natural purposes" of the various societal communities.

Modern Roman Catholic Social Thought

In this light it is not surprising that modern Roman Catholic social theory contains two potentially conflicting tendencies. In the first place, we [126] note an *idea of social order* wholly oriented to the Greek view of the state as the totality of natural society. As a totality, the state must order all of its parts in harmonious cooperation. The Thomist who holds this conception of social order will view the principle of sphere sovereignty as little more than a product of the "revolutionary" Reformation which merely placed the different spheres of life alongside each other and sought their deeper unity only in the *suprarational* religious community of the human race. The Roman Catholic idea of social order, by contrast, conceives of the various life-spheres within the "realm of nature" as *ordered within a natural whole* (the state) which finds its higher perfection in the supranatural community of the church as institute of divine grace.

In the second place, we note the *principle of subsidiarity* which is intended to prevent totalitarian political absolutism by providing for an "ordering" of society not imposed "from above" but developed "from below" so that the central government will leave the task of establishing a socio-economic order as much as possible to the individuals and to the lower communities.

The question as to how these two views are to be reconciled is decisive for the stand Roman Catholicism will take with regard to the postwar issues of social order.

It is not surprising, then, that today one finds Roman Catholic social theory split into two more or less divergent camps. One stream places great emphasis on the whole-part relation it assumes to obtain between the state and the other "natural" life-spheres. It insists on the idea of ordering society without depriving the other life-spheres of their "natural autonomy." But it acknowledges no basic difference, for example, between the position that organized industrial life must occupy within the state and the position constitutionally given to the municipalities and provinces.

This camp is greatly influenced by Othmar Spann [1878-1950], the well-known social theorist from Vienna who called his system "universalism" *[Ganzheitslehre or Allheitslehre]*. The point of departure for his view is the community, not the individual. According to him, whatever is individual or singular can exist only as an expression of the whole, which is realized through its parts in this way. Although even in his view the whole exists only *in* its members and has no existence *apart* from them, the whole does exist *before* its members. Lying at the foundation of its parts, it does not cease to exist when its individual members perish. Thus the whole is "all in all"; everything is in the whole and the whole is in everything. For Spann the individuals and the lower communities of the "realm of nature" are part and parcel [127] of the state, just as the state itself is part of the "community of nations."

The second stream is the so-called solidaristic wing, founded by the Roman Catholic economist and social theorist Heinrich Pesch (1854-1926). In his five-volume work on economic principles Pesch sought to apply the social ethics of solidarism to economics.[1] In his conception society is:

> a whole composed of many and different parts. Each part is by nature directed to a goal of its own and to the fulfillment of a specific social (or political) service. Because of this orientation every part is a unity. Since, however, all these partial goals are many branches of the single perfection of human life, the parts stand in a certain natural relation to each other and to a greater whole. Therefore they must fulfil their task in partnership and in harmonious cooperation, so that the development and well-being of the whole (the state) can be the result of this.[2]

To this point solidarism and universalism are still largely in agreement. But the difference is this: on the basis of the fact that only the individual as a person has independent existence and that the community is only a dependent "unit of order," solidarism infers that the individual cannot

---

1 See Heinrich Pesch, *Lehrbuch der Nationalökonomie*, 5 vols. (Freiburg im Breisgau: Herder and Co, 1922-26).
2 W.M.J. Koenraadt and Max van Poll, *Handboek der Maatschappijleer* [Manual of Sociology] (1937), vol. I, 24f.

be directed to the community in everything or in an ultimate sense, not even on the "natural level." Solidarism does not accept the universalistic thesis that as a natural being an individual is wholly part of the community. It holds that the individual is "older" and prior to the community, and that that individual possesses a "personal sphere" of natural interests over against the state. In *Casti connubii*, the famous encyclical on marriage of 31 December 1930, Pope Pius XI applied these ideas to the problem of sterilization:

> Public magistrates have no direct power over the bodies of their subjects; therefore, where no crime has taken place and there is no cause present for grave punishment, they can never directly harm or tamper with the integrity of the body, either for the reasons of eugenics or for any other reason.[1]

It is consistent with this solidaristic idea that the jurisdiction of government over the "lower communities" be limited as much as possible. On this point the solidaristic wing, which undoubtedly represents the [128] official Roman Catholic view, is more likely to side with Calvinism with its principle of sphere sovereignty over the modern notion of order which views the various life-spheres as merely parts of the state. Still, emphasizing the principle of subsidiarity does not offer a fundamental guarantee against the totalitarianism that continues to threaten society even after the collapse of the national socialistic and fascist regimes. For that matter, even the principle of sphere sovereignty does not arm us against totalitarianism if it is separated from the scriptural motive of creation and thereby robbed of its real intent. Before exploring this further, we shall complete our sketch of Roman Catholic social theory by devoting attention to the realm of human society called "specifically Christian" or "supranatural."

The Roman Catholic View of (Supranatural) Christian Society

The Roman Catholic religious ground-motive (nature and grace) requires an overarching structure of "supranatural" character above the natural substructure of human society. A person possesses not only a *natural* purpose in life (the perfection of his "rational nature") but above that a *supranatural final* purpose through which one's rational nature must be elevated to the sphere of grace.

Within this supranatural realm, where the soul's eternal salvation is at stake, Roman Catholicism calls a halt to the interference of the state. Only the Roman Catholic institutional church can dispense supranatural grace to the believer by means of its sacraments. If, according to the Roman

---
1 Cited from *The Church and the Reconstruction of the Modern World*, ed. with an introduction by Terence McLaughlin (Garden City. N.Y.: Image Books. 1957), 141f.

Catholic conception, natural society is indeed to have a *Christian* character, it must subject itself to the guidance of the church in all matters pertaining to the eternal salvation of the soul. Just as in the realm of nature the state is the perfect community embracing all other natural spheres of life as its parts, so also in the realm of grace the Roman Catholic Church is the *whole of Christian society in its supranatural perfection*. It is the perfect community of Christendom.

Our Roman Catholic fellow-Christians of today are still influenced by the medieval idea of the *corpus Christianum* (Body of Christ), the idea that the institutional church embraces all of Christendom and all of Christian life. This ideal of the Christian community rises far above the Greek conception of the "natural substructure," like an imposing dome. Here too, however, it is not the scriptural ground-motive that governs the Roman Catholic mind. Rather, Roman Catholicism submits to a semi-christianized Greek conception which understands temporal society in [129] terms of the whole-part scheme and which denies the intrinsic nature of the life-spheres as rooted in the divine creation order.

Roman Catholicism looks for the whole – for the total unity – of Christian society in the temporal, institutional church. But according to the ground-motive of God's revelation the true unity of all Christian life is found only in the supratemporal root-community of humankind, which is reborn in Christ. This community is the Kingdom of God, which resides not in a temporal institution but in the hearts of the redeemed. Without a doubt, the church here on earth, in its temporal, institutional organization as community of Christ-believers, can only exist as a *temporal* manifestation of the "Body of Christ." The "visible church" can therefore not be separated from the "invisible church." The latter is the "soul," the "religious root," of the former. But this "temporal manifestation" is not *identical* with the so-called "invisible church" which, as the spiritual Kingdom of Christ Jesus our Lord, *transcends* time and shall exist in all eternity. As one's soul and religious root-unity do not lie in one's temporal existence, so too the spiritual root-unity and true totality of Christian life do not lie in the "visible church," which belongs to temporal society.

It can be noted then that the Roman Catholic view of the church conforms with the scholastic conception of the relation between the body and the soul in human nature. We found earlier that the scholastic view was governed by the Greek religious ground-motive of form and matter. The soul was understood as an abstracted part of a person's temporal existence, the part characterized by the logical function of thought. In opposition to the soul stood the "material body," the matter given form by the soul. Despite its relation to the body, the "rational soul" possessed an independent and immortal existence through its intellectual function.

We saw earlier too that this Greek idea of the soul is radically opposed to the scriptural approach. What is at stake in the issue of the soul is self-knowledge, and self-knowledge depends entirely upon one's knowledge of God. It is only through God's revelation of creation, fall, and redemption that one discovers the religious root, the soul of one's existence. But in the Roman Catholic view of human nature the dualistic, Greek nature motive of form and matter thwarted the spiritual vitality of this biblical ground-motive. Accordingly, the Roman Catholic view lost insight into the spiritual root-unity of human nature. It looked for the "immortal soul" in an abstract part of a person's temporal existence, thereby forfeiting the radical character of the fall and redemption in Jesus Christ.

It is therefore not difficult to understand that Roman Catholicism located the root-unity of Christian society in the temporal, institutional church. As the "perfect community" of the supranatural realm, the [130] church served as the higher "form" with natural society as its "matter." Natural society, climaxed in the state, was related to the supranatural Christian society of the church as the material body was related to the rational soul. *Unintentionally, then, the Greco-Roman conception of the totalitarian state was transferred to the Roman Catholic institutional church.* Roman Catholicism heralded the church as the total, all-embracing community of Christian life.

That is why a Roman Catholic maintains that Christian family life, the Christian school, Christian social action, and even a Christian political party must bear the stamp of the church. Certainly a Roman Catholic does not reject the natural basis of these spheres of life. The argument is that insofar as they operate on the "natural" level they are not part of the church. On this level they possess autonomy. Autonomy holds first of all with respect to the state itself. But with respect to their specifically *Christian* purposes, the state and all the other spheres must subject themselves to the guidance of the church. Marriage too has a "natural substructure"; marriage is the community of husband and wife, founded on natural law, for the purpose of procreation. But it is also a sacrament, and it therefore belongs to the ecclesiastical sphere of grace. And in view of this sacramental character, the church claims the whole regulation of marriage for its canon law, excluding the civil magistrate from this process.

According to the Roman Catholic view, nature and grace cannot be separated in a truly Christian society. This means that the Roman Catholic Church may intervene in the natural realm. Consequently, the relation between the church and the Christian (that is, Roman Catholic) state can never correspond to the relation between two sovereign life-spheres. One might be led to think otherwise when Thomas argued that the state is not subject to intervention from the church in purely natural matters. The illusion is broken, however, when we realize that the church reserves for itself the binding interpretation of "natural morality," to which the Christian magistrate is as bound as any individual church member. In fact, the Roman Catholic Church delimits the boundaries of the autonomy of the Christian state. Thus, when Leo XIII and Pius XI wrote their encyclicals *Rerum novarum* and *Quadragesimo anno*, they offered directives not merely for the "specifically Christian" side of the social and socio-economic issues of the modern day; they also explained the demands of "natural law" and "natural morality" for these problems. On both counts, then, the Roman Catholic Church demands that a Christian government subject itself to ecclesiastical guidance. The state is autonomous only in giving concrete form to the principles of natural law in the determination of so-called positive law. [131]

In conclusion, let us briefly summarize our discussion of the Roman Catholic view of human society. Roman Catholicism cannot recognize the sphere sovereignty of the temporal spheres of life. Influenced by the Greek form-matter motive, it conceives of all temporal society in terms of the whole-part scheme. By virtue of its catholic character ("catholic" means "total" or "all-embracing"), the Roman Catholic institutional church functions as the total community of all of Christian life. The state functions as the total community of "natural life," but in those affairs that, according to the judgment of the church, touch the *supranatural* well-being of the citizen, it must look to the church for guidance.

A Recent Reaffirmation

During the German occupation of Holland a clandestine document appeared entitled *The Glass House. Again a Roman Catholic Party?*[1] It ably expresses the Roman Catholic position in these words:

> The place of church authority in these affairs comes into full view when we consider the question as to who must decide whether a temporal issue is necessarily connected with the salvation of the soul. This competence belongs to the church alone. It alone has the divine mission to guide a person in "matters pertaining to heaven." Thus the church is competent to determine the extent of its actual jurisdiction. Many have taken the church's competence to determine its own competence as the essence of true sovereignty. German jurisprudence calls it *Kompetenz-Kompetenz*. Now, sovereignty in the above sense may be ascribed to the Roman Catholic Church only. It is in this light that the juridical relationship between church and state must be placed. This is not a voluntary cooperation from which the state is free to withdraw or determine as it pleases. The relation is best expressed as follows: an "ordered bond"... must exist between the church and the state, as (Pope) Leo XIII said (in

---

1 A second, expanded edition appeared in 1949. See F.J.F.M. Duynstee, *Het glazen huis. Beschouwingen over den inhoud en den vorm van het staatkundig streven der nederlandse katholieken* [The Glass House. Reflections on the Content and Form of the Political Aims of Dutch Catholics].

the encyclical *Immortale Dei*). Leo compares this bond with the connection between soul and body – a comparison common among the church fathers.

The author cites from the encyclical:

> Whatever, therefore, in things human is of a sacred character, whatever belongs, either of its own nature or by reason of the end to which it is directed, to the salvation of souls, or to the worship of God, is subject to the power and judgment of the Church.[1] [132]

The author concludes that "here then there is juridical authority of the Church over state in the full sense of the word."

The reasoning in *The Glass House* document certainly underscores our observations on the Roman Catholic view of the relation between church and state. A Roman Catholic society acknowledges only one truly *sovereign* authority – that of the institutional church. The other spheres of life, including the state, have only *autonomy*. Although the writer of this document does speak of "sovereignty of the state" in all matters "which fall outside of the religio-ethical sphere," he quickly gives this the correct Roman Catholic meaning by reducing this so-called sovereignty to autonomy.

The author understands the relation of church and state to be analogous to that of soul and body. We have seen that the Roman Catholic view of the soul and the body was Greek, not scriptural, and that it was determined entirely by the Greek ground-motive of form and matter. The *Glass House* writer affirms this influence in his statement:

> The catholic conception of the nature of a person is intimately connected with this: "the human soul cannot be exhaustively defined except in relation to the body, to which the soul bestows life and with which it forms a real and substantial unity," as Antonin Sertillanges says.[2] Redemption, the church, the sacraments, and the resurrection of the flesh are closely connected with this human character. To value the body, material things, the natural, and the rational, as well as the spiritualization of all these through grace – together these witness to the all-encompassing character of Catholicism, to its wonderful harmony.

But because the Church of Rome no longer understood the soul in the scriptural sense as the religious root of human nature, conceiving it instead as an abstract complex of temporal functions, it could only view the "soul" of temporal human society as being in the temporal institutional church.

---

1 Taken from *Social Wellsprings: Fourteen Epochal Documents by Pope Leo XIII*, ed. Joseph Husslein (Milwaukee: The Bruce Publishing Company, 1940), 72.
2 Sertillanges [1863-1948] was one of the most authoritative modern commentators on the philosophy of Thomas Aquinas.

A Parallel: Faith and Philosophy

The official (that is, Thomistic) Roman Catholic view of the relation between faith on the one hand and philosophy and science on the other hand parallels the relation between state and church. In the decades just prior to the Second World War Roman Catholic scholars were preoccupied with the question of whether there can be a Christian philosophy. Whereas from the Augustinian side of scholastic thought this question was answered affirmatively on a number of occasions, the opposite view was dominant among Thomists. As [133] we have already seen, Thomism represents the official Roman Catholic stance.

Unlike Augustine, Thomas defended the "autonomy" of natural thought with respect to the Christian faith. He believed that philosophy must pursue its own task independently of the theology of revelation. It must proceed under the "natural light of reason" alone. If we look closely, we see that this "autonomy" of "natural" science over against the light of revelation is different in principle from the "autonomy" defended by modern humanism. Not recognizing a higher light of revelation, the humanist believes that natural reason is truly sovereign. This notion of the "autonomy of science" is controlled by the humanistic religious ground-motive of nature and freedom, which will be considered in later chapters. In contrast to the humanistic motive, the Thomistic view is rooted in the Roman Catholic ground-motive of nature and grace.

As the Thomists prefer to phrase it, their philosophy "baptized" Aristotle. That is to say, within the field of philosophy it accommodated the Greek thought of Aristotle to ecclesiastical dogma. Greek thought therefore always stands under the control of ecclesiastical dogma, which it may never contradict. According to Thomas, such a contradiction is not even possible if natural understanding reasons purely. If conflicts do arise, they may be the result of errors in thinking which Thomistic philosophy will promptly expose. Hence the Thomist always maintains that the Roman Catholic philosophy of state and society can be accepted by all reasonable human beings independently of the Roman Catholic faith.

But in reality matters are quite different. Orthodox scholasticism is never unprejudiced with respect to religion and church dogma. Philosophy is always determined by a religious ground-motive without which it cannot exist. Forming an inseparable unity with Roman Catholic ecclesiastical belief, Thomistic thought is Roman Catholic in every respect. Thomistic philosophy is the natural stepping-stone to ecclesiastical faith.

Formation of Roman Catholic Political Parties

Whenever Roman Catholicism presents a critical account of its own ground-motive, it will indeed recognize the universal scope of the antithesis established by the Christian religion. However, it understands this antithesis in the light of the religious ground-motive of nature and grace. In this light the antithesis is viewed as an opposition between the *apostate* principle that severs "nature" from church dogma and the Roman Catholic principle that, under the guidance of ecclesiastical authority, places "nature" in the service of "supranatural perfection." [134] Nature and grace (supranature) cannot be *separated* in the Roman Catholic conception. Whoever believes that "natural life" is "sovereign" stands in irreconcilable conflict with Roman Catholicism.

This way of characterizing the antithesis also has implications for social and political activity. The anonymous author of *The Glass House* we cited earlier was quite aware of this. Of course, in a truly Roman Catholic country without a mixed population, Catholics have no need for a political party or social organizations based on Roman Catholic principles. But in a diversified population they normally must accept the antithesis also in the political and social areas. Our writer states:

> One should be aware of the choice: a Roman Catholic political organization is a party whose starting point is the proper relation between church and state; in other words, a party that seeks the true well-being of the citizens insofar as religion offers norms for it. This political party guarantees the basis of every political activity. It is open to the demands and directives of the church that it correct its activities if necessary. The church has the right to demand such correction. This party protects the Catholics from the dangers and conflicts they would experience in parties based on an unacceptable view of politics, that is, in parties where ecclesiastical authority is denied. Only a formal recognition of ecclesiastical authority can guarantee that the concrete political goals of the party, both now and in the future, will agree with extant and future declarations of the church.

"Moreover," our author continues, "reflection on ecclesiastical competence in temporal affairs leads to the conclusion that the question of whether or not a Roman Catholic political organization is necessary, can become an issue subject to the jurisdiction or moral authority of the church." In this connection one might recall the stand taken by the German episcopacy (during the elections of 1929, for instance) in support of the Roman Catholic Center Party. The standpoint of the Dutch episcopacy was very similar, at least before May 1940.[1] Of direct importance is a statement made by Pope Pius XI (to Bishop Aengenent on 3 November 1932): "Political unity among Catholics: before all else, after all else, above all else, and at the cost of all else. One should sacrifice personal opinion and insight to this unity, and count it higher than private interest."

---

1 Shortly after the war the Dutch Roman Catholic episcopacy reiterated its preference for a catholic party on the grounds that it safeguards catholic interests best.

Immediately following the Second World War, a number of Dutch Roman Catholics, called the "Christopher Group," joined the Dutch Labor Party in a conscious effort to break through the Roman Catholic antithesis in the political arena. This Group cannot be considered representative of [135] the official Roman Catholic position, as the most recent elections (1946) made abundantly clear. Moreover, soon after the formation of the Dutch National Movement, influential Roman Catholics, like professors Sassen and Kors, warned against the postwar attempts to eliminate the Roman Catholic antithesis in the political arena. Both strongly defended the inseparable unity of Roman Catholic political practice and the Roman Catholic worldview.

Granted, in certain countries the church may consider the formation of a Roman Catholic Party or labor union undesirable on pragmatic grounds. In the case of Mexico, Pope Pius XI explicitly declared that Mexican Catholics should not establish a party that would call itself "catholic" (2 February 1926). Once again, our anonymous author remarks:

> It is likely that in places where enemies of the church are in power and are prepared to use their power against the church, enemies who accelerate the battle rapidly for no apparent reason, a catholic party would only add fuel to the flames and would therefore be inappropriate. One might say that in an originally catholic country [France is meant] which is currently anticlerical, even though still connected with the church in many ways, a catholic party would cause anticlericalism to spread and would harm the souls of many anticlericalists over whom the church continues to watch. One could also argue that in a country with only slight antipapalism a catholic party might well trigger the promotion of antipapalism, a detriment that would be the more serious if the catholic party were to end up having little power...On these and similar grounds one must conclude that a political party is inappropriate in Mexico and perhaps also in France or England.

But the same author correctly defends the thesis that "a catholic party is in principle the right option wherever the state does not recognize ecclesiastical authority."

The Christopher Group, whose adherents come largely from the southern Roman Catholic provinces of the Netherlands, were perhaps tempted by the anticipation of realizing the ideal of a Roman Catholic society, a society not realizable in the Dutch nation. I take it that they will become more realistic when they discover that they acted on the basis of a nonexistent situation and that they alienated themselves from the majority of their Roman Catholic counterparts. It is not even certain whether the Roman Catholic Party will join the Labor Party in the formation of a coalition cabinet. I am sure of this: if such a coalition is formed – and indeed the weakened position of the Labor Party has created new possibilities for the Roman Catholics – it will be possible only under Roman Catholic leader-

The Great Synthesis

ship. In that event the Labor Party will be in a [136] position only to play second fiddle, merely accompanying the tune set by the Roman Catholic Peoples Party.[1]

Disintegration of the Synthesis

The ground-motive of nature and grace contained the seeds of a "religious dialectic." That is, from the outset the Christian motive of grace and the conception of "nature," which was oriented to the Greek religious ground-motive, stood in irreconcilable opposition and tension. Wherever it had the opportunity to have an impact, this real religious tension drove life and thought from one pole to the other. On the one hand, the danger arose that the nature motive would overrun the motive of grace by summoning the mysteries of grace before the court of natural reason. On the other hand, there was the constant temptation of mysticism which attempted to escape "sinful nature" in a mystical experience of supranatural grace and thus inevitably led to asceticism and world flight. Finally, there was the constant threat that every connection between nature and grace would be systematically cut off in such a way that any point of contact between them would be denied. In the latter case people found themselves straddling an open *split* between "natural life" and the Christian religion, but wanted to accept both in *complete independence* of each other.

Only the doctrinal authority of the Roman Catholic Church was in a position to maintain the apparent synthesis between the Greek and Christian ground-motives. Time and again the church intervened by officially condemning the "heresies" that arose out of the polar tensions within the dualistic ground-motive of nature and grace.

William of Ockham: Herald of a New Age

During the latter part of the Middle Ages (the fourteenth century), when the dominant position of the church in culture began to erode on all sides, a movement arose within scholasticism that broke radically with the ecclesiastical synthesis. This turn of events announced *the beginning of the "modern period."* The leader of this movement was the British Franciscan William of Ockham [c. 1280-1349]. Ockham, a brilliant monk, [137] mercilessly laid bare the inner dualism of the Roman Catholic ground-motive, denying that there was any point of contact between the realm of nature and the realm of grace. He was keenly aware that the Greek view of nature flagrantly contradicted the scriptural mo-

---

1 The 1946 elections gave the Roman Catholic Peoples Party and the Labor Party together a majority in parliament. In the coalition cabinet formed afterwards these two parties shared most of the portfolios under prime minister Louis Beet, a member of the Roman Catholic Party.

tive of creation. Thomas Aquinas had maintained that the natural ordinances were grounded in divine "reason." For him they were eternal "forms" in the mind of God, in accordance with which God had shaped "matter." Ockham, however, rejected this entire position. Intuitively he knew that Thomas's essentially Greek picture could not be reconciled with the confession of a *sovereign* Creator. However, in order to break with the Greek deification of reason he ended up in another extreme. He interpreted the will of the divine Creator as despotic arbitrariness, or *potestas absoluta* (absolute, free power).

In Greek fashion Thomas had identified the decalogue (The Ten Commandments) with a natural, moral law rooted immutably in the rational nature of humankind and in divine reason. For this reason Thomas held that the decalogue could be known apart from revelation by means of the natural light of reason. But for Ockham, the decalogue did not have a rational basis. It was the gift of an arbitrary God, a God who was bound to nothing. God could easily have ordered the opposite. Ockham believed that the Christian must obey the laws of God for the simple reason that God established *these* laws and not others. The Christian could not "calculate" God's sovereign will, for the law was merely the result of God's unlimited arbitrariness. In the realm of "nature" the Christian must blindly obey; in the realm of the supranatural truths of grace one must, without question, accept the dogma of the church.

Ockham abandoned every thought of a "natural preparation" for ecclesiastical faith through "natural knowledge." Likewise, he rejected the idea that the church is competent to give supranatural guidance in natural life. He did not acknowledge, for instance, that science is subordinate to ecclesiastical belief. Neither did he believe that the temporal authorities are subordinate to the pope with respect to the explication of natural morality. In principle he rejected the Roman Catholic view of a "Christian society"; standing entirely independent of the church, secular government in his view was indeed "sovereign."

In short, we may say that Ockham deprived the law of its intrinsic value. Founded in an incalculable, arbitrary God who is bound to nothing, the law only held for the sinful realm of nature. For Ockham, one is never certain that God's will would not change under different circumstances. Radically denying that any point of contact between nature and grace existed, he rejected the official Roman Catholic view of [138] human society, together with its subordination of the natural to the supranatural and of the state to the church.

The attempts of Pope John XXII to stifle the spiritual movement led by Ockham were in vain. The pope's position was very weak; having been forced to flee from Rome, he depended greatly on the king of France during his exile at Avignon. But above all, a new period in history announced itself at this time – a period that signified the end of medieval, ecclesiastical culture. Ockham's critique convinced many that the Roman Catholic synthesis between the Greek view of nature and the Christian religion had been permanently destroyed. The future presented only two options: one could either return to the scriptural ground-motive of the Christian religion or, in line with the new motive of nature severed from the faith of the church, establish a modern view of life concentrated on the religion of human personality. The first path led to the Reformation; the second path led to modern humanism. In both movements aftereffects of the Roman Catholic motive of nature and grace continued to be felt for a long time.

In order to gain a proper insight into the spiritual situation of contemporary Protestantism, it is extremely important to trace the aftereffects of the Roman Catholic ground-motive. In doing this, we will focus our attention especially on the various conceptions concerning the relation between "church" and "world" in Protestant circles. We will be especially interested in "Barthianism," so widely influential today. And, with respect to our overriding theme, we must take note of the resistance against the "antithesis" in the natural realm of science, politics, and social action. This we will attempt to do in the following subsections.

Law and Gospel in Luther

The previous subsection showed how the religious ground-motive of nature and grace held the Christian mind in a polar tension. Near the end of the middle ages this tension ultimately led to Ockham's complete separation of "natural life" from the "Christian life" of grace. Practically speaking, the school of Ockham drove a wedge between creation and redemption in Jesus Christ. We have seen that this had happened earlier, in the first centuries of the Christian church, when the Greek and near-eastern dualistic ground-motives began to overpower the Christian motive. One could detect this not only in Gnosticism but also in Marcion [second century A.D.] as well as in the Greek church fathers.

Although understood in the Greek sense, "natural life" within the framework of nature and grace did refer to God's work of creation. The creation ordinances thus belonged to the realm of nature. As we saw [139] above, Ockham deprived these ordinances of their intrinsic worth. For him the law proceeded from a divine arbitrariness that could change its demands at any moment.

Luther (1483-1546), the great reformer, had been educated in Ockham's circle during his stay at the Erfurt monastery. He himself declared: "I am of Ockham's school." Under Ockham's influence the religious ground-motive of nature and grace continued to permeate Luther's life and thought. Of course, this did not happen in the same way in which this ground-motive was conceived within the Roman Catholic church. The Church of Rome rejected a *division* of nature and grace, considering the former a lower portal to the latter. Rather, Luther was influenced by Ockham's dualistic conception which posited a *sharp divide* between "natural" life and "supranatural" Christian life. For Luther, this conflict between the nature motive and the grace motive expressed itself as the opposition between *law* and *gospel*.

To understand this polarity in Luther's thought, which today plays a central role in Karl Barth and his followers, we must note that Luther returned to a confession which had been rejected by Roman Catholicism: the confession of the radicality of the fall. But within the nature-grace ground-motive, justice could not be done to this truly scriptural teaching. The moment it became embedded in an internally split religious framework, it could not do justice to the meaning of creation. In Luther's thought this shortcoming manifested itself in his view of the law. He depreciated law as the order for "sinful nature" and thus began to view "law" in terms of a religious *antithesis* to "evangelical grace." It might seem that this contrast is identical with the contrast made by the apostle Paul in his teaching on the relation of law to grace in Jesus Christ. Paul expressly proclaimed that one is justified by faith alone, not by the works of the law. Actually, however, Paul's statements do not harmonize in the least with Luther's opposition between law and gospel. Paul always calls God's law *holy* and *good*. But he wants to emphasize strongly that fallen humankind cannot fulfill the law and thus can live only by the grace of God.

Under Ockham's influence, however, Luther robbed the law itself, as creational ordinance, of its intrinsic value. For him the law was harsh and rigid and as such in inner contradiction to the love commandment of the gospel. He maintained that Christians, in their life of love that flows from grace, have nothing to do with the demands of the law. Christians stood above the law. Yet, as long as Christians still existed in this "vale of tears" they were required to adjust themselves to the rigid frame of law, seeking to soften it by permeating it as much as possible with Christian love in their relation to their fellow human beings.

However, the antagonism between law and gospel remains in this line of thought. It is true that Luther spoke of the law as the "taskmaster [140] of Christ" and that he thus granted it some value, but in truly *Christian* life the law remained the counterforce to Christian love. It needed to be broken from within. For Luther the Christian is free not only from the *judgment* of the law, which sin brought upon us, but in the life of grace the Christian is free from the law itself, standing entirely *above* the law.

This view of law was certainly not scriptural and resulted in questionable conclusions. In Luther's thought the scriptural creation motive recedes behind the motive of fall and redemption. He did not acknowledge a single link between nature, taken with its lawful ordinances, and the grace of the gospel. Nature, which was "radically depraved," had to make way for grace. Redemption signified the death of nature rather than its fundamental rebirth. From the ground-motive of Roman Catholicism Luther therefore argued for "nature" to be "swallowed-up" by "grace."

But because of his dualism, Luther could not conclude that the Christian ought to flee from the world. He believed that it was God's will that Christians subject themselves to the ordinances of earthly life. Christians had to serve God also in their worldly calling and office. No one opposed monastic life more vehemently than Luther. Still, nowhere in Luther do we find an intrinsic point of contact between the Christian religion and earthly life. Both stood within an acute dialectical tension between the realm of evangelical freedom and the realm of the law. Luther even contrasted God's will as the Creator, who places a person amidst the natural ordinances, with God's will as the Redeemer, who frees a person from the law. His view of temporal reality was not intrinsically reformed by the scriptural ground-motive of the Christian religion. When in our day Karl Barth denies every point of contact between nature and grace, we face the impact of Luther's opposition between law and gospel.

Birth of Protestant Scholasticism

We have seen how the religious ground-motive of nature and grace influenced Luther in his opposition of law and gospel. For him law was the domain of "sinful nature" while evangelical freedom belonged to the realm of "grace." By viewing "nature" entirely in the light of *sin*, Luther's thought completely suppressed the biblical creation motive. The view of temporal life was not subjected to an inner reformation by the spiritual motive-power of the biblical ground-motive.

Luther remained within the scholastic tradition by considering reason *[Vernunft]* the sole guide in the realm of nature. Unlike Roman Catholicism, however, he did not acknowledge a connection between natural reason and the revelation of God's Word. "The whore reason" *[Die Hure Vernunft]* had to capitulate whenever one desired to understand the voice of the gospel. With respect to the truths of faith, reason was hopelessly blind. But in matters of secular government, justice, and social order a person possessed only the light of reason. It was Ockham's rigorous dualism that sustained Luther's separation of natural reason and the Christian religion.

Clearly, in principle Luther had not severed himself from the dualistic [141] ground-motive. For example, the great reformer expressed no more interest in "profane science" than his scholastic tutor Ockham. Although he fumed against Aristotle and pagan philosophy in general, he did not point the way toward an inner reformation of thought. From his dualistic starting point he did not see that human thinking arises from the religious root of life and that it is therefore always controlled by a religious ground-motive. Similarly, even his new insight into our calling in the world was infected by the dualistic ground-motive. To be sure, his idea that every profession rests upon a divine calling was thoroughly in line with the biblical thrust of the Reformation. And Luther certainly broke with the Roman Catholic view that monastic life had a higher value than worldly life. However, for Luther worldly life belonged exclusively to the realm of law and stood in an inner tension with the gospel of love.

But nowhere was the nature-grace dualism expressed more clearly than in Luther's view of the church. Luther was relatively indifferent to the temporal organization of the church, believing that wherever the Word and the sacrament were found the church was present. He did not grant the church its own exclusive, internal legal sphere of competence. Law and ordinance, according to him, remained "worldly affairs" guided only by "natural reason." He did not, for instance, see an inner connection between the typical qualification of the institutional church as a community of faith and its inherently *ecclesiastical* legal order. What was just belonged to the sphere of the law, to "sinful nature." Only proclamation of the Word and the administration of the sacraments belonged to the realm of grace. Thus it was relatively easy for Luther to leave the juridical organization of the church to the worldly magistrate [*landsheer*] even if this delegation of authority were only "of necessity." Ever since, "regional churches" [*landskerken*] have been a typical characteristic of Lutheran countries.

The peculiar dialectic of the nature-grace ground-motive led Luther's learned friend and co-worker Melanchthon [1497-1560] to attempt a new synthesis between the Christian religion and the spirit of Greek culture.

Unlike Luther, Melanchthon was trained in the literary humanism of his time. He had a great love for classical, Greco-Roman antiquity. Because of his efforts to adapt Greco-Roman thought to the Lutheran articles of faith, the form-matter motive of Greek philosophy soon dominated the Protestant view of nature. Since Luther was basically indifferent to philosophy, the Greek ground-motive had temporarily lost its prominence; with Melanchthon, however, it regained its claim on the [142] view of temporal life and on the view of the relation between soul and body. Melanchthon became the father of *Protestant scholasticism* which even today opposes the truly biblical approach in scientific thought with the unbending resistance of an age-old tradition.

Thus the inherent dialectic of the unscriptural nature-grace ground-motive also infiltrated the Protestant mind. However, there was no pope who could maintain the new synthesis by means of official verdicts and decrees, and soon the unscriptural nature motive was filled with the new religious content of modern humanism, secularizing and absorbing the motive of grace.

Dialectical Theology

It is against the background of the development of the nature-grace ground-motive in the Protestant world of thought that the so-called dialectical theology of Karl Barth [1886-1968] and his initial co-workers (Emil Brunner, Gogarten, and others) must be understood. Dialectical theology sharply opposes the religious antithesis in the area of worldly life, rejecting the idea of Christian politics, of a Christian political party, of a Christian labor organization, and of Christian scholarship.

This new theological movement arose in Switzerland shortly after the first world war. Its adherents forsook the modern humanism that had penetrated German and Swiss theology, having experienced the shocking inner decay of this humanism between the two wars. In harmony with the sixteenth century reformers, dialectical theology seeks to press the incommensurable claim of God's Word against the arrogance of humanism. It is *antihumanistic* in the full sense of the word.

Nevertheless, dialectical theology sustains itself on the dialectical, unscriptural ground-motive of nature and grace. Moreover, the spiritual force of the *humanistic* ground-motive is clearly at work in the view of nature defended by Barth and his immediate followers. They understand nature not in the scholastic-Aristotelian sense but in the modern humanistic sense.

Prior to 1933, when national socialism came to power in Germany, Barth and his school advocated a radical dualism between nature and grace. Like Luther, they identified nature (conceived humanistically) with sin. They separated nature absolutely from the Word of God, which they understood as the "wholly Other" *[ganz Andere]*. Their fundamental depreciation of nature testified to the antihumanistic tendency of this theology. Casting the scriptural creation motive aside, they could not even hint at "points of contact" between nature and grace. However, they left the inner dialectic of this dualistic ground-motive unchecked, and deep divisions soon arose within the circle of dialectical theology.

Briefly, let us consider the historical context behind the development [143] of dialectical theology. In the preceding chapters we have discussed at some length three of the four religious ground-motives that have dominated the development of western culture: the Greek motive of form and matter; the Christian motive of creation, fall, and redemption through Jesus Christ; and finally the motive of nature and grace introduced by Roman Catholicism. We saw that these ground-motives are the hidden, central forces that have lent a sustained direction to the historical development of the West up to this day. As genuinely religious *community* motives, they have controlled the life and thought of Westerners in all areas of life, including those of state and society.

We also saw that the Roman Catholic motive of nature and grace had seemingly bridged the radical antithesis and the irreconcilable contrast between the pagan ground-motive of Greek culture and the ground-motive of the Christian religion. Roman Catholicism conceived of nature in the Greek sense; nature was a cosmos composed of formless, changing matter and of a form that determined the immutable essence of things. Human nature also was viewed as a composition of form and matter; a person's "matter" was the mortal, material body (subject to the stream of becoming and decay), and that a person's "form" was the imperishable, immortal, rational soul, which was characterized by the activity of thought. For Roman Catholicism a supranatural sphere of grace, which was centered in the institutional church, stood above this sphere of nature. Nature formed the independent basis and prelude to grace. Catholicism adapted the church's teaching on creation to the Greek view of nature, which itself was entriely permeated by the pagan religious ground-motive of form and matter. When we exposed the true religious meaning of the Greek ground-motive, we demonstrated that the adaptation and reconciliation were only *apparent*.

We began by establishing that the form-matter motive originated in an irreconcilable conflict within Greek religious consciousness between the older religions of life and the newer culture religion of the Olympian world. The former rested on a deification of the "stream of life," the stream that arose from "mother earth." Although the life stream was without shape or form, whatever possessed individual form and figure arose from it and was subject to decay. Death was the consequence of fate, the blind and cruel *Anangkē* or *Moira*. The life stream itself was eternal. Unceasingly it created new forms from the dead, forms that in turn had to make room for others.

By contrast, the later religion of culture was based on a deification of Greek cultural forms. The new Olympian gods were not formless; they took on personal form and figure. Leaving mother earth, they were enthroned on Mount Olympus, the home of the gods. They stood far [144] removed from the eternally flowing stream of becoming and decay. They were immortal; their form and shape stood above this earth and, although they were invisible to the eye of sense, they were full of light and glory. But the Olympian gods were only deified cultural forces. They had no power over *Anangkē*, the blind fate of death. *Anangkē* remained the self-determining antagonist of the deities of culture. The culture religion, therefore, was able to gain official status only in the Greek city-state; in private life the Greeks remained faithful to the old religion of life with its focus on the problems of life and death.

Harboring the profound conflict between these two religions, the religious ground-motive of form and matter was thoroughly dualistic. It was utterly incompatible with the creation motive of the Word of God, in which God reveals himself as the absolute origin and creator of all things.

The Roman Catholic attempt to bridge the Greek and Christian ground-motives created a new religious dualism. The Greek conception of nature and the Christian teaching of grace were placed over against each other in dialectical tension. Only papal authority could preserve the artificial synthesis between these inherently antagonistic ground-motives. The Reformation limited this papal authority. Thus, to the extent that the ground-motive of nature and grace permeated the Reformation movement, its inner dialectic could unfold itself freely. Hence in the debates concerning the relation between nature and grace within Protestantism, we note the rise of theological trends which denied any point of contact between "natural life" and divine grace in Jesus Christ.

In recent years this tension has grown more extreme in the dialectical theology of Karl Barth who, in his debates with his former ally Emil Brunner [1889-1966], explicitly rejected every point of contact between the Christian faith and natural life. It is said that Barth repudiated the idea of Christian culture. Many feel that Barth, having absolutely separated nature and grace, mortally wounded the Roman Catholic synthesis. In truth, however, dialectical theology in its religious ground-motive remained closely related to Roman Catholicism. Historically speaking, one might say that the Roman Catholic Church had taken revenge on the Reformation by way of the continued impact of its dialectical ground-motive within Protestantism. For this motive had a "unifying" effect only as long as the Roman Catholic idea of the church, with its central papal authority, was accepted. With the rejection of the papacy, the artificial synthesis could not remain intact because of the tension within the ground-motive. The Reformation fragmented into a disconnected diversity of directions, *each identifiable by its particular view of the relation of "nature" and "grace."* It was not the scriptural ground-motive of creation, [145] fall, and redemption that led to this division within the Reformation but the continual influence of the dialectical ground-motive of Roman Catholicism.

Dialectical theology had of course severed itself from the Greek and scholastic conception of nature. By incorporating the new humanistic view of nature in its dialectical tension with the humanistic view of freedom, dialectical theology evinced that it was influenced by humanism. Here the difference also becomes apparent. Whereas the Roman Catholic Church accepted the Greek view of nature in a *positive* sense by attempting a reconciliation with the Christian creation motive, *Barth allowed the creation motive to recede from sight*, sacrificing it to the motives of fall and redemption in Jesus Christ. The great master of dialectical theology had no use at all for creation ordinances that might serve as guidelines in our "natural life." According to Barth the fall corrupted "nature" so thoroughly that the knowledge of the *creation ordinances* was completely lost.

Brunner was of a different mind on this point. He believed that the creation ordinances were valid as expressions of "common grace." At the same time, however, he depreciated these ordinances by placing them in a dialectical polarity with the divine love commandment which he understood as the "demand of the hour" *[Gebot der Stunde]*. Because of their *general* character, the creation ordinances are cold and loveless. They form the realm of the *law* which stands in dialectical opposition to the freedom of the *gospel* in Jesus Christ who was free from the law. In Brunner too one clearly sees the continuation of the Lutheran contrast between law and gospel. This contrast is merely a different expression of the dialectical opposition between nature and grace which in this form – gospel vs. law – had made its first appearance in late-medieval scholasticism.

For Brunner the law, the cold and rigid framework in which God confines sinful "nature," must really be broken through by the evangelical commandment of love. This commandment knows no general rule and is valid only in and for the moment. For example, marriage – a creation ordinance – cannot be dissolved; but the command of love can break through this rigid, general structure as the "demand of the hour." Brunner held that God is indeed the author of the creation order, but as "law" the creation order is not the authentic will of God, which manifests itself only in the evangelical love commandment.

Thus it is still the same ground-motive of nature and grace which brought division even within the camp of dialectical theology. In Barthianism it led to such a rigorous dualism that the scriptural ground-motive, the dynamic power of the Christian life in this world, was cut off at its root. Christian scholarship, Christian political life, Christian art, [146] Christian social action – Barth, and to a lesser degree Brunner, considered them impossible. In their eyes, such efforts compromise the very name of Christ and express the synthesis scheme of Rome which proceeds from a hierarchic continuity between nature and grace.

In its religious root, dialectical theology persistently demonstrates the inherent dialectic of the Roman Catholic ground-motive in a modern way. The nature motive of dialectical theology embraces the humanist view of reality, and this view is immediately brought into "crisis" because it expresses a person's "sinful nature." The "Word of God," wholly unilaterally, lashes into this "self-determining nature" like a lightning flash, bringing all of life, including so-called "Christian culture," into a crisis under the divine judgment. Barth did not see any connection whatsoever between natural life *as one knows it* and creation. For him natural life must be viewed exclusively in terms of the fall. Although Brunner admitted that a connection exists between them, he too depreciated creation. Without a doubt, an unmistakable Gnostic tendency asserted itself in dialectical theology. Dialectical theology drove a wedge into the ground-motive of Scripture, dividing creation and redemption and separating God's will as the Creator from God's will as the Redeemer.

Since dialectical theology incorporated both the Roman Catholic and the modern humanistic ground-motives (the second within the framework of the first), it is necessary that we explore in detail the humanistic ground-motive of *nature* and *freedom*. We will trace the dialectical development of the modern ground-motive from its inception to the present day. In this way we hope to provide a thorough picture of the great spiritual movement of humanism. [147]

Chapter 6

Classical Humanism

The fourth religious ground-motive to gain hold of western culture was that of nature and freedom. Introduced into the historical development of the West by the great humanistic spiritual movement of the modern period, this motive gradually acquired undisputed leadership that lasted until the end of the nineteenth century. At that time humanism itself began to experience a fundamental spiritual crisis while the powers of the Reformation and of Roman Catholicism freed themselves from the substrata of culture and renewed their participation in the great spiritual struggle for the future of western civilization. Today antihumanistic and anti-Christian forces have joined the conflict, the outcome of which we cannot yet predict.

It is humanism that first demands our attention. Particularly since the German occupation of Holland the relationship of humanism to Christianity has been a crucial question. How must we understand humanism's religious ground-motive of nature and freedom? Against what background did humanism arise, and how did it develop? What led to its current crisis? These are fundamental questions which we shall attempt to answer.

The Ground-Motive of Nature and Freedom

We saw earlier that Roman Catholicism underwent a severe crisis at the close of the Middle Ages. The power position of the church, which embraced the whole of medieval society, began to fall apart. One life [148] sphere after another wrested itself loose from the church's power. Rooted in the ground-motive of nature and grace, ecclesiastically unified culture began to disintegrate. In short, numerous indications pointed clearly to the dawning of a new age.

In this critical period a movement arose within late-medieval scholasticism that fractured the church's artificial synthesis between the Greek view of nature and the Christian religion. This proved to be of decisive significance for the modern period. Denying any point of contact between nature and grace, this movement exposed the deep rift between the Christian religion and the Greek view of nature. Western culture seemed presented with two options: it could either pursue the "natural" direction which ultimately would lead to a complete emancipation of a person from the faith of the church, or return to the pure ground-motive of Scripture, namely, creation, fall, and redemption through Jesus Christ. The Renaissance movement, the early forerunner of humanism, followed the first path; with varying consistency, the Reformation followed the second.

The Renaissance was basically concerned with a "rebirth" of humankind in an exclusively natural sense. The "new age" that dawned required a "new people" who would take their fate into their own hands and would no longer be faithfully devoted to the authorities. This is the ideal of the risorgimento, the ideal of rebirth in the sense of the Renaissance. Rebirth was to occur through a revitalized participation in Greco-Roman culture, freed from the damage it had incurred in its accommodation to Christianity. But the Renaissance did not return to the original Greek religious ground-motive. The deepest religious root of the Renaissance movement was the humanistic religion of human personality in its freedom (from every faith that claims allegiance) and in its autonomy (that is, the pretension that human personality is a law unto itself).

From the beginning the Renaissance revealed the inevitable conflicts between the Christian religion and the natural religion of human personality. For instance, the Italian Niccolo Machiavelli [1469-1527] was a fierce adversary of Christianity. The Christian message that one should love one's enemy contradicted human virtu, human initiative and heroism. Virtu expressed the ideal of the heroic Renaissance person who could make Fortuna, blind fortune, serve his or her own ends.

However, humanism did not reveal itself in its first representatives in terms of these anti-Christian tendencies. Men like Erasmus [1466-1536], Rodolphus Agricola [1443 or 1444-1485], and Hugo Grotius [1583-1645] represented a "biblical humanism"; along with their admiration for the Greek and Roman classics they also pleaded for a free study and exegesis of Scripture. They certainly did not attack the abiding doctrines of the [149] Christian faith. To all appearances their sharp criticism of medieval scholasticism was intended as a return to the simple teachings of the gospel, and they greatly admired the church fathers, many of whom, after all, had also been steeped in classical culture.

But a more careful examination reveals that the real spiritual force behind "biblical humanism" was not the ground-motive of the Christian religion. The biblical humanists viewed the Christian religion more as a moral code than as the revealed path of salvation for a human race lost in sin and spiritual death. Already among them the dignity of human personality stood at the center of religious attention. When Erasmus, who remained a Roman Catholic, defended the moral freedom of the human will against Luther, his civilized and dispassionate argument must have compared favorably with Luther's heated prose which expressed the basic convictions of the latter's faith. But Erasmus lacked the profound Christian earnestness that moved the German Reformer. Humanism began to reveal its true intentions even before its emancipation from the authority of Scripture was complete.

The new motive of freedom was inseparably linked to a new view of nature. As we saw earlier, in the Greek view of human nature the mysterious matter motive with its stress on inexorable fate had been the continuous and tragic counterforce to the optimistic form motive which emphasized the good and the beautiful in the cosmos. Likewise, the scriptural view of reality, which contained the teaching of a radical fall, cut off any superficial optimism about nature at the root. But humanism approached nature from a completely different frame of mind. Already the early Renaissance detached its conception of nature from both the Greek idea of fate and the Christian doctrine of radical depravity. Proudly conscious of its autonomy and freedom, modern humankind saw "nature" as an expansive arena for the explorations of its free personality, as a field of infinite possibilities in which the sovereignty of human personality must be revealed by a complete mastery of the phenomena of nature.

Copernicus's discovery of the earth's dual motion – around its own axis and around the sun – revolutionized the traditional Aristotelian and Ptolemaic picture of the world, which viewed the earth as the fixed center of the universe. Unjustifiably, the church continued to defend the old conception for many years, considering the centrality of the world in the history of salvation indispensable to the faith. In view of this, humanism proclaimed the Copernican worldview as a new kind of gospel, turning against the authority of the church and scholasticism with revolutionary passion. When Galileo and Newton later laid the foundations for mathematical physics, thereby demonstrating that one [150] could indeed control nature by discovering the fixed laws to which moving things are subject, humanism, driven by its religious personality ideal, embraced the new scientific method and elevated it to a science ideal that should be accepted as the directive in every area of science, an ideal that pretended to disclose the true coherence of the whole of reality.

The religious motive of the absolute freedom and autonomy of human personality did not permit scientific thought to proceed from a given creation order. The creation motive of the Christian religion gave way to faith in the creative power of scientific thought which seeks its ground of certainty only within itself. With this change, the idea of the autonomy of science was given a completely different meaning from that of Thomistic scholasticism. Although Thomas Aquinas had also taught that natural reason is autonomous with respect to the Christian faith and divine revelation, his position was wholly embedded in the Roman Catholic ground-motive of nature and grace. Nature was merely the preamble to grace, and natural reason itself was brought to a higher stage of perfection by the supernatural gift of grace. As long as reason operates in a purely scientific manner, it can never lead to conclusions in the area of natural knowledge that conflict with the supranatural means of revelation. If seeming conflicts do arise, they are attributed to logical errors of thought, as Thomas promptly points out. Wherever Thomas followed Aristotle's Greek view of nature, his idea of the autonomy of natural reason continually led him to adapt Aristotelian theory to Roman Catholic doctrine.

But the humanistic approach was very different. Humanism was controlled not by the Roman Catholic ground-motive of nature and grace but by the modern motive of nature and freedom. Faith in the absolute autonomy of free personality could not tolerate a distinction between natural and supranatural truths. It could not endorse the Roman Catholic adaptation of autonomously discovered natural truths to the authoritatively binding teachings of the church.

By the same token, humanism also broke with the Greek view that the order of reality is anchored in an invisible world of forms. The humanistic science ideal could not possibly subscribe to the Greek "forms" which for Aristotle constituted the essence of perishable things. The Greek form-matter motive communicated nothing to a modern person. For in that motive, the contemplative reflection of a "beautiful world of forms" which brings measure and harmony to chaotic "matter" was but idle speculation. After all, the driving force of modern humankind's scientific research was the ideal of complete mastery of nature by means of which the autonomous freedom of human personality – that is, its independence from supranatural powers – could be revealed. [151]

It would soon be clear, however, that the new nature motive stood in religious conflict with the humanistic freedom motive, a conflict similar to the tension within the Greek motive of form and matter and the Roman Catholic motive of nature and grace.

Dialectical Tensions

The religious ground-motive of humanism is just as internally divided as the Greek and Roman Catholic ground-motives were. It too bears a so-called dialectical character; that is, it consists of two religious motives which are in inner conflict with each other and which alternately drive the stance and worldview of humanism from one pole to the other.

In essence, the nature motive of modern humanism is a motive of control. The control motive is intensely and religiously tied to the new freedom motive which originated in the humanistic religion of personality, the cult of autonomous humankind which desires to make itself absolutely independent of every authority and of every "supranatural power" in order to take its fate into its own hands. Like Copernicus, who brought about a revolution in the traditional picture of the universe with the earth at its center, so humanism brought about a revolution in the religious valuation of human personality. In the humanistic conception, this personality is the measure of all things, including religion. As the great philosopher Immanuel Kant declared near the end of the eighteenth century (in the preface to the first edition of his *Critique of Pure Reason*):

> Our age is, in a special degree, the age of criticism, and to criticism everything must submit. Religion through its sanctity, and law-giving through its majesty, may seek to exempt themselves from it. But they then awaken the just suspicion, and cannot claim the sincere respect which reason accords only to that which has been able to sustain the test of free and open examination.

When the motive of control arose out of the new religion of personality (with its motive of freedom), the conflict between "nature" and "freedom" soon began to reveal itself. For the control motive of autonomous humanity aims at subjecting "nature" and all of its unlimited possibilities to humankind by means of the new method of mathematical science. Nowhere in reality does it tolerate the validity of limits to the operation of the natural-scientific method. The motive of control thus expressed itself in the new science ideal which sought to grasp all of reality in a closed chain of cause and effect, a chain determined by the universal [152] laws of mechanical motion. It will not accept the validity of anything as "truly real" if it does not fit into this chain of mechanical cause and effect. The firm ground of theoretical inquiry lies neither in a divine creation order nor in a realm of the eternal forms of being, as the Greek philosophers thought. The humanistic freedom motive sanctioned no other basis for theoretical thought than mathematical natural-scientific thinking itself. There was a profound conviction that the certainty of mathematics lay within mathematics itself with its exact methods of proof. Autonomous humankind trusts the certainty of its thought and depends on it.

But it was precisely when the new science ideal was taken seriously that a problem presented itself. It became apparent that when science determined all of reality as an uninterrupted chain of cause and effect, there would no longer be room anywhere in that reality for human freedom. Human willing, thinking, and acting required the same mechanical explanation as did the motions of a machine. For if the human person itself belongs to nature, then it cannot possibly be free and autonomous. "Nature" and "freedom," science ideal and personality ideal turned out to oppose each other as declared enemies. A genuinely inner reconciliation between these antagonistic motives was impossible, since both were religious and thus absolute. Although the freedom motive had evoked the new motive of nature, each motive excluded the other. Humanism had no choice but to assign religious priority or primacy to one or the other.

Humanism's self-conscious point of departure during the first period of its development (dating from the sixteenth to the seventeenth and the greater part of the eighteenth centuries) was the primacy of the new science ideal. Humanism believed that science would make modern humankind truly free and would raise it above the dogmatic prejudices of church doctrine. Science would bring true enlightenment that could oust pagan barbarism and the dark realm of medieval superstition. True freedom was sought where the foundation of modern science had been found – in autonomous, lucid, and distinguishing thought.

But again, it was here that obstacles arose. Did not the new science ideal require that thinking itself be explained in terms of the mechanism of the soul's motions? Indeed – at least if this science ideal with its new nature motive would be consistently applied. But already here some humanistic thinkers raised objections. The motive of freedom required that at least mathematical thought, the core and center of free personality, be exempt from natural-scientific explanation.

Descartes and Hobbes

Along these lines the founder of humanistic philosophy, the famous Frenchman René Descartes [1596-1650], drew a firm line between the [153] bodily or material world and the human soul. Descartes limited "nature" to the material world. In this world the new science ideal reigned supreme; here it could explain all phenomena mechanistically. But the "human soul" was considered independent of the "natural body" as a substance or as a self-sufficient entity which depends on nothing outside of itself for its existence.

In Descartes's estimation it was necessary that mathematical thinking be entirely free and autonomous. Finding its ground and validity in itself alone, mathematics was independent of sensory impressions received from the "external, bodily world." According to Descartes and his followers, mathematical concepts do not arise from sensory perceptions of material things; rather, they find their guarantee in themselves.

Thus, in conformity with the dualistic motive of nature and freedom, Descartes split human existence into two rigorously separated parts: the material body and the thinking soul. The ultimate ground of scientific certitude and, for that matter, of moral freedom, lay in consciousness, in the "I think."

But Descartes did not succeed in consistently maintaining this strict division between material reality and the thinking soul. Under the leadership of the famous Englishman Thomas Hobbes [1588-1679], another stream of humanistic thought directed itself against Descartes's dualistic view of reality which limited the nature motive in favor of the freedom motive. Hobbes, who witnessed both the revolution of England under Cromwell and the restoration of the British royal house, concurred entirely with Descartes in the humanistic ground-motive that governed their thought. Confidently declaring war between modern science and the "kingdom of darkness," Hobbes was an early apostle of the Enlightenment.

But in contrast to Descartes, Hobbes did not call a halt to the application of the new science ideal to what was believed to be the seat of human freedom, namely, autonomous thought and free will. Well-versed in the new natural-scientific method of the great Italian scientist Galileo, with whom he had made personal contact during his travels, Hobbes aimed at applying Galileo's method consistently, utilizing it in the areas of morality, law, political life, and even the motions of the human soul.

Like Descartes, Hobbes began his main philosophical work by expressing universal doubt in the reality that presents itself in daily experience. He suggested the following experiment to his readers. One should begin by mentally breaking down the whole of that reality to the extent that its truth is not guaranteed by scientific inquiry. Then – with a conscious allusion to the creation story – he argued that scientific thought must shed light upon the chaos and must systematically rebuild the world again by means of the exact scientific method. For Hobbes such a reconstruction [154] required the simplest possible tools: strictly mathematically defined concepts. The new science of nature, which initially approaches reality exclusively in terms of its aspect of mechanical motion, must reduce all natural phenomena within its special field of investigation to phenomena of motion. In this way Hobbes analyzed sensorily perceived phenomena into their simplest components; counted, measured, weighed, and described in mathematical formulas, these components were the stepping-stones toward explaining more complex phenomena.

In Hobbes's opinion this exact method provided the key to explaining all of reality. For this reason he could not acknowledge a boundary between "body" and "soul." He reduced everything – including mathematical thinking – to the motions of material things. The fact that this reduction eliminated the basis for the human freedom of the will, did not trouble him. Scientific integrity demanded that mathematical concepts themselves be understood as products of the mechanical motions of the soul, motions caused by the impressions of bodies in one's psychical life. Clearly, then, the nature motive was dominant in Hobbes. And yet his vision that only the new science would chart the way toward human freedom testified to his solidarity with Descartes.

Hobbes's system is commonly called "materialism." This, however, was a modern and humanistic materialism, one driven by the religious force of a humanistic freedom motive that had dissolved itself into the nature motive. His materialism and the ancient materialism of the Greek nature philosophers had only their name in common. In the Greek philosophy of nature, "matter" signified the eternally flowing, formless stream of life. Giving birth to whatever possessed individual shape and form, this life stream was understood as the divine origin of things. The modern concept of a mechanical law of nature was entirely unknown to the Greeks. While the modern concept of a natural law originated from the humanistic motive of nature and freedom, the Greek concept was governed entirely by the form motive of culture religion. Before the humanistic concept of natural laws could arise it was necessary that the modern view of nature be discovered; "nature" needed liberation from both the Greek idea of fate and the Christian idea of the fall into sin. "Nature" had to be deprived of its "soul" before it could be subjected to human control.

We see, then, that humanism entangled itself in the dialectic of its own ground-motive already at its first stormy appearance. Nature and freedom soon began to reveal their inherent conflict as religious motives. The first philosophical conflict between Descartes and Hobbes pointed towards the further development of this dialectic. At this stage, however, humanism still had the vitality of its youth. It was aware that the future of the West lay in its hands. Gradually, both Roman Catholicism [155] and the Reformation were forced onto the defensive, surrendering more and more of western culture to humanism. The sun of humanism was rising, and an optimistic faith in humanity's creative power inspired its leading figures.

Humanism has human-ized the Christian ground-motive of creation, fall, and redemption within its own ground-motive. Hence humanism is not a paganism; it passed through Christianity which it changed into a religion of human personality. Soon it also assimilated the ground-motives of Greek culture and Roman Catholicism.

Political Theories of the Modern Age

The new humanistic ground-motive soon made its impact felt on the process of differentiation in society that had begun with the Renaissance. After the breakup of medieval ecclesiastical culture, the idea of the state began to break through in various countries in the form of absolute monarchies. Gradually absolute monarchs regained for the crown many of the prerogatives that had fallen into the hands of private lords under the feudal system. The new humanistic science ideal suggested an exact method by means of which this could best be done.

State Absolutism

Humanism did not acknowledge that governmental authority is limited intrinsically by societal spheres grounded in the creation order. Such a recognition contradicted the autonomy and freedom of human personality, which humanism interpreted in accordance with its own religious ground-motive. As long as modern humankind expected freedom and independence through the advance of the new exact sciences, the motive of nature or control would also govern its view of society. The "modern age" demanded a "new construction." Humanistic thought directed itself particularly to the construction of the state. The new state, which was unknown in medieval society, was designed as an instrument of control that could gather all power to itself. Humanism assumed that science was as competent to construct this state as it was to manufacture the mechanical tools controlling the forces of nature. All current knowledge of society, which was still relatively incomplete, was consciously adapted to this constructionistic science ideal.

In sixteenth century France, Jean Bodin [1530-1596] laid the foundations for a humanistic political theory in his absolutistic concept of sovereignty. This concept formed the methodological starting point and [156] cornerstone for his entire political theory. For Bodin the essential characteristic of sovereignty lay in its absolute competence or power unlimited by positive juridical boundaries. Although in conscience the government might indeed be bound by natural and divine law, it nevertheless stands above all positive rules of law which derive their validity only from the will of the government itself. No law-giver *[rechtsvormer]* in the nonstate spheres of life can appeal to a ground of authority that lies outside of the power of the state's sovereign legislator. In the whole of society the formation of law must depend solely on the will of the state's legislator, the only sovereign. Even customary law or common law, which in the Middle Ages was more significant than statutory law, was subject to either the implicit or explicit approval of the sovereign. The necessity of this requirement was understandable, since customary law clearly bore the stamp of an undifferentiated feudal system, the mortal enemy of the modern state.

The humanistic concept of sovereignty did not merely declare war on the undifferentiated societal relationships of the "Dark Ages." Inspired by the modern ideal of science, it also aimed at guiding the incipient process of differentiation in order to guarantee the absolute sovereignty of the state over all the remaining life-spheres. Among the differentiated societal bonds, the church had been the state's most powerful rival. But now the time had arrived to bring the church under the sovereignty of the state. The Reformation and subsequent conflicts within Protestantism had excited denominational passions, and the unrest of the churches spilled over into politics, threatening the peace and unity of the state. Political humanism had only one remedy for this, namely intervention by the state in the internal affairs of the church in order to force the church into a position of "tolerance" which would bring peace and unity back into the body politic.

This was also the solution offered by Hugo Grotius, an adherent of Bodin's concept of sovereignty. Grotius was not only a representative of "biblical humanism," but also the founder of the humanistic theory of natural law. This new doctrine of natural law was also one of the heralds of the modern age. It became the champion for the reconstruction of the legal system necessitated by the breakthrough of the modern idea of the state. It sought a point of contact with classical Roman law with its sharp distinction between public law and private civil law, and, like the Roman jurists, based the latter in a law of nature whose basic principles were the inherent freedom and equality of all human beings. This humanistic doctrine of natural law stood in clear opposition to the undifferentiated indigenous law of the Germanic nations which was viewed as being in conflict with "natural reason." Over against this, Grotius and his immediate [157] followers intended to derive a comprehensive system of legal rules from the "rational, social nature" of humankind. Independently of human institutionalization, these rules were to hold for all times and all nations. To this end they employed the new mathematical and scientific method, the ground and certainty of modern humanity. In reality, however, it was largely classical Roman law that furnished the "rules of natural law." Grotius sought an autonomous basis for his doctrine of natural law, independent of ecclesiastical authority. As he himself declared, this foundation would hold even if God did not exist. As a "biblical humanist" he hastily added that denying the existence of God is reprehensible; but this admonition did not alter the fact that for him an appeal to the "natural, social nature" of a person was sufficient for the validity of natural law.

Grotius's standpoint was completely different from the position of Thomas Aquinas which was based on the Roman Catholic ground-motive of nature and grace. Thomas indeed taught that a person can know certain principles of natural law and natural morality by the natural light of reason independent of divine revelation. But in the final analysis Thomas always referred these principles back to the "rational" wisdom of God the Creator. Thomas and the other scholastics would never think of searching for an autonomously valid ground of natural law in "natural human reason" alone, a ground independent of even the existence of God. Only in the heretical trends of late scholasticism, which completely separated nature and grace, did these tendencies appear. Grotius's conception of the basis of natural law as independent of the existence of God was a harbinger of the process of emancipation and secularization which came to fruition during the Enlightenment. The new humanistic freedom motive was the starting point of this process.

Characteristic of the new doctrine of natural law was its individualistic construction of societal spheres, particularly the sphere of the state. As long as the motive of nature and control was dominant in the humanistic doctrine of natural law, theorists unanimously defended Bodin's absolutistic concept of sovereignty. Because its consistent application left no room for the free personality, the concept of sovereignty was made acceptable through the construction of a "social contract." It was argued that by means of a social compact the originally free and equal individuals had surrendered their natural freedom voluntarily in order to bind themselves as a body politic. This was generally followed by a contract of authority and subjection, in which the people conferred authority to a sovereign and pledged obedience. In this way the free and autonomous individual consented to the absolute sovereignty of a ruler. Such an individual could therefore never complain of injustice. [158]

Critical Turning Point
When humanism accentuated the natural-scientific motive of control rather than the motive of freedom, it sought the ultimate ground of certainty in mathematical and natural-scientific thinking. Humanists were convinced that only the method of thought developed by modern mathematics and natural science teaches human beings to know reality as it is "in itself," stripped of all the subjective additions and errors of human consciousness which victimize us in the naive experience of daily life. The new ideal of science came with great pretensions! It alone could unveil the true order and coherence of reality.

However, precisely at this point the first misgivings about the value of the exact sciences arose. The location of the ground of certainty lay in the exact concepts of subjective consciousness. But the more human beings explored this subjective consciousness itself, the more insistent the question of the actual origin of mathematical and natural-scientific concepts became. From where did these concepts derive their content? One could not deny that children and primitive peoples did not possess them. They must therefore have originated in the course of time. But from what did we form them? Here the problem of theoretical knowledge was immediately cast into psychological terms. It was assumed that inner human consciousness had only one window to the reality of the "external world." This window was sensory perception as it functioned in the aspect of feeling. If consistently carried through, this assumption implies that the origin of mathematical and natural-scientific concepts can only lie in the sense impressions of the external world. But from these impressions one could derive neither exact mathematical relationships nor the mechanical laws of cause and effect that constituted the foundation of classical mechanics. Perception merely taught that there is a temporal sequence of sense impressions from fact A to fact B. It never demonstrated that B always and necessarily follows A, and yet this demonstration was what the laws of physical science required.

Faced with this predicament, the conclusion was reached that we cannot know to what extent the exact natural sciences assist us in understanding reality. Why then, we may ask, do we still accept the laws of causality? At this point humanism showed that it was unwilling to abandon its new science ideal. Its solution was as follows: if the law of cause and effect does not make us understand the coherence of reality as it is in itself, then this law must at least refer to a mechanical connection between our sense impressions.

David Hume's well-known theory of the association of impressions and representations was the model for this view. The Scottish thinker [159] Hume [1711-1776] explained the sequence of cause and effect entirely in terms of psychical association, arguing that if we repeatedly observe fact B following fact A, then at our next perception of A we necessarily connect A with the representation of B.

The critique of scientific thought begun by John Locke and continued by David Hume struck a serious blow to the "metaphysical" pretensions of the deterministic science ideal which claimed that science could furnish knowledge of reality as it is "in itself," that is, independent of human consciousness. It seemed that the freedom motive, which had suffered under the overextension of the nature motive, might get the chance to free itself from the deterministic ideal of science. If the natural-scientific laws do not correspond with objective reality, then science cannot claim the right to deny the freedom of one's thought and will. But were modern people prepared to pay this price for reinstating their awareness of freedom and autonomy? Would they sacrifice the foundations of their science ideal to this end?

The epistemological attack on the science ideal was only a prelude to a widespread and critical reversal within the humanistic thought – and life-orientation. After their initial intoxication with science, modern thinkers began to reflect on the deepest religious root and motive in their lives. This deepest root was not modern natural science but the humanistic religion of personality with its motive of freedom. If the deterministic science ideal was unable to give the autonomous freedom of a person its just due, then it should not occupy the dominant place in the humanistic life- and worldview. If this is the case, then it is erroneous to search for the essence of a person in scientific thought; and then it is imperative that the motive of control, the dynamic behind the science ideal, be deprived of its religious priority. Primacy belongs to the freedom motive instead.

It was Jean-Jacques Rousseau [1712-1778] who called humanism to this critical self-examination. In 1750 he became famous overnight by submitting a paper in response to a competition organized by the University of Dijon. The topic was a favorite Enlightenment theme: what have modern science and culture contributed to the freedom and happiness of humanity? Rousseau's answer was a fierce, passionate attack both on the supremacy of science in life and on all of modern, rationalistic culture. Rousseau argued that science had exchanged freedom and equality for slavery. Also in his later writings Rousseau remained a spokesman for the humanistic freedom motive. For him the root of human personality lay not in exact scientific thought but in the feeling of freedom.

Rousseau's humanistic religion was not one of reason but of feeling. When he claimed that religion resides in the heart rather than in the [160] mind, he regarded the "heart" not as the religious root of human life, as the Scriptures teach, but as the seat of feeling. He also interpreted the nature motive in terms of a natural feeling of freedom. The original natural state of human beings was a condition of innocence and happiness; individuals lived in freedom and in equality. But rationalistic culture brought humankind into slavery and misery. It created inequality and subjected nations to the rule of kings. As a result, no trace was left of the free and autonomous human personality.

Nevertheless, Rousseau did not believe that a return to the happy state of nature was possible. He had no desire to abandon the modern idea of the state. Rather, he sought to conceive of a body politic that would conform fully to the freedom motive of modern humanity. He envisioned a state in which individuals, after relinquishing their natural freedom and equality, could regain them in a higher form.

Certainly, in the first phase of humanism, Grotius, Hobbes, and other proponents of natural law attempted to justify the absolute sovereignty of the ruler before the forum of the humanistic freedom motive. Their point of departure too was a "state of nature" characterized by freedom and equality. The notion of a social contract was required to justify governmental authority – whether or not followed by a contract of super- and subordination between people and government. Under such a contract individuals voluntarily surrender their natural freedom and equality. In complete autonomy, they place themselves under a government. In this way, individuals can transfer their natural authority to the government, retaining nothing for themselves. *Volenti non fit iniuria:* no injustice is done to one who wills it. One cannot complain of injustice if one agreed to the institution of absolute government.

John Locke [1632-1704] was among the first modern thinkers not satisfied with this natural-law construction of an absolute state. His starting points were the inalienable rights of life, property, and freedom, which could not be surrendered even in a contract. From the outset, therefore, Locke limited the content of the social contract to the goal of the peaceful enjoyment of one's natural human rights in a civil state. Individuals relinquished to the government only their natural competence to defend their rights on their own behalf against intrusion from others. In this way Locke laid the basis for the classical liberal view of the state. According to this liberal approach the state is a limited liability company (corporation) organized to protect the civil rights of life, liberty, and property.

Thus already in Locke's classical liberal idea of the state we discover a reaction of the freedom motive against the nature motive which had governed the earlier conceptions of natural law. Rousseau, however, was not satisfied with this reaction. Like Locke, he proceeded from the [161] free and inalienable rights of a person. But Rousseau went beyond the essentially private-legal human rights, which constitute the foundation of civil private law, to the public-legal guarantee of the freedom and autonomy of human personality in the inalienable rights of the citizen. In this way Rousseau is the founder of the classical humanistic idea of democracy which soon clashed with the classical liberal conception of the state.

Classical Liberalism

"Freedom and equality!" This was the indivisible slogan of the French Revolution, the death warrant for the remnants of the old regime *[ançien régime]*. It was inscribed in blood. Both during and after the Restoration period many spoke of the hollow and unrealistic tone of these revolutionary concepts. Such criticisms, however, were misplaced, and as a result many arrows missed the mark in attempts made to refute the principles of the French Revolution.

Undoubtedly, the principles of the French Revolution were governed by the humanistic ground-motive. Locke and Rousseau were its apostles. However, the "natural-law" theories of these thinkers aimed at two concrete goals: a) the breakthrough of the idea of the state in terms of the final breakdown of the undifferentiated feudal structures; and b) the breakthrough of the fundamental idea of civil law, i.e., the idea of human rights. These goals could indeed be realized because they were entirely in line with the process of differentiation which had begun in western society after the Middle Ages and which was, as we have argued in an earlier context, founded in the divine order for human history. Both goals presupposed the realization of freedom and equality in a specifically juridical sense, and not, for example, in an economic or social sense. Further, both belonged together; a civil-legal order cannot exist without the order of the state.

An authentic state is not really present as long as the authority to govern in effect belongs, as a feudal right, to the private prerogatives of a ruler who in turn can convey, pawn, or lend them to officials belonging to the ruler's realm or even to private persons. According to its nature and inner structure, the state is a *res publica,* a "public entity." It is an institution qualified by public law, a community of government and subjects founded typically on a monopoly of sword power within a given territory. As Groen van Prinsterer declared in his second period of intellectual development, every true state has a republican character.

Thus the division of the forms of the state into monarchies and republics commonly made since Machiavelli is basically incorrect. The word *re-*

public indicates nothing whatsoever about the form of government. It merely signifies that the state is a public rather than a private [162] institution. But the word *monarchy* does pertain to a form of government; the government here is monarchical, that is, a single person is the head of government. Conversely, the word *monarchy* does not relate to the question of whether a monarchy complies with the character of the state as a republic. Throughout the course of history many monarchies have lacked the character of a state, since governmental authority functioned not as an office serving the *res publica* but as the private property of a particular ruler. Governmental jurisdiction was an undifferentiated feudal prerogative. In such cases one should speak not of a state but of a realm (regnum), which was the property of a king. Not every realm is a state.

Nevertheless, the monarchical form of government is not incompatible with the character of a republic. Royal authority can function as the highest office within the *res publica*. The opposition between "monarchy" and "republic" arose only because the undifferentiated view of royal authority, as a private prerogative of the ruler, was maintained for such a long time precisely in the monarchical setting. This is also the reason why so many natural-law theorists in the humanist tradition linked the idea of the state to the idea of popular sovereignty. It seemed that only the sovereignty of the people complied with the view that the state is a *res publica*. Furthermore, in the light of the religious ground-motive of humanism, popular sovereignty seemed the only way to justify governmental authority before the forum of the free and autonomous human personality.

Thomas Hobbes, with his keen intellect, quickly detected the weakness in the conception of popular sovereignty in which the people and the state were identified (seen as one). After all, in this construction the "people" was but an aggregate of individuals who contracted with each other to relinquish their freedom and equality and thus entered a state relationship. But Hobbes clearly saw that without a government this "people" cannot form a political unity, a state. Only in the person of the government does the people become a corporate body capable of acting on its own. The government represents the unity of the people. For this reason Hobbes rejected the notion that people and government can be viewed as two equal parties that enter into a contract to settle the content of governmental authority. In view of this, Hobbes had no use for the notion of popular sovereignty which supposedly existed prior to and apart from the body politic. Only the government, as representative of the unity of the people, is the true sovereign. The people could never protest against the sovereign's injustice, since its actions comprised the actions of the people. Although Hobbes first attempted to justify the absolute monarchy of the Stuarts, he had little difficulty in isolating his position from [163] the monarchical form of government when the Puritan Revolution temporarily unseated the Stuarts, establishing the authority of the English parliament. Sovereignty could also be vested in a body like parliament.

John Locke's classical liberal political theory was directed against Hobbes's absolutistic concept of sovereignty that left the people unprotected from their ruler. Locke reinstated popular sovereignty as the basis for the republican character of the state. However, he did not commit the error of linking popular sovereignty to a specific form of government, arguing only that the democratic form of government in the sense of a representative government guarantees the people's freedom best. For Locke the crown merely represented the sovereign people even in an autocratic, monarchical form of government. If it was clear that the king no longer promoted the cause of the people and the common good, and if the people lacked democratic and parliamentary institutions, then the people could resort to revolution. In such a case the people only exercise their original right of sovereignty, for a despotic monarch who merely pursues his private interests is not the head of state but just a private person.

Thus in Locke the idea of the representation of the people acquired a republican sense that was genuinely related to the idea of the state. This republican feature distinguished the modern idea of representation from the feudal practices of the Middle Ages, when the estates (knighthood, clergy, and townsmen) acted as the representatives of their respective "subjects" before their lords. For here the republican basis was lacking.

Locke's political theory is a prime example of classical liberalism because he views the state as an association among individuals entered into for the purpose of establishing organized protection of the natural, inalienable human rights, i.e., liberty in the sense of private autonomy, property, and life. These natural human rights constitute the basis for the sphere of civil private law where all individuals without discrimination can enjoy legal freedom and equality. These rights were not transferred to the state in the social contract. The social compact transfers to the state only one's natural freedom to defend one's right to life, liberty, and property. In civil society every person is free, by means of labor, to acquire private property and to dispose of it autonomously. This freedom is guaranteed by the power of the state and subject to limitations required by the common good in accordance with the law.

The social contract is thus the avenue by means of which individuals decide to enter into the body politic for a specific and limited purpose. But the social contract also comprises a contract of authority whereby these individuals subject themselves once and for all to the will of the [164] majority in the exercise of the most prominent right of sovereignty, viz., the institution of the power of legislation. The sovereign people thus possess what French theorists describe as the *pouvoir constituant*, the original legal power to institute a legislative body. The people exercise this legislative power only by means of representation, not directly as Rousseau argued in his radical democratic conception.

Locke's liberal conception of the state did not imply a universal right to vote on the part of every citizen. He was perfectly satisfied with a limitation of the franchise to a socially privileged class, as was the case in the English constitutional monarchy of his day. Freedom and equality in "civil society," in the private-legal order, did not at all imply equality in the political rights of the citizens, and certainly not a so-called "economic democracy." Locke's democratic ideal did not extend beyond the demands that the king exercise legislative power only through parliament, the constitutional representative of the people, and that the king be subject to all of parliament's laws. His democratic ideal directed itself only against the private prerogative and divine right *[droit divin]* of the monarch, since both contradicted the humanistic idea of freedom and autonomy of the human personality, oriented to what the English call "the rule of law." Locke's ideal must be understood against the background of the constitutional monarchy of William of Orange. Later this ideal itself came into conflict with the notion of radical democracy, the political gospel preached by Rousseau on the eve of the French Revolution.

For classical liberalism democracy was not an end in itself. Rather, it was a means to protect private civil rights. When democracy was later elevated to be an end in itself *[Selbstzweck]* on the basis of the humanistic freedom motive, democracy developed in an antiliberal manner. This line of development was Rousseau's.

After Locke, the classical liberal idea of democracy was linked with the idea of the separation and balance of the legislative, executive, and judicial powers of the state. The French thinker Montesquieu [1689-1755] was a major advocate of this doctrine. Taken together, then, the following configuration of ideas comprises the classical liberal idea of the just state [law state; *rechtsstaat*[1]]: the state is a representative democracy founded in popular sovereignty, subject to the constitutional supremacy of the legislature though with the greatest possible separation and balance of the state's three powers, and organized to protect the individual's civil [165] rights. One can find a penetrating analysis of this position in the excellent dissertation by J.P.A. Mekkes, entitled *The Development of the Humanistic Theories of the Constitutional [Just] State.*[2]

The humanistic freedom motive distinctly inspired the liberal idea of democracy. But in the context of classical liberalism this motive was expressed only in the doctrine of inalienable human rights, in the principles of civil legal freedom and equality. As we noted above, the political

---

1 *General Editor's note*: The term *rechtsstaat* will as a rule be translated as "just state."
2 J.P.A. Mekkes, *Proeve eener critische beschouwing van de ontwikkeling der humanistische rechtsstaatstheorieën (Utrecht/Rotterdam: Libertas, 1940).*

equality of citizens was definitely not a part of liberalism. The doctrine of the inalienable rights of citizens, in the sense of Rousseau's radical democratic theory, is not of liberal origin.

But does this liberal conception of the constitutional state embody the principle of pure democracy as seen in accordance with the humanistic freedom motive? Not at all! The entire principle of representation, especially when it is severed from the notion of universal franchise, is inherently at odds with the principle of pure democracy. Unquestionably, the liberal idea presupposed an aristocratic and elite foundation. The legislature merely represented the people within the republic. With or without the cooperation of a monarch, it exercised legislative authority independently of its constituents. The legislature was a people's elite chosen according to the liberal standards of intellectual ability and wealth. The voters themselves belonged to an elite. According to liberal criteria, only they were capable of fulfilling this special political function. In view of his radically democratic standpoint, Rousseau's judgment of this highly esteemed English liberalism was surprisingly mild when he wrote: "the English people believe that they are free. But they are mistaken. They are free only while choosing members of Parliament."

In reality, the impact of classical liberalism on the development of the modern constitutional state is a direct result of the absence of a consistent application of the democratic principle. This does not mean that liberalism – with its individualistic, humanistic basis and application – is acceptable to us. But we appreciate its blend of monarchic, aristocratic, and democratic elements which Calvin already recommended as a basis for the relatively best form of the state. Moreover, the principle of the independence of parliament over against the electorate is fully in harmony with the state as *res publica* as we have explained it. Further, the principle of an elite – when divorced from its indefensible ties to land ownership, capital, or the intellect – is an aristocratic element which the modern literature on democracy increasingly recognizes as a necessary counterforce to the anarchistic influence of the "masses" in government policy. Finally, Montesquieu's famous teaching on separation and balance of powers [166] within the state contains an important kernel of political wisdom which is easily overlooked by those critics who only see the untenability of this theory.

Certainly, little effort was needed to demonstrate the impossibility of an absolute separation of the legislature, the executive, and the judiciary powers in the persons who occupied these offices. Opponents quickly pointed out that the separation of powers was not found in the English constitution, as Montesquieu had claimed. In our day some have attempted to salvage Montesquieu's theory on the separation of powers by interpreting it as a mere separation of constitutional functions which could be combined in the same office-bearer. But this "correction" cuts the heart out of Montesquieu's theory by interpreting it in a purely legal sense while it was intended as a political guideline. The French thinker aimed at a balance of political powers within the structure of the state. He sought to achieve this balance by placing the "aristo-democratic" power of the people in the legislature and the "aristo-cratic" or monarchic power in the actual administration of the country's affairs. It was clear that in his conception, judicial power as such could have no political significance. For this reason he referred to this power as a kind of "nullity" *[en quelque façon nulle]* and as the mere "mouthpiece of the law" *[la bouche de la loi]*. From a constitutional point of view this of course cannot be maintained. The power of the judiciary, itself devoid of political significance, should not however be subject to the political influence of either the legislature or the executive. It had to function in the "balance" of powers for the protection of the rights of the individuals.

Viewed in this light, we see that Montesquieu merely elaborated the principle of "moderation" *[modération]* in democracy by a balanced blend of monarchical and aristocratic political forms. This was entirely in keeping with the liberal framework of Locke's representative democracy. Locke too considered a balance of political powers essential, which was quite in harmony with the juridical supremacy of the legislator. He attempted to achieve this balance by limiting the frequency and duration of the legislative sessions, so that the executive branch in fulfilling its task would not be unduly influenced by political pressure from parliament. Although he did not include the judiciary in his triad of powers, Locke explicitly maintained that the independence and impartiality of the courts are necessary conditions for guaranteeing the liberties and rights of the individual.

What also deserves our attention is that the parliamentarism which developed in England under the foreign House of Hanover did not agree with the classical liberal idea of democracy. The political hegemony given to parliament and, behind it, to the political party electorally victorious under its "leader," was clearly in conflict with the liberal idea [167] of balancing political powers. Parliamentarism in England was curbed by the nation's self-discipline, adherence to tradition, sportsmanlike spirit of "fair play," respect for individual rights, and acceptance of the principle of elitism. But in a country like France parliamentarism was easily transformed into a full-fledged radical democracy. The executive was reduced to a political tool of the assembly, and in turn the assembly became degraded to a political tool of the masses.

Radical Democracy

Modern commentators on democracy are fond of contrasting liberalism and democracy. Liberalism, they argue, is based on the principle of freedom; democracy, by contrast, on the principle of equality. When they battled their common foe – namely, the remnants of feudalism – the contrast between these two basic principles was not yet clear. As a result, the French Revolution was waged under the slogan of freedom, equality, and brotherhood.

But this approach is certainly based on a misunderstanding. It is an error caused by a lack of insight into the classical humanistic meaning of the concepts of freedom and equality. To be sure, a fundamental contrast exists between liberalism and radical democracy, as we have dicovered above. Liberalism advocates a moderate democracy tempered by representative institutions, a balance between the monarchical power of the ruler and the legislative power of the assembly or parliament, and the independence of the judiciary to guarantee the individual citizen's private rights of freedom.

Radical democracy could accept neither the representative system nor the liberal idea of separating and balancing political powers. Nevertheless, as long as radical democracy rested on its classical humanistic basis, it too was driven, in an even more fundamental way, by the humanistic motive of freedom. Rousseau, the apostle of radical democracy, was also the spokesman for the humanistic ideal of freedom. He was the first thinker to attach religious primacy to the humanistic freedom motive, above the humanistic nature motive. To him autonomy, the free self-determination of human personality, was the highest religious good which far surpassed the classical science ideal of controlling natural phenomena through the natural-scientific research methods of the mind. In Rousseau's radically democratic idea of the state, equality of citizens constituted a radical application of the humanistic principle of freedom in the structuring of the state.

For Locke, the father of classical liberalism, democracy was not an end in itself. It was merely a means to protect the private autonomy of the individual in the free disposition of the property rights of such a person. Equality in his view belongs to the private-legal sphere of civil law. [168] The conception of natural law during his day was primarily concerned with retaining as much natural freedom as possible, the freedom that one enjoyed before the state was instituted. Locke made no radical attempt to apply the humanistic freedom motive to the exercise of political rights. He never referred to inalienable constitutional rights of citizens or to constitutional equality of citizens. For him it was self-evident that an elite composed of the educated and of the rich should be the active participants in legislation. Even the election of legislators was limited to an elite. A large majority of citizens was expected to be content with a passive role in politics.

But for Rousseau the crucial issue was political freedom. He concerned himself with the inalienable rights of the citizen *[droits du citoyen]*, in which the rights of human beings *[droits de l'homme]* were to be given public-legal expression. Rousseau was as it were religiously obsessed with guaranteeing the autonomous freedom of human personality within the constraints of the state. No element of free self-determination could be lost when individuals made the transition from the state of nature to the state of citizenship. If one surrendered but a part of one's natural freedom in the social contract without receiving it again in the higher form of the inalienable rights of active citizenship, then self-determination was unattainable. To Rousseau a representative system like England's assaulted the free self-determination of humankind. Sovereign people cannot be "represented," for representation forces the people to surrender their rights of free self-determination to an elite which can then impose its own will on the people again and thus enslave them.

The liberal idea of separating political powers was entirely unacceptable to Rousseau for the same reason. The sovereignty of the people is indivisible, since the people's inalienable right of free and sovereign self-determination is itself indivisible. What does it profit people – in Rousseau's humanistic frame of reference – if they retain part of their private, natural freedom over against the state, but then subject themselves to laws not of their own free making in their public position as citizens? A state of this kind is clearly illegitimate over against the inalienable claims of human personality. It remains an institution of slavery. Only in a state based on suppression and domination – a state therefore which is illegal before the tribunal of the humanistic ideal of personality – does the need arise to protect the private rights of individuals, the need to keep intact the remnant of natural liberties over against the tyrant.

But a state which is an authentic expression of the humanistic idea of freedom cannot possibly recognize the private freedom of the individual over against itself. Such a state must completely absorb the natural freedom of a person into the higher form of political freedom, of active citizenship rights which inherently belong to all citizens equally and not [169] merely to an elite among them. In a truly free state the individual cannot possess rights and liberties over against the *res publica* because in such a state the total freedom of the individual must come to expression.

In Rousseau's natural-law conception of radical democracy, the individuals surrender all their natural freedom to the body politic in order to receive this freedom back, in a higher political sense, as members of the state. In a free state every citizen without distinction becomes a part of the sovereign people, a body which sets the law for itself. The right of legislation cannot be transferred; it is the primary right of the sovereign people itself. The law must be the expression of the truly autonomous communal will, the *volonté générale*, which is never oriented to a private interest but always serves the public interest *[salut public]*. A true law cannot grant privileges to particular persons or groups, as in the feudal system. If the law imposes public burdens, they must affect all citizens equally. Here too the freedom of the body politic requires that all citizens be equal before the law. The government of the land can possess neither political power nor legal authority of its own. As magistrates, the rulers are merely servants of the sovereign people, removed at will.

Like Hobbes's Leviathan, Rousseau's radical democracy is totalitarian in every respect. It expresses the humanistic motive of freedom in a radically political way, in absolute antithesis to the biblical creation motive underlying the principle of sphere sovereignty. The notion of radical democracy contains the paradoxical conclusion that the highest freedom of a person lies in the utter absolutism of the state. As Rousseau declared: "a person must be forced to be free" *[On les forcera d'être libre]*.

But this criticism may not blind us to the important elements of truth in Rousseau's classical humanistic conception of democracy. In distinction from the undifferentiated feudal notions of governmental authority, Rousseau's idea of the state pointedly brought the res-publica conception to the foreground. He still viewed equality, the foundation of democracy, in a strictly political sense as an outgrowth of the citizen's freedom within the state. Rousseau was not a victim of the inner decay of the democratic idea that we see around us today when people rob the principle of equality of its typically political meaning by applying it indiscriminately to all relationships of life. Indeed, some of these leveling tendencies were noticeable among certain revolutionary groups during the French Revolution. Communism had already begun to announce its presence. But these trends could not persevere as long as the classical idea of the state, though itself a humanistic absolutization, retained its hard won hold on the minds of people. The battle between "freedom" and "equality" could begin only when the idea of the state itself was drawn into humanism's latest process of decay. [170]

Separation of Science from Faith

We have sketched the development of humanism's life- and worldview from its beginnings to its first inner crisis. We have seen that humanism was rooted in the religious ground-motive of nature and freedom, a motive containing an irresolvable dualism.

Unquestionably, the freedom motive was humanism's deeper driving force. This motive embodied itself in the modern ideal of the personality, the cult of the human person understood as an end in itself. Freed from all faith in given authority, human personality attempted to establish the law for itself in complete autonomy and according to its own rational standards.

The new view of nature itself was rooted in the freedom motive. It was not inspired by the Greek motive of form and matter. It also withdrew itself from both the ground-motive of divine revelation, that of creation, fall and redemption through Jesus Christ, and the Roman Catholic ground-motive of nature and grace (supra-nature). Modern humanity saw "nature" as unrelated to and uninfluenced by "supranatural" powers; "nature" was conceived of as reality within space and time to be completely controlled by natural science and technology. It was believed that human freedom would achieve its highest expression in its mastery over nature. It was this belief that called forth the classical humanistic science ideal, which declared that the natural-scientific method could analyze and reconstruct reality as a completely determined and closed chain of cause and effect. This assumption was the basis of the classical humanistic motive of nature.

But we also saw that the consistent application of the nature motive left no place in reality for human freedom and autonomy. From the outset "nature" and "freedom" stood in an irreconcilable conflict. It was the growing awareness of this conflict that caused the first crisis of humanism. In solving the tensions between "nature" and "freedom," some attempted to moderate the pretensions of the old ideal of science by limiting the validity of the laws of nature to sensorily perceivable phenomena. Above this sensory realm of "nature" there existed a "supra-sensory" realm of moral freedom which was not governed by mechanical laws of nature but by norms or rules of conduct which presuppose the autonomy of human personality.

This was the solution to the basic religious issue of humanism prepared by the great German thinker Immanuel Kant (1724-1804) near the end of the eighteenth century, the "Age of Enlightenment." Like Rousseau, Kant gave religious priority to the freedom motive of the modern personality ideal. Freedom, according to Kant, cannot be scientifically proven. For him science is always bound to sensory experience, to [171] "natural reality" as understood in the limited context of Kant's own conceptions. Freedom and autonomy of personality do not lie in sensory nature. They are practical ideas of a person's "reason"; their supra-sensory reality remains a matter of faith. Such a belief is not the old faith rooted in ecclesiastical authority or in divine revelation; for faith subject to authority does not agree with the motive of freedom in modern humanism. Rather, as Kant formulated it, this is a "rational faith." Rooted in autonomous reason itself, it is entirely in keeping with the autonomy of the human personality.

In Kant's thought the chasm dividing science and faith runs parallel to the chasm separating nature from freedom. This deserves special attention because it clearly demonstrates that the modern division between faith and science, which in line with Kant many accept as a kind of gospel, is itself religious throughout. This must be clearly understood because this division between faith and science is used to disqualify every attempt at a biblically motivated inner reformation of scientific thought as an "attack on science itself." But the separation itself is religious. Inspired by humanistic faith, this pretended division clashes with the true state of affairs. Wrestling to find its religious anchorage and to locate the firm ground of its life, modern humankind sought ultimate meaning in its autonomy and freedom, in its rational and moral disposition. But this religious ground threatened to sink from under its feet since the classical science ideal left it no room. The first attempt to escape from this religious crisis consisted therefore in the separation of faith from science.

The religious passion that characterizes today's defence of the "neutrality of science" reveals the true origin of this modern attitude toward science. The latter is rooted in the humanistic motive of freedom. It built itself a "realm of nature" according to the view of reality prescribed by the classical science ideal.

The science ideal – even in Kant's limited sense – had simply taken the place of the divine creation order in the modern humanistic consciousness. It proceeded from a conception which denied the given nature of the many aspects of reality, their particular character and the different laws which govern these respective aspects. This science ideal gave rise to the construction of a "mechanistic worldview" which, though in recent years discredited by the facts themselves, still vitally shapes the outlook of many. The mechanistic standpoint rests on an overestimation and an absolutization of the mechanical phenomena that present themselves only in the aspect of motion, and then only in the so-called macro-processes, the large-scale processes which in an objective sense are accessible also to sensory perception. But when one [172] conceives of the other distinct aspects of reality – such as the organic, the logical, the historical, etc. – in terms of mechanical motion, then the unrealistic picture of the classical science ideal results. One is then predisposed to think that all other sciences must operate according to the methods of mechanical physics, believing that organic processes, emotional feeling, the historical development of culture, logical processes, economic processes, and so forth must be scientifically approached and explained as processes of mechanical motion which are determined entirely within the chain of cause and effect. Under these assumptions the humanistic nature motive indeed has a free hand in the unfolding of science and will leave no room for the humanistic freedom motive. The classical ideal of science does not take into account the order of reality set by God the Creator. In this order we detect the great diversity of aspects, each with its own irreducible nature and law, which proclaims the astonishing richness and harmony of God's creative wisdom. The classical science ideal rejects this great diversity in the order of reality.

When Kant called a halt to the further expansion of the science ideal by keeping it out of the "supra-sensory realm of freedom" – the shelter of the humanistic personality ideal – he was motivated not by a respect for God's creation order but by the humanistic freedom motive. This freedom motive could tolerate limits no more than the classical ideal of science could.

The ideal picture of reality designed in accordance with the mechanistic science motive was colorless and monotonous. It was as it were a modern Moloch which devoured whatever became a victim of its suggestive power. Even the rarefied atmosphere of Kant's world of ideas in the supra-sensory realm of freedom could not withstand the influence of this view of reality. Under a different guise, the science ideal regained its former supremacy in the nineteenth century.

We have also seen how this science ideal influenced political theory to create a society after science's own image. We have seen that the state was dissolved into an aggregate of individuals under the influence of the natural-scientific way of thinking. Binding themselves together contractually, the individuals subjected themselves to an absolutely sovereign authority. The modern state was constructed according to the mechanistic model of a machine – an instrument of control, as in the natural-law theory of Thomas Hobbes, the humanistic contemporary of Oliver Cromwell.

We also noted that the freedom motive in the humanistic theory of natural law reacted against this mechanistic and absolutistic picture of the state. Classical liberalism, defended also by Kant, sought to place the [173] state in the service of individual freedom. But even the "free individual" remained an "element" of society. Kant displayed the unmistakable signs of natural-scientific thought of the day. Because of its overestimation of the individual, liberalism became unrealistic, colorless, and alien to social reality.

Nevertheless, the humanistic teaching of natural law had great significance for the evolution of both the modern idea of the state and the idea of civil private law with its basic principles of human rights, freedom, and equality before the law. The same must be said for the various conceptions of democracy developed on a humanistic basis: representative democracy and radical or direct democracy.

It is necessary that we keep the whole panorama of the first phase of humanism's development clearly in view in order to understand the enormous reaction of the freedom motive against the classical way of thinking in humanism's subsequent period. [174]

Chapter 7

Romantic Redirection

The French Revolution finally translated the individualistic notions in the humanistic theory of natural law into political reality. However, the Revolution was soon followed by the great reaction of the Restoration period. The Restoration period initiated a new spiritual upheaval within the humanistic worldview. It was a time of ferment and spiritual confusion in which many again dreamed of a synthesis between Christianity and humanism, as in our own postwar period. But in actual reality humanism maintained the absolute spiritual leadership in western culture.

The New Personality Ideal

The religious turn within humanism's worldview occurred from out of its deepest dynamic; namely, the freedom motive of the personality ideal. During the Restoration period the personality ideal began to emancipate itself from the influences of the classical nature motive and its mechanistic world picture. The personality ideal acquired a new and irrational form which assimilated and reinterpreted many familiar Christian motives in a humanistic fashion. Even prominent Christian thinkers and statesmen, Roman Catholic as well as Protestant, were misled by this and mistook the new spiritual movement as a dependable ally in their fundamental battle against the revolutionary principles. We shall attempt to sketch this new spiritual movement within humanism in terms of the inner dialectic of humanism's own ground-motive. [175]

As we saw earlier, Kant had confined the classical ideal of science and its mechanistic view of nature to the area of sensorily perceptible phenomena. But within this limited realm of "nature" he had completely accepted the science ideal. In his conception, "nature" and "freedom" were separated from each other by an unbridgeable gap, though he granted religious priority to the freedom motive. However, even in Kant's view of the freedom and autonomy of human personality, one can clearly detect the influence of the natural-scientific attitude of the Enlightenment. After all, he retained the Enlightenment's *individualistic* and *rationalistic* orientation in his own view of human personality.

In the rationalistic view of nature maintained by the classical science ideal there was no place for a proper recognition of the *true individuality of things*. After all, irreducible individuality did not fit a view of nature in which all complex phenomena are dissolved into their simplest and colorless "elements" and wholly determined by universal laws of nature. In this view a particular phenomenon can be reduced to a specific instance that exemplifies the validity of a universal law or rule.

In Kant's conception of human personality one can still detect this type of rationalism. In his characterization of the autonomy of human personality, the true human *autos* (the selfhood or the ego) is known only by means of the universal form of the moral law (the *nomos*). Kant's rigorous ethics of law left no room for recognizing the value of *individual* disposition. With respect to the universal, moral law, all people are merely indistinct "individuals" who lack real individuality.

Conversely, this rationalistic and individualistic view of the personality ideal did not grant the true idea of *community* its rightful place. Kant shared with the entire Enlightenment the individualistic view of society produced by the overextension of the natural-scientific way of thinking. For him the state is an aggregate of individuals joined together under general legal rules of conduct by means of a social contract. For him even marriage is not a true community. He viewed it merely as a contract between two individuals of different sex for the mutual and lasting possession of each other's bodies.

Romanticism and the "Storm and Stress" *[Sturm und Drang]* movement bitterly opposed this rationalistic and individualistic view of the personality ideal. For Romanticism the motive of freedom demanded a different understanding of personality. Kant's "bourgeois morality" was ridiculed already in the early years of the Romantic era. The Romantics did not wish to interpret the autonomy of the person in such a way that the human *autos*, the true self, would lose itself in the *nomos*, the universal moral law. On the contrary, for them the *nomos*, the rule for human conduct, must find its origin in the full individuality of the *autos*, [176] in one's individual disposition. Human personality must indeed be a law unto itself! But if this is taken seriously, then the law must be wholly *individual*, in harmony with each person's disposition and special calling.

Early Romanticism placed this "ethics of genius" over against "bourgeois ethics." The thesis that general laws are completely opposed to true morality typified the change from a rationalistic to an irrationalistic conception of the autonomous personality. Humanism's turn to the other extreme, a turn that completely dismissed the validity of binding universal laws, led to dangerously anarchistic consequences, particularly in the area of sexual relationships.

Early Romanticism developed the "morality of genius" especially in an aesthetic direction. For Kant, individuality was just as valid in the realm of art as in the realm of organic life. But Kant did not understand this validity in a scientific way, which is directed at determining *objective* states of affairs in reality. Rather, the claims of the individual with respect to art were made on the grounds of a person's *subjective* power of judgment which cannot claim to grasp reality objectively but makes judgments only on the basis of the subjective impressions of a purposeful arrangement nature makes on one's faculty of judgment. Only in relation to this restriction did Kant treat the genius of the artist and did he speak of the impression of the "harmonious relation between nature and freedom" which the work of art makes on one's aesthetic faculty of judgment.

Romanticism made this conception of the work of art its starting point and transferred it to its "ethics of genius." For instance, the sexual surrender of a woman to a man out of spontaneous love – quite apart from the civil bond of marriage – was glorified as aesthetic harmony between "sensuous nature" and "spiritual freedom." Friedrich Schlegel's romance, *Lucinde*, glorified this kind of "free love" which is guided only by the harmony of the sensual and spiritual inclinations of the individual man and woman.[1] Johann Fichte [1762-1814] also defended this "free love" in one period of his thought.

The Romantic glorification of sexual love was characteristic of a new type of individualism which arose as a result of a shift from rationalism to irrationalism. Romanticism summoned its adherents to express this subjective, individual inclination in an aesthetic harmony between sensual *nature* and spiritual *freedom* in total disregard for the general rules of ethics established to guide the spiritless "masses." [177]

In order to escape the anarchistic implications of its new personality ideal, irrationalistic Romanticism needed to discover *limits* for the individual freedom of the autonomous personality. But such limits could of course not be sought in a universally valid moral law. They could only be found by viewing the individual person as a member of an all-embracing *community* which itself possesses a uniquely individual disposition and personality. The rationalistic conception of the person as a nondescript individual – a conception in which only the *general idea* of freedom and autonomy demanded practical realization – had to yield to an irrationalistic conception of the free personality as a wholly individual member of *the spiritual community of humankind* which differentiates itself in a variety of individual *partial* communities such as the peoples and nations of the world.

---

1 *Friedrich von Schlegel's Lucinde and the Fragments*, trans. with an intro. Peter Firchow (Minneapolis: University of Minnesota Press, 1971). *Lucinde* was first published in 1799.

It seemed that with this change Romanticism had given the old, abstract, and rationalistic idea of world citizenship a much richer content, filled with individuality. Autonomous and free personality could now express its individual inclination fully. But this individuality of any particular person is co-determined by that person's family, people, and the national community of which she is a member. Romanticism no longer acknowledged the existence of "a universal human being" as a nondescript individual with human rights; it viewed the individual personality only as a member of this individual national whole.

The humanistic personality ideal thus deepened and broadened itself as a *community ideal*. In its irrationalistic turn it simultaneously acquired a universalistic character. Freedom and autonomy were conceived of as the freedom and autonomy of the individual community of persons. This universalism is the ideology of community.

Ideology of Community

We have now become acquainted with the universalistic conception of the humanistic personality ideal. We have seen how Romanticism, which acquired its spiritual influence after the French Revolution, resisted the individualistic understanding of the humanistic freedom motive. That understanding had been influenced by the classical humanistic science ideal, which explicated all complex natural phenomena in terms of their simplest elements in accordance with the natural-scientific method. Human society too was seen in terms of its elementary components. The free, autonomous individual was viewed as this elementary component which thus constituted the point of departure for the modern conception of the law of nature and the natural-law construction of human society. As we saw [178] earlier, this individualistic theory was *rationalistic*; that is, the theory attempted to dissolve what was irrational – namely, the incomprehensible individuality of subjective human life – into rationally intelligible and transparent instances of universal law-conformities. The model and guide for this attempt had been the natural-scientific thought of the day. The classical science ideal sought to accomplish a rational control of "nature" by discovering the general laws that govern phenomena. To this end it was essential that the "components," in terms of which complex phenomena were to be understood, be stripped of any irrational characteristics so that they could be grasped in clear and transparent universal concepts.

Thus the "autonomous individual," in terms of whom complex societal phenomena were constructed, was the *rational* component of all social relations, stripped of all authentic individuality and endowed only with the *universal* faculties of reason and will which were viewed as autonomous and free in accordance with the humanistic freedom motive. This was the background of the proclamation of the French Revolution: freedom and equality for all human individuals.

In opposition to this individualistic and rationalistic view of the humanistic personality ideal, Romanticism posited its universalistic and irrationalistic conception. For Romanticism the autonomous freedom of the human personality cannot be understood in terms of a universal colorless individual constituted by rational lawful relationships, but rather in terms of the fully individual disposition of a person. In accordance with the humanistic ground-motive, a person's individual and irrational disposition is a law unto itself. The individual and ultimately irrational disposition of a person cannot be grasped in terms of any universal concept of understanding. Yet, in accordance with the humanistic ground-motive, it must be a law unto itself. A genius like Napoleon, for example, cannot be judged in terms of universal standards. The autonomous freedom of humankind requires that genius be understood in a strictly individual sense.

In order to avoid the anarchistic implications of this break with universal laws and norms for judgment, Romanticism needed new ties to restrict the individual personality in some fashion. The limits to the expression of personality were found not in a general law judging all human beings but only in the individual's membership in a higher human community which had a completely individual disposition itself. Romanticism enthroned the national community and its utterly individual, national spirit *[volksgeest]*. This community replaced the indistinct individual of humanistic natural law and of the French Revolution. Abstract individuals, instances of the general concept of "a human being," do not exist. Individual Germans, Frenchmen, Englishmen, Dutchmen do exist; and their individuality is determined by the individual character of the *volk* to which they belong. They share in that character because they have organically *[naturwüchsig]* come forth out of [179] a specific people. The wholly individual character or spirit of a people is also the free and autonomous source of its culture, state, legal system, art, social customs, and moral standards. In other words, moral rules and positive laws valid for societal relationships are the autonomous products of the spirit of an individual people and therefore cannot serve as the normative standards for other peoples which possess a different individual character or disposition. This is thus the irrationalistic and universalistic change in the humanistic freedom motive.

A new *ideology of community* was the immediate result of this change. Romanticism replaced the gospel of the autonomous and nondescript *individual* with the gospel of the autonomous and individual *community*. Both Romanticism and all of post-Kantian "freedom idealism" clung to the idea of a "community of humankind" of which all other communities are individual parts. This idea constituted Romanticism's "idea of humanity" or, in Goethe's words, respect for whatever "bears the human countenance" *[was Menschenantlitz trägt]*. But the community of humankind remained an eternal, supratemporal ideal which manifests itself in temporal society only in individual, national communities.

I trust that by now the intrinsically humanistic origin of this new community ideology is evident. This is a crucial matter since this ideology again poses a dangerous threat in our own day, as it is irreconcilably engaged in a battle against the scriptural ground-motive of creation, fall, and redemption in Jesus Christ.

The community ideology clearly conflicts with the scriptural motive of creation. Those who take the biblical creation motive seriously will never be guided by the idea of an autonomous national spirit which in its absolute individuality is its own law and standard. They will never view a *temporal* community as the totality of all human relationships of which the other societal spheres are merely dependent parts. On the contrary, they will accept the sovereignty of these spheres, all of which have a distinct character of their own because of their created inner nature. They will never attempt to reduce the horizontal societal interlinkages [*maatschapsbetrekkingen;* coordinational relationships] between distinct communities or between individual persons in their coordinate relations to communal bonds. In other words, they will be on guard against any overextension or absolutization of a temporal community at the expense of societal relations which, because of their inherent nature, are noncommunal in nature. In short, whoever takes the biblical creation motive seriously will never be able to accept the dilemma between individualism and universalism, the exaltation of either the "autarkic individual" or the "autonomous community." [180]

For some it is difficult to understand that universalism, with its community ideology, is essentially unscriptural. Why is it that many Christians condemn individualism but believe that universalism, which views temporal society as a total community of organic parts, is basically a Christian notion? The solution to this riddle is not difficult. They appeal to biblical statements which teach that God made all humankind "of one blood." [Acts 17:26; KJV.] Scripture itself proclaims that humankind is one great community, originating in Adam and Eve. Isn't this precisely the claim of the universalistic theory of society? Certainly not! The *genetic* origin or the way in which the human race originated with respect to its bodily existence sheds no light on the internal character and structure of the temporally distinct spheres of life in which God placed us.

If we carry the idea of Christian acceptance of universalism to its logical conclusion, the argument would proceed as follows. The temporal society of humankind is one large *familial* community founded on the bonds of blood. This familial community is a temporal totality of which all specific life-spheres are merely organic parts. Thus kinship bonds, individual families, states, ecclesiastical communities, economic structures, trade and industry are all equally parts of the familial community of humankind. Since parts must obey the law of the whole, the principle of the family is the true law for every specific life-sphere.

But, we must ask, is it indeed in harmony with Scripture to subject the life of the state to the law that governs the family? And is it possible to operate a modern industrial concern according to the example of the family? Clearly, whoever thinks in terms of this kind of universalism must begin by eliminating the internal natures of the various life-spheres that exist independently of the manner in which the human race takes on bodily form in the course of time.

But even a thinker like Abraham Kuyper, the great champion of the principle of sphere sovereignty, occasionally strayed into this universalistic trap by appealing to the genesis of humankind out of "one blood." Where in his works he started to follow this universalistic direction, he proved at the same time to be once again susceptible to the universalistic theory of the "national community" understood as an individual whole embracing all of the human societal spheres. Then the doctrine of sphere sovereignty is given a turn in which the clear, scriptural contours of his famous speech *Sphere Sovereignty*[1] can hardly [181] be recognized. Then "nation" and "government" are proclaimed to be two sovereign spheres of life: the nation *[volk]* as the individual, total community embracing every natural, "organically grown" societal relationship; and the government as a mechanistic, "surgical" device which must not tamper with the rights of a "sovereign people." Then the inner nature of the state is once again denied when the other, nonpolitical spheres of society, as autonomous elements of the natural life of the people *[volk]*, are infused into it. Then we note the appearance of the dangerous theory of "organic franchise" and the defence of a system in which "corporate" as well as "political" interests are represented. Then "sphere sovereignty" is reduced to the constitutional guarantee of parliamentary representation against usurpations of power on the part of the government. A meagre guarantee indeed!

In contrast, the Word of God teaches us to see all temporal spheres of society in terms of the created root-community *[wortel-gemeenschap]* of humankind that fell from God in Adam, but that was restored to communion with God in Jesus Christ. But this root-community of humankind, revealed to us in the Word of God, is not *temporal* in nature. It bears a *spiritual, central-religious* character. It touches the relation of humankind to God.

If we take our point of departure in the revelation of the spiritual root-community of humankind, then we stand in implacable antithesis to

---

1 Abraham Kuyper, *Souvereiniteit in eigen kring* (Amsterdam: J.H. Kruyt, 1880). This address was delivered at the opening of the Free University of Amsterdam.

every universalistic community ideology that considers a temporal community to be the totality of all societal relationships. Only the spiritual root-community in Jesus Christ bears a genuinely *totalitarian* character. Every other community ideology originates in the spirit of darkness.

The New Science Ideal

We have now traced in some detail the redirection in the conception of the humanistic freedom motive. The universalistic approach pushed the individualistic view to the background. Rationalism, which attempted to construe society out of its simplest elements – individuals – and which tried to reduce all individuality to a universal, conceptually definable rule or regularity, gave way to an *irrationalism* which did the opposite: it elevated the individual disposition or spirit of a people to the status of a special rule which cannot be applied to other peoples and nations.

It is a matter of course that this new conception of the freedom motive would also have definite repercussions in the realm of science. The natural-scientific standpoint of the classical science ideal had lost its attraction; the new universalistic approach rejected the scientific method [182] that divided a complex phenomenon into its simplest "elements." Instead, taking its point of departure from the individual whole, the new universalism proceeded to understand the peculiar place and function of the parts in terms of the whole. Its focus was constantly on the individuality of phenomena.

The science of history lent itself particularly to the application of this new method, since the historian sought theoretical insight into what was individual and unique *[einmalig]*. When attempting to describe historical phenomena, the concern of historians was to grasp the phenomena in the historical context of a given period. When analyzing the High Renaissance, for instance, they dealt with a historical *whole* of a completely individual character which immediately differentiated itself according to the national peculiarities of the different peoples. In this kind of study the historian is not concerned with finding universal laws which determine the course of individual events, as had been the procedure by which classical natural science sought to determine natural phenomena.

It seemed, then, that the new historical way of thinking opposed the natural-scientific method in every respect. For example, the historical approach implied that one must see the present as dependent upon the past. Cultural development occurs only in conformity with the line of historical continuity. Historical tradition is the link which ties the present to the past. Tradition embodies itself in cultural treasures which are not acquired by isolated "individuals" but in the course of generations. This historical tradition again is not identical for every nation but presents individual variants in accordance with the individual character or spirit of a people *[Volksgeist]*.

From the vantage point of the humanistic ground-motive, it seemed that historical development constituted a "dialectic" link between "nature" and "freedom." (*Dialectic* then refers to the process of breaking through contrasts.) At first sight "culture" seems to be the free and autonomous product of an "individual national spirit." But further reflection makes clear that this individual "creative freedom" has its reverse side in a hidden "natural necessity." Unlike the thinkers of the French Revolution, the new historical thinkers could not view "freedom" in a rationalistic and individualistic fashion. The leaders of the Revolution believed that they were free of the past and that they could thus seek to realize their revolutionary ideas for all times and peoples. They thought they could begin with a "clean slate" and introduced the revolutionary calendar with the year one. But the historical way of thought brought to the fore the dependence of every national spirit upon its own individual past and upon its own tradition. A "hidden law" was at work in this dependence. The Romantics were fond of calling this law "divine [183] providence." But just as often they called it – without reference to the familiar Christian terminology – the *destiny [Schicksal]* of a people.

This new historical way of thought, which we have already examined in an earlier context, was elevated to the status of a *new science ideal* which demanded recognition not only in the science of history but in every area of scientific inquiry. *Historicism*, the new humanistic view of reality, originated in this way. Just as the classical science ideal of humanism viewed all of reality from the perspective of natural science, so historicism viewed all of reality from the perspective of historical development. Just as the classical science ideal absolutized the aspect of mechanical motion, so the historical science ideal absolutized the aspect of history.

In the estimation of historicism the earlier natural-scientific way of thinking was not even valid in the area of natural phenomena. Nature as well as culture required historical analysis; for, like human culture, the earth, the heavens, plants, and animals were products of development. "Natural history" prefaced "cultural history," the history of humanity. Nature itself contained the hidden traces of "creative freedom." Physicists had recently discovered electrical phenomena which could not easily be explained in terms of the model of mechanical motion. To the Romantics this inadequacy of the mechanistic framework proved that even in "nature" the concept of "mechanical causation" could not be maintained consistently since "individual freedom" operated even in the phenomena of physics.

The Romantics saw a gradual increase in the "creative freedom" within "nature," especially with reference to the world of "living organisms" which were preeminently suited to the universalistic way of thinking. The organism was investigated not as a mechanical aggregate of atoms but as a whole composed of organic parts whose specific function could be understood only with reference to the individual whole. Thus "nature" itself revealed a dialectical interplay between "freedom" and "necessity" which seemed to cohere with the historical character of the whole of reality. In this way the link between universalism and historicism was established over the entire spectrum.

Like the classical science ideal, the new historical science ideal arose from the freedom motive of humanism. The historical approach merely gave the freedom motive a new universalistic and "irrational" direction. But the new science ideal did not overcome the inner conflict within the religious ground-motive of humanism. In time it too would come into conflict with the freedom motive. As a matter of fact, the historicistic way of thought would eventually cause an inner crisis within the humanistic worldview. In our day this crisis displays itself in the *spiritual* [184] *uprootedness* of those who seek to live out of the humanistic ground-motive.

However, before we turn to the most recent course of development within humanism, we must pay attention to two significant matters. In the first place, we must take note of the deplorable influence of historicism on those Christian thinkers and statesmen who had taken a position against the principles of the French Revolution. In the second place, we must deal with the alliance between historicism and modern sociology (the science of human society) and point to the dangers which began to threaten Christian thought from this angle.

Counter-revolution and Christianity

Clearly, humanism's shift to the historical way of thinking and to the universalistic overestimation of the community was a reactionary phenomenon in the history of the West. The real meaning of the so-called Restoration period, which followed upon the fall of Napoleon, was deeply permeated by these new humanistic motives. The Restoration clearly displayed the nature-freedom polarity of the humanistic religious ground-motive. Overestimation of the autonomous community followed the absolutization of free and autonomous individuals in the previous period of humanism. Irrationalism countered the rationalistic overemphasis on lawfulness or on the universal rule by overemphasizing individuality and the utterly unique. And overextension of historicistic thinking replaced overextension of natural-scientific thinking.

The new current within humanism was *conservative* in every respect. It defended tradition against the irrepressible urge for renewal felt by those more progressively inclined, those who represented the spirits of the Enlightenment and the French Revolution. The conservative character of this direction within humanism must be clearly seen. The eighteenth century Enlightenment and the French Revolution were indeed renewing and progressive forces in historical development. Although rooted in the humanistic ground-motive, they fulfilled a task of their own with respect to the disclosure of western culture. The idea of human rights and the idea that the state is a republican institution serving the common good were the inspiring slogans in the battle against the undifferentiated conditions of feudal society.

In an earlier context I explained that the first unmistakable indications of genuine historical *progress* are to be found in the breaking up of the undifferentiated spheres of life which embrace persons in all of their [185] relations and which always have the character of totalitarian communities. As soon as the process of differentiation begins, undifferentiated communities are doomed to disappear. They then break up into differentiated spheres, each of which has its own specific destination but none of which – in terms of its inner nature – can then pretend to be the totalitarian community which embraces individuals in every area of their lives. Only with this process of differentiation is room created for the recognition of the *rights of individuals as such*, independent of a person's membership in particular communities like kinship bonds, nation, family, or church. What is called civil private law is a product of this process of development. In terms of its inner nature, civil private law is based on the rights of individuals and cannot tolerate dependence on race or nationality. Freedom and equality in a civil-legal sense were thus clearly not just hollow slogans of the French Revolution.

Such human rights did not exist in either primitive Germanic law or in feudal society. Under nazism we have experienced what it means when civil-legal freedom and equality are abolished and when a person's legal status depends upon the community of "blood and soil." A system of private civil law can only be realized when the state has been established as *res publica,* as a public institution, to terminate the rule of private feudal lords and to make all of its members equally subjects of public governmental authority in public-legal freedom and equality. Both of these institutions – the system of the state and the system of civil private law – were first fully introduced by the French Revolution.

However, because of the revolutionary principles underlying the Revolution, these fruits were not produced without blemish. Humanistic individualism led to overextending the civil-legal and the public-legal idea of freedom and equality. Hence it did not recognize the rights of the private, nonstate *communities* in society. It respected only free and autonomous *individuals* and their counterpart, the *state*, which was founded on the treacherous, individualistic grounds of popular sovereignty and social contract. This revolutionary individualism, which rejected not only the sovereignty of God but also the sphere sovereignty based on it, had no feeling for historical continuity in culture and could not provide a stable foundation for governmental authority. The idea of the state, hardly realized, became the victim of the revolutionary consequences of the principle of popular sovereignty. France presented Europe with the spectacle of permanent revolution that could be smothered only temporarily by the iron fist of a dictator.

The Restoration period appealed to the new historical and universalistic [186] trend within humanism for support against this revolutionary, rationalistic individualism, placing itself on the side of historical tradition and presenting itself as the force of preservation and conservation. It did not display truly progressive and renewing tendencies. Its primary significance lay in its new insight into historical development, its stress on the national individuality of peoples, and its emphasis upon the community over against the rationalistic individualism of the French Revolution which neglected the significance of genuine communal relationships.

But the Restoration's reaction against the unhistorical, rationalistic, and individualistic traits of the Enlightenment contained great dangers. The new historicism encouraged a view of human society that excluded the acceptance of firm norms and clear limits between societal structures. The Restoration impeded a correct insight into the significance of the French Revolution for western culture by relativizing the basic differences between the differentiated and undifferentiated structure of society. Its universalistic thought pattern led to a dangerous community ideology which no longer recognized the essential import of human rights nor the inner nature of civil private law. The Historical School advocated the false notion that civil law is really folk law *[volksrecht]* and thus paved the way for national socialism with its *volk* ideology.

Regrettably, leading Christian thinkers and statesmen of the Restoration period did not perceive the humanistic ground-motive of the new spiritual movement. Both Roman Catholic and protestant thinkers sought support from the new universalism and historicism in battling the principles of the French Revolution. Roman Catholic thinkers like Louis de Bonald [1754-1840], Joseph de Maistre [1753-1821], and Pierre Ballanche [1776-1847] drew inspiration from the new humanistic movement in order to glorify the mystical beauty of medieval society and to denounce the cold rationalism and individualism of the French Revolution. They claimed that medieval society had realized the true community ideal. "Natural" life, formed organically in guilds and medieval towns, was overarched by the "supranatural" community of the church, headed by the Vicar of Christ. With these thinkers the historical way of thought displayed definite reactionary tendencies.

Although protestants rejected the typically Roman Catholic characteristics of this reactionary social idea, they too appealed to the undifferentiated relationships of feudal society. Counter-revolutionary tendencies became apparent here which rejected civil-legal freedom and equality and the republican idea of the state as fruits of the revolutionary spirit.

The well-known book by the Swiss nobleman Ludwig von Haller, [187] *Restauration der Staatswissenschaften*,[1] even led Groen van Prinsterer into this error during the first phase of his intellectual development. The dangerous origin of historicism was not fathomed. The very founders of the Historical School in Germany were devout Lutherans. And the manner in which the Romantics, particularly the philosopher Friedrich Schelling [1775-1854], were able to link historicism with the familiar doctrine of divine providence, blinded many believers. The Romantics no longer ridiculed the Christian faith. Near the end of his life Schelling wrote *Philosophie der Offenbarung*, which seemed to restore orthodox Christian dogmatics to its place of honor by rejecting the narrow-minded, rationalistic criticism of Scripture developed during the Enlightenment. Schelling blamed Christian theology for its fearful retreat from the conceited critique of rationalism.

Who at that time could recognize that Schelling's point of departure was not the Christian religion but *Vernunft*, the new historicistic and universalistic direction of the personality ideal? Schelling warned his readers in advance that his *Philosophie der Offenbarung* should be understood rationally; it should not be viewed as some sort of "Christian philosophy," for which he had no respect. His new so-called "positive philosophy" intended to show only that it too could comprehend the Christian truths in a rational manner.

Nonetheless, this unnatural bond between the Christian faith and universalistic historicism took hold. It persists even today, hampering seriously the proper impact of the scriptural motive of creation, fall, and redemption. [188]

---

[1] Ludwig von Haller, *Restauration der Staatswissenschaften*, 2 vols. (second edition, 1820-1825).

Chapter 8

The Rise of Social Thought

When in the first half of the nineteenth century Christianity and the new universalistic direction within humanism formed a dangerous alliance against the principles of the French Revolution, a third party entered the scene. It was greeted with suspicion by the others, for it did not suit the conservative orientation of the Restoration period. Romanticism and freedom idealism had clothed themselves in Christian garments, but the new ally clearly was neither Christian nor idealistic. To be sure, it did react with cynical criticism to the "ideology" of the French Revolution, and it did adapt itself to the historicistic and universalistic thinking of the Restoration. But the new ally believed that traditional Christianity was a historical phenomenon that had outlived itself. Likewise, it countered idealistic humanism with a program of a so-called "positive philosophy" whose task it was to discover the general laws governing the historical development of society. This program called for an exact investigation of brute social facts, free of idealistic prejudice. This menacing party and hybrid was modern sociology. Originating in France, it claimed that it was the new science of society – a claim that was indeed justified.

Birth of Modern Sociology

It is true that the phenomena of human society had drawn the attention of thinkers since Greek and Roman antiquity. But until the nineteenth century these phenomena had always been treated within the framework of political theory because the state was considered the "perfect [189] society" which embraced all other communities that were rooted in the rational, social nature of human beings. The later humanistic theory of the state, dating from the sixteenth century, did not depart from this traditional approach to societal relationships. Humanistic political theory displayed two trends. In the first place we note a more empirical tendency, which was oriented to an inquiry into factual social phenomena. And in the second place we detect a more aprioristic tendency, especially in the natural-law tradition, which attempted to construe and justify all social bonds in terms of a social contract between individuals.

Similarly, the Historical School never taught that the investigation of human society should be the concern of "sociology" understood as an independent science. The Historical School merely introduced a new "sociological attitude" which maintained that the various aspects of society (such as the juridical, the economic, the lingual, the aesthetic, and the moral) should be understood in terms of a mutual historical coherence as expressions of the same historical national character or spirit of a people [volk].

The founder of the Historical School in legal science, the famous German jurist Friedrich Karl von Savigny [1779-1861], emphasized that morals, language, law, art, and so on are merely dependent aspects of "culture." The latter emerges as a strictly individual configuration of a national spirit. For him these aspects grow out of a national spirit; originally developing unconsciously, they mature and finally perish when the source of the particular national spirit has "withered." In this way Savigny opposed the unhistorical and aprioristic view of law defended by the natural-law theorists.

The Historical School aimed at applying the new "historico-sociological" way of thought to all the special sciences concerned with social relationships, using the new approach not only in the science of law but also in linguistics, economics, aesthetics, and ethics. Much of the convincing force of historicism is indebted to this new sociological way of thinking. Teaching that language, law, morals, art, and so forth are dependent cultural aspects of an individual national community, the Historical School left the impression that historicism itself was grounded in concrete reality. If the Historical School had claimed that law, language, morals, and so on are only aspects of the "evolution of history," its absolutization of the historical aspect of reality would have been immediately clear. But the snare of historicism lay in the fact that its starting point lay in a concrete national community conceived of as a comprehensible social entity.

In the Restoration period many were prepared to admit that language, law, morals, economics, and so forth were only dependent aspects of the culture of a national community which displays a "nature" [190] or a "spirit" of its own. On the authority of the new historical approach, many readily accepted the thesis that the national community itself is also a phenomenon of purely historical development. They did not see that the historical point of view focuses on only one aspect of the national community and that it is impermissible to reduce the other aspects to the historical. The national community, they argued, is a social reality, not an abstract aspect of society.

Nevertheless, as we noted, the Historical School did not give birth to a special science of human society. Instead, it aimed at permeating existing scientific disciplines with its new sociological and universalistic way of thinking. To the Historical School the sociological and the historical approaches were identical.

But the intentions of modern sociology were entirely different from those of historicism. Modern sociology was based on a remarkable and inherently contradictory connection between the universalistic thought of the Restoration and the older natural-scientific thought of the Enlightenment. As we saw earlier, the classical humanistic science ideal aimed at controlling nature by discovering the general laws which explain phenomena in their causal coherence. To this end the natural-scientific method was elevated as the model for all scientific inquiry, although the method was not applied to the phenomena of human society to any significant extent.

Precisely this latter application was the goal of modern sociology. Its early proponents reproached the leaders of the French Revolution for experimenting with society in the light of their "natural-law ideologies" of freedom and equality without having the slightest notion of the real laws which govern social life. "Let us continue the solid tradition of the work of Galileo and Newton." These were the words of Auguste Comte [1798-1857], the founder of the new sociology. This meant that the revolutionary experiments should give way to sound policies based on knowledge of the social facts instead of hollow metaphysical speculation. Sociology is the science of these facts. Hence Comte believed that it would become the most important science in the hierarchy of positive sciences. It would chart the course for the happiness of a new humanity that would overcome the blood and tears caused by the ignorance of the earlier leaders. This entire motive of modern sociology was thus nothing but the unadulterated nature motive of the classical humanistic science ideal. It displayed the same optimistic rationalism.

But the founders of the new science also drew from the historico-sociological approach of the Restoration period. They attempted to link the natural-scientific method with the universalistic conception of human society, concurring with the Historical School that society is an organic [191] whole in which the various relationships function only as parts. They readily conceded that constant structures do not exist in society and that societal relationships are purely historical in character. In particular, they were convinced that language, law, economics, art, morality, and religion cannot be studied abstractly, since these can be comprehended only as non-self-sufficient facets of the "social whole" which relate to each other in indissoluble interaction. Unlike the Historical School, however, they sought this social whole not in a national community but in what they called "society" *[la société]*.

Modern sociology emphatically rejected the irrationalistic traits of historicism, since these did not mesh with its own rationalistic approach. Because of this the new sociology held that the science of history had inherent shortcomings. The Historical School had argued that the search for general laws in historical development is at odds with the nature of historical inquiry itself. According to the Historical School historians focus their inquiry on the absolutely individual, unique phenomenon which never repeats itself in the same way and which can only be understood in similarly individual coherences. If historians can detect a definite direction in the course of history, they must ascribe it to a "hidden law" of an "individual spirit of a people" which we must refer back to divine providence as the destiny *[Schicksal]* of a people.

Modern sociology rejected this irrationalistic turn within the humanistic motive of science and freedom. At this juncture it intended to continue the rationalistic tradition of the classical science ideal. Believing that genuine science searched for a clear formulation of universal laws which could explain particular phenomena, the new sociology claimed that it would for the first time initiate an authentic science of history. Thus historicism was given a rationalistic redirection in modern sociology which in the second half of the nineteenth century completely overcame the earlier irrationalism.

Distinction between State and Society

As we have pointed out, modern sociology, as it emerged in France at the beginning of the nineteenth century, gave itself the task of explaining societal relationships in terms of their causes. In doing this, it continued the Enlightenment tradition of the natural-scientific method which had been elevated to the classical humanistic science ideal. Thus in the religious ground-motive of humanism, the nature motive, which was directed to the mastery of reality, once again regained ascendancy. At the same time, however, modern sociology attempted to connect the natural-scientific method of investigation with the universalistic view of human society defended by [192] Romanticism and by the Historical School. This means that "society" was interpreted as an "organic whole" whose parts are inextricably interwoven and thus comprehended, in their typical function and significance, only in terms of that organic whole.

This synthesis between the natural-scientific method of the Enlightenment and the universalistic approach of the Restoration period was internally contradictory. As we have seen, the universalistic position was the result of an irrationalistic shift of the freedom motive. The point of departure for universalism was not the abstract, rational "individual" but the individual community. The universalistic way of thought, which had always viewed temporal society as an individual whole, arose as a rival to the natural-scientific view of reality. Its source was not the nature motive but the freedom motive of humanism.

Natural science always attempted to dissolve complex phenomena into their simplest elements, explaining these elements by means of general laws. When this procedure was applied to social relationships, such collective entities as the state, the church, and the family were reduced to mere interactions among "individuals," society's simplest elements. Consequently, "individuals" were divorced from all their genuinely individual, irreducible characteristics as neutral examples of the genus "rational, free human beings."

Universalism and historicism objected to this abstract, leveling, and atomistic approach by highlighting the total individuality of a person and the wholly unique inclination of such a person as determined by the individual character of the national community of which one is a member. This universalistic approach did not acknowledge general laws which govern society. The individual whole – that is, the national community – was given primacy. This community could not be explained in a natural-scientific fashion as a constellation of elements; rather, it could only be accepted as an irreducible, individual whole. This whole determined the nature of its members in an absolutely individual way.

Consequently, when modern sociology sought to reconcile the opposite approaches of the Enlightenment and the Restoration, it entangled itself in an antinomy. The insoluble dualism within the humanistic ground-motive again expressed itself in an internal contradiction within scientific thought.

For how did modern sociology understand the whole of society? It conceived of the whole not as an individual national community, as Romanticism and the Historical School had done, but as "society." To grasp the meaning of "society" correctly we must consider the distinction between "state" and "society" which arose first in the eighteenth century, even before the French Revolution.

We have already pointed out that prior to the nineteenth century the [193] problems of human society were treated within the framework of political theory. The distinction between state and society was unknown in antiquity and in the Middle Ages. Among the Greeks and the Romans the lack of such a distinction was due to a totalitarian conception of the state which was simultaneously regarded as a religious community. Hence the Christian religion, which accepted only Christ's kingship in the church, was seen as an enemy of the state. The scholastic literature of the Middle Ages preserved the totalitarian idea of the state, although it did not of course accept the state as a religious community. In conformity with the

Roman Catholic ground-motive of nature and grace, the scholastics viewed the state as the total community only in the realm of nature. Above it stood the church, the supranatural institution of grace and the total community embracing all of Christian life.

Both the Greco-Roman and the scholastic way of thinking were essentially universalistic. The Roman Catholic nature motive sought to synthesize the Christian ground-motive of creation, fall, and redemption with the Greek ground-motive of form and matter. Along with the Greek ground-motive Roman Catholicism adopted the Greek view of society, but accommodated it to its view of the church. The idea of the state had not become a reality during the Middle Ages because the "natural substructure" of society was still largely undifferentiated. Nevertheless, great scholastics like Thomas Aquinas continued to theorize in terms of the Greek and Roman conception of the state.

During the sixteenth and seventeenth centuries, when the state began to develop in the form of an absolute monarchy, humanistic political theory once again linked itself to the Greco-Roman idea of the totalitarian state. But at this stage the new political theory came under the influence of the humanistic ground-motive of nature and freedom. In the first centuries of the modern period, attempts were made to justify an absolute state that would absorb all the other spheres of life. The classical humanistic ideal of science provided the theoretical framework for the absolute state according to the model of the natural-scientific method. It built the state from its "elements" in such a way that all spheres of life came under the state's absolute sovereignty and control. In this way definite attempts were made to dismantle the feudal structure of medieval society in which governmental authority lay in the hands of private lords. In the modern period the humanistic motive of control inspired the idea that the state is an instrument of domination. The mastery motive was the motive of nature in its classical humanistic sense.

In its first period the humanistic theory of natural law also accommodated itself to this motive of control. Hugo Grotius, Thomas Hobbes, and the German jurist Samuel Pufendorff [1632-1694] accepted Bodin's absolutistic concept of sovereignty as he elaborated it by the end of the sixteenth century. As long as this concept dominated [194] humanistic political theory, the state was seen in the Greco-Roman manner as the totality structure embracing the whole of human society. As a result, a fundamental distinction between state and society could not emerge.

This began to change when in England the humanistic freedom motive assumed predominance over the nature motive in political theory. In an earlier context we noted how the classical liberal idea of the just state [*rechsstaat*] spread from England. John Locke brought about a fundamental change in the natural-law construction of the state at the transition from the seventeenth to the eighteenth century. Hugo Grotius and his followers interpreted the social contract, in which "free and equal individuals" left the state of nature in order to enter the body politic, as the transferal by these individuals of all their "natural freedoms" to the political sovereign. From the outset Locke gave the social contract a much more limited scope. In his view individuals did not thereby surrender their innate and absolute human rights to the state. On the contrary, they associated themselves in a body politic for the sole purpose of protecting their natural rights of freedom, life, and property. These natural human rights – the foundation of civil private law – defined the inalienable sphere of the individual's freedom. The social contract thus did not transfer these natural rights to the state. The only right that was transferred consisted in the legal power to maintain and guarantee these civil freedom rights by means of the arms of the state. For this purpose the individuals had to relinquish their natural right to protect themselves and their property on their own. This conception, which we have come to describe as the classical liberal idea of the state, for the first time opened up the possibility for the principial distinction between "civil society" and the "state." Civil society would then comprise the sphere of the individual's civil freedom, a sphere free from state intervention.

This conception of society became more clearly defined with the rise of the science of economics at the end of the eighteenth century. Both the Physiocrats and the Classical School within the fledgling science appealed to Locke's doctrine of natural law and his liberal idea of the state. Both schools of thought taught that economic life is served best when individuals pursue their own economic interests within the legal framework of their inalienable rights to life, liberty, and property. They maintained that economic life is governed by eternal, unchangeable natural laws that harmonize beautifully with the "natural rights" of the individual. Everyone knows their economic self-interest best. If the state does not interfere with the free play of economic and social forces, then a "natural harmony" should reign among individual interests, resulting [195] in the greatest level of societal good. "Civil society" was therefore seen as the free play of socio-economic interests within the legal framework of the inalienable civil private rights of individuals.

In the following section we will see how modern sociology attached itself to this conception of civil society.

Civil Society and Class Conflict

Classical liberal political theory, in close cooperation with the new science of economics (the physiocratic and the so-called Classical School), was therefore the first to make a basic distinction between state and civil society. Both of these new theories, dominated by the humanistic ground--

motive of nature and freedom, enjoyed exceptional success. This occurred first in England, where the so-called mercantilist policies, which had led to complete government control of trade and industry, were abolished; next in France, where the French Revolution had cleared away the last remnants of feudalism. As a result, the structure of the state began to distinguish itself clearly from the private spheres of life. In accordance with the revolutionary program, which did not tolerate an intermediary between the state and the individual, not only old guilds but also new social organizations were forbidden, even when new structures were a proper response to the differentiation of society. Consequently, "civil society" acquired a thoroughly individualistic character that satisfied the requirements of the liberal economic ideas of the Physiocrats and the Classical School. Within a short time a new type of person appeared on the scene: the free entrepreneur who was no longer hampered in any of his undertakings. Economic life entered upon a period of immense expansion. But at the same time untold suffering awaited the laborers.

The position of the worker was drastically altered at this time by the structural changes introduced into the process of production. The development of large-scale manufacturing firms brought with it an intense division of labor among a massive contingent of laborers working within a single factory. Later, when machinery was introduced into the factory, giant industries began to appear. In the first volume of his famous *Das Kapital*, Karl Marx presented a sociological analysis of the influences of these structural changes on contemporary life as a whole. His analysis is still extremely important.

These structural changes could not have taken place in the earlier systems of production. The old guild system of production had effectively prevented the change of an individual guild master into a large scale capitalistic entrepreneur by rigorously limiting the number of journeymen [196] a guild master was permitted to employ. Moreover, guild masters were allowed to hire journeymen only for the trade in which they themselves were masters. There were other impediments as well. The trade guilds systematically prevented the intervention of merchant capital – the only free form of capital available from the outside – into their own affairs. Merchants were allowed to buy any commodity – except labor as a "commodity." They were tolerated only in the business of retailing finished products. If external circumstances made further division of labor necessary, then existing guilds were split up or new guilds originated next to the old ones. But none of these changes led to a concentration of different trades within one factory. As Marx correctly observed, the guild system excluded any division of labor that separated the workers from their means of production and that made these means the monopolistic property of the investor of capital.

This economic framework changed radically, first in the period of large-scale manufacturing and even more drastically in the subsequent period of mechanized industrialization. These structural changes in the process of production contributed greatly to the development of new class tensions. They appeared in "civil society" which had been left to its own devices and had been structured in an individualistic manner. The class conflicts occurred between the urban labor proletariat, which was the victim of limitless exploitation, and the entrepreneur, who owned the capital. The individualistic structure of civil society had indeed debased labor to a "commodity." And the new forms of production had enormous repercussions within the liberal system of uninhibited competition against which the goodwill of a solitary entrepreneur was entirely powerless.

It seemed as if an iron necessity controlled these repercussions. David Ricardo [1772-1823], the great systematician in Adam Smith's Classical School of economics, concluded in *The Principles of Political Economy and Taxation* that machinery and labor move in a continual relation of rivalry.[1] If labor is made into a free commodity, it will become unsalable and thus worthless as soon as the introduction of new machinery makes it superfluous. That segment of the labor class, which in this sense has become a "superfluous" part of the population, faces two possibilities. It can either be destroyed in the unequal battle between obsolete forms of production and new mechanized forms of industrialization, or it can spill over into more easily accessible branches of industry. In either case the price of labor will be pushed down. For the [197] process of mechanization also requires an ever cheaper labor force and an extension of the hours of work. Adult laborers are therefore gradually replaced by women and children who must be exploited as long as possible. Family life is torn asunder and a general "pauperization" *[Verelendung]* of the proletariat sets in. Marx was again the first one to state that "civil society" – the focus of modern sociology – was a true image of the picture Thomas Hobbes had drawn of humankind's "state of nature" – *bellum omnium contra omnes*, a war of all against all! Civil society displayed an economically qualified structure, and the civil-legal order with its basic principles of freedom and equality seemed to be but a legal cover for the deathly class struggle waged in "society."

It should therefore come as no surprise that modern sociology, established on a positivistic foundation and interested – in accordance with the model of the natural sciences – in discovering the laws determining the historical development of society, believed that it had found in "civil society," with its frightening processes of dissolution, those hidden forces

---

1 David Ricardo, *The Principles of Political Economy and Taxation,* (Homewood, Ill.: R.D. Irwin Inc., 1963). The reference is to the third edition of 1821, p. 479.

which are of decisive causal significance for the historical form of society as a whole. The state itself, as defined by liberalism and the French Revolution, seemed to be nothing but an instrument of the ruling class for the suppression of the working class. The state must therefore not be understood as an institution independent of civil society nor, as earlier political theories had taught, as the total community embracing the whole of society. To the contrary, "society" itself must be seen as the whole which gives birth to the state as a political instrument of domination.

This signified a fundamental break with both the classical liberal, natural-law distinction of state and society as well as the earlier identification of the two. The new science of sociology had indeed made a revolutionary discovery which fundamentally undermined both the idea of the state as *res publica* – the institution which embodies the public interest – and the idea of civil law with its principles of freedom and equality. Both ideas had come to expression in eighteenth century society. But the focus of the new sociology was not on these ideas. Rather, the class contrasts as the driving forces in the historical process of society – these seemed to be the positive social facts. The classical idea of the state and the idea of civil private law seemed to be but "ideologies" of a bygone era characterized by metaphysical speculation. These ideologies only served to conceal the truly valid laws governing society. Quite understandably, therefore, the conservative Restoration movement eyed the new ally in its battle against the ideas of the French Revolution with suspicion.

Yet, the French founders of modern sociology did not fully comprehend the frightening speed with which the class contrast between labor [198] and capital was growing. In this respect they still lived in the past; using the example of youthful America, they believed that it was possible for an intelligent laborer to rise to the status of an entrepreneur. In their minds the class conflict in modern society existed only between those who drew "laborless income" and the actual working class in whose hands lay the future of society. Those with "laborless income" were the speculators who during the French Revolution purchased the estates of the nobility and the clergy for virtually nothing; those in the working class were the managers and the industrialists who were kept from government posts by the court elite of the Bourbons. Hence Marxist sociology disparagingly dismissed these French optimists.

Nevertheless, the concept of the classes – destined to play a fundamental part in the science of society – was discovered not by Marx but by Henri de Saint-Simon [1760-1825] and Auguste Comte. After we have explained their use of the new discovery in the following pages, we need to set out in a fundamental way our own standpoint with respect to the concept of social classes.

The Class Concept

As Saint-Simon remarked, France drafted no less than ten different constitutions in the short span from 1789 to 1815. Society, however, remained the same, for human beings do not change so rapidly. This discrepancy caused Saint-Simon, one of the founders of modern sociology, to observe that constitutional frameworks could not possibly form the heart of social life. He wrote:

> We ascribe too much weight to the forms of government. The law determining both governmental authority and the form of government is not as important and has less influence on the happiness of the nations than the law determining the rights of property and the exercise of these rights. The form of parliamentary government is merely a form; property is the heart. It is therefore the regulation of property which in truth lies at the foundation of society.

Wealth, he said, is the true and only foundation of every political influence. For this reason politics must be based on the positive science of the production process, which in turn is based on economic science. Saint Simon apparently proceeded from the assumption that economic production and the regulation of property are mutually interdependent. Changes in both the form of production and the regulation of property give rise to the formation of social classes. This formation of classes governs the entire development of human society. [199]

With reference especially to the history of France but in part also to the history of England, Saint-Simon attempted to explain the significance of class formation as the real causal force in the entire development of social institutions. With respect to France he argued that after the invasion of the Franks into Gaul two classes emerged: the Franks as lords and the native Gauls as slaves. The slaves cultivated the land for their owners and labored in every branch of work. Like the ancient Roman slaves, according to Saint-Simon, they received a small amount of money *(peculium)*, which they carefully hid. The Crusades and resultant affluence created a great need for money on the part of the Frankish masters who were thus forced to sell "freedoms" *(franchises)* to their slaves. But the same luxury heightened the social significance of the artisans, tradesmen, and merchants, who had to satisfy new needs. Louis XI, who preferred the title "King of the Gauls" to "Head of the Franks," formed an alliance with the communes, the laboring Gauls in the cities and in the country, in order to subject the Frankish princes to his authority. Since the monarchy deprived the princes, the ruling noble class, of political power, and since as a result the princes were enticed to settle in the cities, they lost all political significance. Under Louis XIV they became the servants of the king. And, during the reign of the "Sun King" the increasing exchange of products led to the rise of a new class, that of the bankers.

The French Revolution, Saint-Simon maintained, was launched by the bourgeoisie, the middle stratum of the population that had risen from the communes to the rank of the "privileged" but that had still felt discriminated against in comparison with the old nobility. The bourgeoisie consisted of the nonaristocratic jurists, military personnel of middle class background, and property owners who were neither managers nor laborers in the production process (i.e., who were not *industriels*). For Saint-Simon the true purpose of the revolution of 1789 was the establishment of an "industrial system." He believed that the final phase of the revolution had not yet arrived; the revolution would be complete when the *industriels*, the truly productive members of the population, including the entrepreneurs who give leadership in the process of production, gained political leadership. In Saint-Simon's estimation, the first step toward this goal was the well-known loan made to the government of France in 1817. The loan was not negotiated in the "barbarian" manner of the eighteenth century but was closed after peaceful talks between two equal partners, the government and the important class of bankers.

In this way Saint-Simon attempted to give a causal explanation of the entire development of society in terms of class formation and class conflict. His attempt testified to the natural-scientific approach in his [200] sociology which was directly inspired by the classical humanistic science ideal: the control of reality by a discovery of the laws which explain its causal coherence.

Over against this tendency in Saint-Simon's thought we detect a contradictory one. He also explained societal development in terms of the history of ideas and worldviews. Here we encounter the impact of the humanistic freedom motive on Saint-Simon's interpretation of the social process. In an earlier context we noticed a similar impact on the social thought of the Romantics, the Historical School of jurisprudence and German idealism. And, quite in harmony with this second trend in his thought, he argued that the rise of the political system of the future – the "industrial" system – would be entirely dependent upon a prior breakthrough of positive sociology and its proclaimed ideas. Finally, this trend of thought also helps explain Saint-Simon's universalistic conception of "society" as an organic whole whose parts are intimately united and kept together only by means of common ideas.

Saint-Simon's concept of social classes on the other hand is individualistic in nature, and thus contradicts the notion of community inherent in the universalistic view of society. Saint-Simon interpreted "classes" as "components" of society which drive it apart in diverging directions. The concept of class is a concept of conflict. Wherever classes exist, unreconciled social oppositions dominate and lead to a struggle for power, he argued.

How should we respond to Saint-Simon's emphasis on the significance of classes in the development of society? Classes can be formed only in what we describe as the coordinational societal interlinkages *[maatschapsverhoudingen]* which must be distinguished from communal relationships *[gemeenschapsverhoudingen]*. In the latter, human beings are bound together into a solidary unity within which persons function as members. [201] In the coordinational relationships, however, human beings function next to each other in a side-by-side manner, either in a relation of neutrality, in mutual cooperation, or in a conflict situation.[1]

Moreover, classes belong to the intrinsically economically qualified or characterized relationships of conflict. They are a growth in the tissues of society and must thus be sharply distinguished from the different estates or "stations" *[standen;* German: *Stände]* in society, which are qualified or characterized by the aspect of social intercourse and which represent a normal differentiation in social life.

The question we now face is this: is it really possible to explain the structuring of society in terms of class divisions? Are they, for instance, indeed the causal forces of the development of the internal life of the state? In this connection it is of little consequence that Saint-Simon's sketch of the history of class tensions in France, and of the political development determined by these tensions, simply does not meet the criteria of a rigorous scientific inquiry. For at a later time scholars attempted to prove the accuracy of class analysis with much more dependable scientific tools and thereby also presented a much more precise delineation of the class concept. Here we are exclusively concerned with the sociological problem raised in a fundamental manner by Saint-Simon: the significance of class conflict for the life of the state and the whole of society.

---

1   These distinctions are fundamental to Dooyeweerd's sociology. He defines *community* as "any more or less durable societal relationship which has the character of a whole joining its members into a social unity, irrespective of the degree of intensity of the communal bond." See Herman Dooyeweerd, *A New Critique of Theoretical Thought*, vol. 3 (reprint, Lewiston, NY: The Edwin Mellen Press, 1997), 177. For Dooyeweerd communities comprise the undifferentiated structures like tribes, clans, or guilds, and the differentiated structures of marriage, family, state, church, and the voluntary associations (business enterprises, political parties, recreational clubs, etc).

   Dooyeweerd defines *societal interlinkages* (or the "interindividual and intercommunal relationships," which is his translation of *maatschapsverhoudingen*) as those relationships "in which individual persons or communities function in coordination without being united into a solidary whole. Such relationships may show the character of mutual neutrality, of approachment, free cooperation or antagonism, competition or contest." (Ibid.) As examples of societal interlinkages he mentions: "Free market relations, publicity, the differentiated fashions (in dress, recreation, conversation, etc.), theatrical performances, private philanthropy, diplomacy, international political relations, electioneering propaganda of political parties, missionary activity, etc." (Ibid., 588f.)

This problem is still intensely relevant and demands a fundamental analysis. We cannot rid ourselves of this issue by way of blanket generalizations. It calls for further serious consideration on our part.

Estates and Classes

In our last sections we focused on the rise of modern sociology as a component in the general redirection of humanistic thought since the beginning of the last century. I attempted to explain how Saint-Simon, who, with Auguste Comte, is considered the founder of sociology as an independent science, viewed the entire historical development of western society as a history of class struggle. Class struggle was seen as the real motor of the whole process of social development, as indeed the cause of the rise of the state and of all political revolutions. The state, in fact, was regarded as nothing but the instrument wielded by the ruling class to keep the dominated class in a state of subjection. [202] When the class struggle would finally come to an end in the "new industrial era" as a result of the leading role of the new sociology, then also the state would automatically wither away. "Governance of persons" would then gradually yield to "administration of things." This doctrine was formulated by Saint-Simon, well before Karl Marx and the famous Communist Manifesto of 1848 in which the Marxist doctrine of class struggle found its classical, though popularized expression.

While the doctrine of class struggle as the real "cause" of social development may have been a "discovery" of Saint-Simon, he derived the class concept from the then recently developed science of economics. In earlier discussions we saw in detail how the entire distinction between the state and civil society goes back to the combined influence exerted by Locke's liberal humanistic doctrine of natural law and the so-called Physiocratic School in economic theory. The French Revolution and the early industrialization of economic life first gave concrete expression to these humanistic ideas.

The French physician François Quesnay [1694-1774], founder of the Physiocratic School, in his theory had divided the population into different classes. Next to the nonpropertied class of wage earners he posited a class of independent entrepreneurs which, in turn, was subdivided into three classes; namely, the productive class of farmers, the nonproductive class of merchants and industrialists, and finally, the class of landowners. In other words, the class concept had its origin in economic theory. In turn, under the influence of this theory, the newly developing science of social life began to regard civil society as a constellation which in essence was controlled by economic forces. Here Quesnay's theoretical class divisions were not adopted; however, that was not significant for the new conception of civil society itself.

The new science of economics, with its distinctly liberalistic orientation, was further developed in the so-called Classical School of Adam Smith, Ricardo, J.B. Say, and others, and had a pervasive influence on the sociological conception of civil society *[bürgerliche Gesellschaft]*. Its influence can even be detected in Hegel, the greatest representative of humanistic freedom idealism after Kant. Hegel himself did not regard sociology as a separate science of human societal relations. And, quite independently of the French sociologists, he presented a penetrating analysis of modern civil society, in which he clearly brought to light the role of the machine as a mechanization of labor. Like the Classical School, he too regarded economic self-interest as the primary impulse in this process; but, at the same time, he posited the increasing interdependence among individuals, resulting from the continually increasing division of labor, as a curbing factor. It is the cunning of Reason which forces individuals, in a seemingly limitless and arbitrary pursuit after [203] satisfaction of their own needs, to accommodate themselves to the interests of others. In his idealistic framework of thinking, Hegel continued to adhere to the concept of a state which is not the subservient instrument of economic class domination, but which is the true embodiment of the ethical idea in the new universalistic turn which humanism had given to its personality ideal.

Civil society, in which individuals with their private civil rights still regard their economic self-interest as being in opposition to the universal norms of morality and justice to which this society subjects itself of necessity, is to be taken up *[aufgehoben]* in the all-encompassing state which Hegel deified as the Greeks had done. In this state the individual and the group are ordered as parts of a higher ethical whole and acknowledge the general interest as their true self-interest.

In his picture of civil society we see that Hegel did not use the "class concept" of the French sociologists but employed the concept of "estates" *[Stände]*. His pupil, Lorenz von Stein, who sought to establish a connection between Hegel's conception of the state and society and the theories of the French sociologists, was the first to again make Saint Simon's class concept the focal point of his analysis of civil society without, however, sacrificing the Hegelian concept of estate.

In this way both the concept of class and the concept of estate have become part and parcel of the conceptual framework of modern sociology, and they have been the subject of extensive studies, in particular by the German sociologist Ferdinand Tönnies. However, the way in which these undoubtedly important concepts were shaped and used in sociology clearly betrays their humanist origin. An uncritical adoption of them in their current sociological meaning within a Christian view of society is therefore quite irresponsible. Particularly in the political arena these concepts have been manipulated in an extremely dangerous fashion.

Humanist theory and ideology continually attempted to present a view of social reality as an unbiased account of the social facts themselves. In reality, however, this approach was strictly determined by the religious ground-motive of humanism – the ground-motive of nature and freedom – with its irreconcilable tension between the classical science ideal, which seeks to control all of reality after the model of natural-scientific thought, and the personality ideal which upholds the values of human freedom, autonomy, and dignity.

The class concept used in early French sociology was in harmony with the natural-scientific pattern of thought of the Enlightenment. It only suited an individualistic conception of society which regards the economic self-interest of the individual as the real cause and driving force of societal development. If the entire history of society is nothing [204] but the history of class struggle, then no room exists in such a society for a true community. In that case, the state too can be considered only as an instrument of class domination.

The Physiocratic and the Classical Schools in economics simply had not arrived at a theory of class struggle because they dreamt of a "natural harmony" among individual interests and because they had allied themselves with the humanistic natural-law theory of inalienable rights in which the humanist personality ideal, in its individualistic shape, had found expression. In distinction from this, the early French sociologists had broken with these "idealistic speculations." They rejected the theory of natural rights as "idle metaphysics" in order to concentrate exclusively on a natural-scientific explanation of the social facts. These facts did not point to a "natural harmony" in economic life but to a harsh and pitiless struggle between the propertied and nonpropertied classes.

Hegel's concept of estate, on the other hand, originated from a universalistic view of civil society which had arisen out of the new conception of the humanistic motive of freedom. His limited recognition of the individualistic tendencies at work in modern civil society was only a point of transition toward his universalistic conception of society. This universalistic conception regarded individuals again as members of "occupational estates" *[beroepsstanden]* to which they had to belong if they were to unfold their individuality. For only in a community can individuals realize themselves and experience authentic existence. An "occupational estate" upholds its own honor without which an individual cannot possibly attain dignified economic existence. These "occupational estates," as the highest expression of communal consciousness in civil society, must thus in turn be embodied again as autonomous corporations in the state, which is the "ethical totality."

In this manner the concepts estate and class must be seen as expressions of the polar tendencies within the humanistic understanding of society.

Both were oriented to a notion of civil society which in a general sense elevated the economic aspect to the starting point of the entire conception of society in total disregard of the real structural principles of society.

Universalistic sociology would later attach itself to the concept of estates so that it could construct society again as an "organic whole" in which the newly proclaimed revolutionary tendencies might be rendered harmless. Over against that, individualistic society would further elaborate the class concept which later, in Marxism, became the instrument of "social revolution." The concept of estates belonged to the conservative realm of thought. The class concept was permeated with the combative ardor of the spirit of social revolution, which, after first [205] smouldering quite gently, would flare up with fearful intensity in the Communist Manifesto.

The Christian theory of the state and society, especially in Germany, in its opposition to the revolutionary Marxist doctrine of class struggle, sought support from the universalistic conception of "occupational estates," just as in an earlier phase it had sought support from the Historical School in its battle against the ideas of the French Revolution. In both cases a fundamental mistake was made. A Christian conception of the social order should not look for a home in the conservative camp, nor in the revolutionary, the universalistic, or the individualistic thought patterns of humanistic sociology. However, the spirit of accommodation again prevented the ripening of a truly scriptural, reformational outlook on human society.

Basic Problems in Sociology

When sociology began to present itself at the beginning of the nineteenth century as an independent science, it was immediately confronted with a series of fundamental problems. Unfortunately, from the very outset the new science failed even to formulate these problems properly, and, although twentieth century sociologists tend to look down upon the French founders of their science with a certain air of condescension, they have not thus far made any progress even in the correct formulation of these basic questions.

Alleged Value-free Character

On the contrary, many contemporary sociologists evince a definite antipathy to this task. Their argument is that sociology is still a young science which has had to endure numerous fundamental assaults from outsiders who have reproached it for its failure to stake out an independent field of research. However, so their argument continues, sociology has gone quietly ahead and, through the results of its researches, has in fact proved its right to exist. In this respect it has taken the road which has also been followed by the other empirical sciences (that is, the sciences which are concerned with the study of phenomena encountered in experience). All these sciences gradually detached themselves from the illusion that they must first delimit their respective fields of research in an a priori fashion. This, they said, was an impossible demand, imposed by philosophy. Sociology, like the other empirical sciences, has also dissociated itself from this philosophical, a priori approach. Empirical research itself must first show the way, and only then will it be [206] possible to distinguish the contours of the field of sociological inquiry in progressively clearer outline. After proper progress has been made in such research, philosophical reflection is certainly bound to follow.

This reasoning seems very attractive and convincing, but it disregards a number of basic realities. In the first place, it ignores the problem of empirical research in sociology itself. From the outset it has been wrongly supposed that "social facts" present themselves to our perception in an objective manner similar to that which supposedly applies to the objective phenomena of the natural sciences. In order that these social facts may be grasped as objective data, it is necessary to suspend all norms and standards of evaluation. Science, after all, is not concerned with the state of affairs that ought to prevail in society, but with the reality that is. This position has remained the great dogma of modern sociology, even after the hegemony of the methodology of the natural sciences had been shattered in this century and, in the footsteps of Max Weber [1864-1920], the historical or "cultural-scientific" method began to be applied to societal phenomena.

After my earlier discussions, the reader will immediately observe that this substitution of the historical ideal for the classical ideal of science, which had aimed at control over nature, remained rooted in the same humanistic ground-motive of nature and freedom. In neither case, therefore, could one speak of a presuppositionless, unbiased scientific methodology. Both under the supremacy of the methodology of the natural sciences and under the supremacy of the historical attitude, sociology began to eliminate, as a matter of principle, all those constant structures of society, grounded in the order of creation, which in fact make possible our experience of the variable social phenomena. The religious ground-motive of humanism demanded such a conception of "true science."

In order to understand this clearly, one must realize that societal relations always presuppose norms (rules of how it ought to be) without which such relations simply cannot exist. For example, if sociologists wish to launch a study of marital relations in different societies, they are immediately confronted with the question of what has to be understood as "marriage." Marriage is in principle different from concubinage or any other extramarital sexual relation. However, without the application of social norms this fundamental difference cannot be determined. Let us take another example. If someone seeks to study the nature of the state from a sociological point of view, the question of what a state is cannot be eluded. Can one already call the primitive communities of sib, clan, or family "states?" Were the feudal realms and demesnes in fact states? Can one consider an organized band of robbers a "state?" Anyone who discusses monarchy, parliament, ministers, etc. is concerned [208] with social realities which cannot be experienced as such unless one takes into account their authority or competence. However, authority and legal competence are essentially normative states of affairs, which presuppose the validity of social norms. Authority and legal competence cannot be perceived objectively by our senses, like the claws of a predatory animal or the muscular strength of an athlete.

Social classes and estates (which I discussed earlier) are also as such not sensorily perceptible entities. Anyone who speaks of "propertied" and "nonpropertied" classes presupposes the notion of ownership, which rests upon the validity of legal norms. Moreover, the division of the entire population of a country into "propertied" and "nonpropertied" is a construction which makes sense only if we accept ownership of the means of production as our criterion; and we can determine what a means of production is only if we employ economic norms. When one speaks of "estates" as categories of persons bound together by a consciousness of "social honor," then one is concerned with social realities which cannot exist without the validity of norms of social intercourse.

What "social facts," then, would be left if one took seriously the dogma that sociology, being an empirical science, must suspend all norms and standards of evaluation? The answer will surely be: "None!" Without norms human society cannot really exist. Reality that is accessible to our experience displays a large number of normative aspects in which it is subjected to laws or rules of what ought to be. It is exactly these normative aspects which first characterize human societal relationships, even though these relationships also function within aspects in which reality is not subjected to norms but to the so-called laws of nature.

It has been said, of course, that as an empirical science sociology ought to direct its theoretical focus to a gang of robbers no less than to legitimate organizations, and that therefore the question as to whether a specific social group formation acts in harmony with a valid legal order is irrelevant as far as sociology is concerned. But if sociologists really wish to study a gang of robbers in its organization and operation, then they certainly will have to take into account the distinction between a criminal and a noncriminal organization. Otherwise I truly would not know how one could manage to investigate sociologically a gang of robbers and not perhaps mistakenly honor a charitable organization, a church, or a state with one's attention as a scientist. However, if one takes seriously the dogma that, in making such distinctions, sociology has to suspend all norms and standards of evaluation, from what source will one then derive a criterion for detecting an actual gang of robbers?

One might reply that social norms themselves, too, can be treated scientifically as pure social facts, observing that these are recognized as valid within a particular society without, however, investigating the [208] question as to whether these norms really ought to have any validity. The task of sociology is then limited to scientific inquiry into the factual circumstances through which these particular norms have achieved such recognition. In other words, the social norms themselves have to be causally explained by the sociologist as factual states of affairs arising out of social circumstances of a non-normative character. In this manner sociological science supposedly is able to suspend all normative standards of evaluation in order to study social facts without prejudice or bias.

What are we to think of this? Here we have obviously touched upon the heart of the question with which we are concerned. Since we are dealing with a problem of cardinal importance for our whole scientific understanding of sociology, we will have to devote especially close attention to this turn which has been given to the dogma of scientific neutrality or lack of bias.

Sociologists who think they can really suspend all normative points of view speak of social norms only in the sense of rules of behavior according to which on the average, persons factually conduct themselves. Here it would be irrelevant whether such a factual regularity in human behavior is also in accordance with the official legal order and morality. It is, of course, assumed that over a period of time this factual regularity creates a feeling of "ought to be" in the members of a social group. This is then referred to as the "normative power of facts." Thus this factual behavioral regularity itself is not explained on the basis of a feeling of "social ought," but on the basis of other "social facts," such as the increasing division of labor and the accompanying increase in solidarity and mutual dependence among the members of society.

It is certain that one may observe in a social group (to adopt this empty sounding sociological term) patterns of behavior which by themselves never imply a feeling of "social ought." One might think, for example, of the lamentable increase since the period of German occupation in petty theft committed by employees, as well as of other "bad habits." Such "bad habits" can only operate negatively, by undermining, within certain limits, the general consciousness of norms and standards. In other words, they may contribute toward the feeling in the wrongdoer that what is done "is not all that bad," but no such person would ever maintain that "this is how it ought to be." Why not? The answer is that "bad habits," such as those just mentioned, can never generate "social order" but bear the stigma of being "anti-social" and anti-normative. Only authentic social norms, which order societal relationships in a truly lasting manner, can, when they are followed, bring about a feeling of "social ought." In other words, a feeling of ought presupposes a norm and therefore can never exist as the "cause" or "origin" of [209] the latter, just as the factual regularity in behavior can never by itself be a "cause" of a "feeling of ought."

This rather simple situation (one might call it simple since anyone can check it) leads us to further reflection on the core of the problem we have raised; that is, the question regarding the meaning of causal explanation in sociology and the relation between an "explanatory" and a "normative" view of societal relationships.

Causal Explanation versus Normative Evaluation
The current opposition between causal explanation and normative evaluation is deeply rooted in the religious ground-motive of the humanistic view of reality, the motive of nature and freedom. The concept of causality with which nineteenth century sociology operated was that of the classical humanistic ideal of science which, in turn, had derived it from classical physics. This concept bore a strongly deterministic character and thus left no room for the autonomous freedom of human personality.

Saint-Simon and Comte, the two founders of modern sociology as an independent science, had attempted to link this natural-scientific way of thinking with the universalistic perspective of Romanticism and the Historical School. Thus they regarded society as an organic whole and even taught that ultimately society was held together only by communal ideas. But the link that was established between the rationalistic way of thinking of the natural sciences and the irrationalistic perspective of historicism revealed an inner antinomy. The first way of thinking attempted to analyze all complex social phenomena into their simplest "elements" and to establish, on the basis of general laws of cause and effect, a connection between these elements. This method inevitably led to an individualistic view of human society. The second way of thinking, on the other hand, attempted to understand all social relations as individual parts of an individual whole, and thus led inevitably to a rejection of the natural-scientific concept of causality as well as of any acceptance of universal laws for the development of human society.

However, in the second half of the nineteenth century the influence of German freedom idealism, with its universalistic and irrationalistic view of reality, began to decline. The discovery of the cell as the supposed basic "element" of organic life inaugurated a new era of supremacy for the rationalistic natural-scientific way of thinking. Commencing in England, the theory of evolution began its triumphant procession. Under the initiative of the English thinker Herbert Spencer [1820-1903], the biological school gained a foothold in sociology. This school had completely divorced itself from the universalistic and idealistic strains in the system of Saint-Simon and Comte. Human society was entirely seen [210] from a biological point of view and, in accordance with the new evolutionistic way of thinking, was once again explained on the basis of its "simplest elementary components." Thus for the time being the mechanical concept of causality of classical natural science gained sole hegemony in sociological thought.

Only toward the end of the nineteenth century do we find a new and decisive reaction, inspired by the humanistic motive of freedom, to this mechanical way of thinking. The psychology of human behavior began to attract the center of attention, and the insight developed that the psychological motives of human action cannot be grasped in terms of the mechanical concept of causality characteristic of evolutionistic biology. At the same time, a resurgence of Kant's critical philosophy along so-called neo-Kantian lines led to a renewed reflection on the limits inherent in the natural-scientific method of thought. A line of demarcation was drawn between the natural sciences and the humanities [*Geisteswissenschaften;* "spiritual" sciences], with the latter founded in a psychology belonging to the humanities [*geisteswissenschaftliche Psychologie*]. This contrast was further complicated by a distinction between the natural and the cultural sciences; in the latter the method of historical science was elevated as the model of thought. Starting from the irrationalistic way of thinking of Romanticism and the Historical School, the neo-Kantian thinker Heinrich Rickert [1863-1936] formulated this distinction as follows: the natural-scientific method is concerned with the discovery of general laws and views all phenomena completely apart from any values and evaluations; the cultural sciences, on the contrary, are especially interested in the individuality of phenomena and seek to relate this to values (e.g., beauty, justice, and power) acknowledged in society.

All of this was followed in the twentieth century by a great revolution in physics itself when it appeared that micro-phenomena in physical processes are basically not subject to the mechanical concept of causality and that the so-called natural laws of classical physics can only be maintained as statistical regularities for phenomena appearing on a large scale. With this the era of supremacy for the classical humanistic ideal of science finally had come to an end. However, this did not mean a return to the speculative, a priori philosophical systems of German freedom idealism (Fichte, Schelling, and Hegel). It was no longer possible to find a firm basis for the humanistic freedom motive in the old faith in the eternal ideas of human dignity and autonomy. To the extent that one wished to safeguard the freedom of human personality over against the claims of the classical, deterministic concept of causality, one looked for an "empirical" basis in the more recent research of psychology.

The unshakable faith of idealism had been uprooted. And after the [211] revolution in twentieth century physics which we just described, the entire problem of freedom receded into the background. Irrationalistic historicism, which had detached itself from its spiritual roots in freedom idealism, gained the upper hand everywhere. In this way the process of the religious uprooting of humanism was set in motion.

Sociological science was swept along in this process before it had formulated properly the really fundamental questions as to what its field of research in fact was. Under these circumstances we cannot expect sociologists to have arrived at any clear view concerning the meaning of the concept of causality as employed by them. We will therefore attempt to clarify this issue and demonstrate at the same time that the current distinction made in sociology between the explanatory and the normative point of view – a distinction which rests upon the humanistic ground-motive of nature and freedom – is in sharp conflict with the order of reality.

The concept of causality, if it is to be applied in order to offer a scientific explanation of observable phenomena, requires above all a possibility for comparison between cause and effect. It must be possible to subsume "cause and effect" under a single denominator which lies within the reach of scientific determination. The concept of causality of classical physics fulfilled this requirement completely since it established causal relations only between phenomena which occurred within the same aspect of reality – the aspect of physical energy motion *[energie- beweging]*. Thus heat and mechanical motion, for example, were indeed comparable entities when viewed under this abstract aspect. However, an entirely different situation arises when an attempt is made to establish a causal nexus between the physico-chemical aspect of phenomena and the aspect of organic life. Such an application of the concept of causality can be meaningful only for someone who thinks that the phenomena of organic life can ultimately be reduced to processes of a purely physical and chemical character. However, such thinking rests upon a "materialistic" presupposition or bias which does not have the least basis in reality as we experience it, but which is wholly inspired by the classical humanistic ideal of science and remains rooted in the religious ground-motive of humanism.

Dual Structure of Reality
For the truth is this, that the different aspects of reality, such as physical motion, organic life, feeling, historical development, law, morality, etc., cannot be subsumed under the same scientific denominator. They are mutually irreducible aspects of being, in which reality manifests itself to us. It is therefore impossible that they should stand in mutual relations of cause and effect to one another. Thus in sociology it is scientifically

[212] meaningless to state that the legal order has its cause in a feeling for justice or that economic valuations are "caused" by feelings of pleasure and pain, for the aspect of feeling of society is fundamentally different from the jural or the economic aspect. When viewed under the aspect of feeling, phenomena evince a character entirely different from that which appears when investigated under the jural or the economic aspect. Therefore, no scientific explanation is offered at all when one tries to establish a causal connection between the various aspects distinguishable in reality, for we are concerned here with aspects of reality which do not – in a scientific sense – admit of any comparison.

Superficially, of course, one might object to this position that everyone in fact assumes such causal relations. For instance, if someone is struck and killed by a lightning bolt, or if someone commits suicide by taking poison, is it not assumed without question that a causal connection exists between purely physical and chemical processes and the phenomena of organic life? Or, if someone is driven by hunger to steal bread, is it not assumed, again without question, that a causal connection exists between emotional drives and illegal conduct? However, the objection would hold only if also in our everyday thinking – the basis for such opinions – we viewed phenomena under various isolated aspects. But, of course, this is not at all true. In the nonscientific experience of our daily life, we perceive and grasp things and events in their concrete reality, and there they function in all aspects without exception. To put it differently, purely physico-chemical processes do not exist. Similarly, there are no phenomena in reality which are contained entirely within the aspect of organic life or the aspect of feeling. The entities studied by physics and chemistry under their physical aspect, function no less in the aspects of organic life, conscious feeling, historical culture, and economic or juridical life. Thus we cannot speak of "poisons" within that aspect, of being isolated by physics and chemistry. Only within the aspect of organic life can certain substances be poisonous; that is, in relation to the vital functioning of plants, animals, and human beings. Similarly, within the subjective life of feeling these substances can operate as causes only to the extent that they themselves function within the aspect of feeling of reality. But what then are the functions which these substances can fulfill in the aspects of organic life, feeling, etc.? After all, we assume that substances – like poisons – by themselves do not possess organic life, or a faculty of feeling or logical thinking. Are these substances then not really of an exclusively physical and chemical character, so that only physics and chemistry can teach us what they really are? If this is indeed your opinion, then I invite you to put it to the test.

In our everyday manner of experiencing reality, a bird's nest is, without a doubt, a truly existing thing, and you know, of course, that [213] this nest is built from materials which by themselves have no organic life. But, if chemistry provided you with the exact chemical formulas of the building materials, the complete reality of the bird's nest would not be fully grasped. We are dealing with an animal product which fulfills a typical function in a bird's existence, a function which in this product has manifested itself in an objective fashion. This is the function of an object, an object-function, as we would term it. This object-function characterizes the nest only in its relation to the subject-function of organic life which characterizes the bird and its nestlings. Thus in the bird's nest we are confronted with a typical relation between subject and object, which is an essential component of the reality of this product. It is a relation which is already expressed in the very term *bird's nest*. If we disregard this relation, in order to study the nest exclusively according to the physical and chemical aspects of its materials, then the bird's nest as such vanishes from our view and we are left with nothing but a scientific abstraction.

This will become even clearer when we observe the role played in society by things which are composed of inorganic materials. Houses, offices, factories, museums, streets, highways, automobiles, trains, airplanes, etc., only have real existence in a subject-object relation within society. Without exception they function in all aspects of reality: in the physical aspect, in the aspect of organic life, in the psychical aspect of feeling (in their sensorily perceptible properties), in the logical aspect (by virtue of their objective logical characteristics), in the historical aspect of cultural development (they are all products of human culture), in the aspect of language (they possess an objective symbolical meaning), in the aspect of social intercourse, in the aspect of economic valuation (they are all economic goods), in the aesthetic aspect (they are all objects of aesthetic appreciation), in the jural aspect (they are all objects of human rights and legal transactions), etc.

But, no one ever experiences the reality of these things as the simple sum total of the functions they possess within the different aspects of reality. Rather, we experience them exclusively as typical totality structures, in which their various distinct aspects are arranged in typical fashion to form an individual whole. Therefore, these typical totality structures of concrete things are to be clearly distinguished from the constant structures displayed by the specific aspects of reality which we call modal structures because they pertain to a particular mode or way of being within a specific aspect of reality. Without a proper insight into these modal structures, it becomes impossible to achieve scientific insight into the typical totality structures of reality. And without insight into this dual structure of reality, it is impossible in sociology to use the concept of causality in a sound scientific manner. [214]

Modern sociology, however, has actually attempted to "explain" the phenomena of human society after it had – as a matter of principle – discarded these structures which make possible these very phenomena as well as our experience of them. Therefore, the first basic requirement for a Christian sociology is to detach itself from the humanistic understandings of reality to which the various schools tacitly adhere. In view of this we will attempt to uncover the underlying structures of reality to which we have already pointed and which, under the influence of the humanistic ground-motive, have been banished from the perspective of science. The difficulty of this undertaking should not deter any reader who is equally convinced with us of the urgent necessity of a Christian sociology. Such a sociology can be developed only in a gradual fashion, but never without a radical conversion of our entire scientific understanding of reality, a conversion which must be brought about by the spiritual dynamic of the ground-motive of God's Word-revelation – creation, fall into sin, and redemption through Jesus Christ.

Ideal Types and Creational Structures

Ultimately, all the fundamental problems of sociology seem to converge in the question of how it is possible to bring together in a comprehensive theoretical perspective the great diversity of modal aspects revealed by society. The various special sciences concerned with social relationships, such as social biology, social psychology, history, linguistics, economics, legal theory, etc., may restrict themselves to study these relationships under a specific modal aspect, such as the aspect of organic life, the aspect of feeling, the historical aspect, the aspect of language, the economic, or the jural aspect. However, sociology cannot adopt this restricted perspective of a special science. Rather, it is the essential task of sociology to bring together all these aspects in a typical comprehensive theoretical perspective. This presupposes that one has an idea of the mutual interrelation and coherence of the aspects, the respective place which each of them occupies in the entire order of the aspects, and, finally, the manner in which the aspects are arranged within the typical totality structures of reality to form individual wholes.

In other words, our whole theoretical understanding of the underlying structures of reality is at stake here. The fundamental problems we have raised are indubitably of an intrinsically philosophical nature. But sociology gains nothing if it tries to brush these questions aside with a sweeping gesture, proclaiming that it is content to conduct research into empirical phenomena, while the philosophical root problems can be left to a social philosophy. After all, is it not exactly the question of the empirical character of the reality of social relationships which is at issue [215] here? The typical structures within which empirical social relationships are ordered – such as the structure of marriage, nuclear family, lineal family, state, church, business, school, labor organization, social intercourse, relations of war, etc. – are not sensorily perceptible entities presented to us in an objective space of sense perception. In principle, these typical structures embrace all modal aspects of reality without exception, they arrange or group these aspects in a typical manner to form individual totalities, and they make possible our experience of the concrete and temporally variable societal phenomena. The question regarding the inner nature of these societal structures simply cannot be evaded if one wishes to investigate empirical phenomena in a truly scientific manner.

Let us take an example from a socio-historical inquiry into the factual development of the life of the state. Is it not imperative first to reflect on what one understands by a "state?" Were the primitive kinship communities, clans, sibs, and tribal communities really "states?" Is it correct to apply the term state to the medieval fiefdom of the bishopric of Utrecht? Did the state have its origins in the family or in conquest? Is the state merely the instrument of power wielded by the ruling class in order to keep the oppressed class in subjection? How are the physical, biotic, psychical, historical, economic, jural, ethical, and other aspects interrelated within the structure of the state? Does law play the same role in the state as in other social structures, or, in its empirical reality, is the state nothing but an organization of historical power, while the enforcement of the legal order represents only one of the numerous purposes of the state and as such is extraneous to a sociological understanding of the state? Can all these questions be answered objectively on the basis of sense perception? Surely, anyone who has retained a measure of critical awareness will not assert that this is the case!

Is there an alternative solution? Are we to operate in sociology with so-called "ideal-type" concepts which we have extracted in arbitrary fashion from the variable social phenomena as these are presented to us under the historical aspect of reality? Such "ideal types" ultimately are nothing but subjective constructions which cannot contribute anything to our insight into the typical totality structures of reality. Max Weber, the well-known German scholar who introduced these so-called ideal types into the conceptual framework of sociology, expressly acknowledged their relatively arbitrary and derivative character and only wished to utilize them as aids toward a better understanding of the historical individuality of phenomena, especially of the subjective socio-historical meaning of human action. He explained that "ideal types" are achieved by consciously exaggerating certain traits within "historical [216] reality" and abstracting these from all other traits. He readily admitted that one will never simply come across such an ideal type within reality itself. As example one can point to the ideal type of *homo economicus*, the fantasy image of a person who is driven only and exclusively by personal economic self-interest and of someone who chooses, in a strictly rational fashion, the means whereby these goals could be realized. In a similar manner, one might construct an ideal type of the modern bureaucratic state, of church and sect, of the medieval city, of medieval crafts, etc. However, the real structural problem we have brought to light has not even been raised here; that is, the question of how the various aspects which manifest themselves in society are arranged within the distinctly typical totality structures to form wholly unique individual entities. Yet this is the basic question of all sociology. One reads a great deal in various writings and daily newspapers about the "structures" of society and about structural changes. But it is far from clear what exactly is understood by this. Quite often these terms conceal a scientifically defended notion that economic factors are really decisive and determine the entire coherence of a "society." It is also quite common that the expression "social structure" conceals a pseudo-scientific conception of society as an "equilibrium of forces" whose disruption will necessarily effect structural changes.

Those who have seen the urgent necessity for the development of a sociology based on a spiritual-Christian foundation must inevitably assume a skeptical attitude toward this pseudo-scientific methodology which eliminates the real structures of reality, for they understand that these structures are grounded in the creation order. We have seen, of course, that modern sociology did not receive its spiritual dynamic from the ground-motive of Christianity – creation, fall into sin, and salvation through Jesus Christ – but from the humanistic ideal of science, either in its classical natural-scientific form, or in its modern historicistic form. And this ideal of science depended throughout upon humankind's faith in its own autonomy understood in characteristic humanistic fashion. This faith could not tolerate the acceptance of a creation order to which individuals, quite independently of their own subjective thinking and volition, are subject. Thus society, inspired by this ideal of science, began immediately to eliminate the modal structures of the aspects and thought that it could grasp the empirical reality of society apart from its underlying structural matrix.

The elimination of a normative perspective from social reality led, of necessity, to the elimination of all those aspects of reality which, in accordance with their modal structure, bear a normative character. As we have emphasized, after such elimination one is not left with an [217] empirical social reality, but with an arbitrary, abstract, and scientifically unsound construction of that reality. The elimination of the modal structures of the aspects directly implied the elimination of the typical totality structures or individuality-structures of social reality, since the latter depend on the former. Therefore, since our first objective must be to acquire insight into the typical totality structures of society and into the different ways these structures are mutually intertwined, we must begin our own inquiry with an analysis of the modal structures of the various distinct aspects of society. We will see how such an analysis will, in a surprising manner, provide us with insight into the entire sequence of these aspects and thus into the place each aspect occupies in this sequence.[1] [218]

---

1. This was Dooyeweerd's last contribution to *Nieuw Nederland*. It was published in the issue dated May 13, 1948. The reader who desires to pursue Dooyeweerd's argument can consult the following publications in English and German: Herman Dooyeweerd,"Historicism and the Sense of History," in *In the Twilight of Western Thought*, ed. Jamie Smith, The Collected Works of Herman Dooyeweerd, gen. ed. D.F.M. Strauss, (Lewiston: The Edwin Mellen Press, 1999), series B, vol. 2: 43-76; and "Die Philosophie der Gesetzesidee und ihre Bedeutung für die Rechts- un Sozialphilosophie," *Archiv für Rechts- und Sozialphilosophie*, vol. 53 (1967): 1-20 and 465-513. Dooyeweerd's most elaborate explication of the so-called modal structures of reality and the totality structures of society is contained in the second and third volumes of his *A New Critique of Theoretical Thought*, trans. David H. Freeman and William S. Young, The Collected Works of Herman Dooyeweerd, gen. ed. D.F.M. Strauss, (reprint, Lewiston: The Edwin Mellen Press, 1997). A nearly exhaustive bibliography of Dooyeweerd's publications in English, French, and German before 1975, as well as a list of writings about him issued before that date can be found in L. Kalsbeek, *Contours of a Christian Philosophy: An Introduction to Herman Dooyeweerd's Thought*, ed. Bernard Zylstra and Josina Zylstra (Toronto: Wedge, 1975), 307-313.

Translator's Preface (1979 edition)

A few months after the Second World War, in August 1945, Herman Dooyeweerd became editor of a weekly paper named *Nieuw Nederland*. During the next three years he contributed to it regularly, thus in his own highly distinctive way sounding the note of Reformation amidst serious and dedicated attempts at postwar renewal and even reconstruction of the social and political order in the Netherlands. That note needed to be sounded with the greatest possible clarity. The spiritual crisis demanded a diagnosis based on a sustained systematic analysis of the religious roots of western culture. Dooyeweerd's articles attempted to do just that. A brief sketch of the background against which they were written may help to clarify this.

Since the days of Guillaume Groen van Prinsterer and Abraham Kuyper, just before the turn of the century, Calvinism had been a way of life and one of the very pillars of the Dutch social order. Far from being a theological system along rationalist lines, continuing a dead or at least stifling tradition, as has by and large been the case in Anglo-Saxon countries, Dutch Calvinism addressed itself relevantly and incisively to every sphere of life. One need but read Kuyper's *Stone Lectures* on Calvinism presented at Princeton in 1898 to sense something of the tremendous vitality and broadness of scope inherent in "the Calvinist world and life view."

But in the course of the twenties a spiritual apathy crept into the Reformed community. The battle for public recognition and governmental support of Christian schools had been won; in the political arena the Calvinist Anti-revolutionary Party was firmly established; in public and private life the Calvinist was thoroughly respectable. But the great leaders were gone, and it seemed to some that the rigor with which the central principles ("antithesis" and "sphere sovereignty") were maintained and put into practice was not entirely unlike rigor mortis.

At that time Dooyeweerd, who was born in 1894, had completed his formal studies in law at the Free University and had served in a variety of governmental positions. Because he recognized the need to engage in foundational studies, in 1922 he was invited to become head of the Kuyper Institute in The Hague – the research center of the Anti-revolutionary Party. In this capacity he launched an ambitious publication program aimed at outlining the foundation of Christian political theory and practice. In many ways one can draw a parallel between those efforts of the twenties and the focus of the collection now before us. Then, too, his intent was to call people to reflection on the vital strength of the biblical ordering principles for the whole of societal life, drawing on the work of

Abraham Kuyper who in turn had depended greatly on the Calvinist tradition – particularly on John Calvin himself – to inspire truly Christian action and organization. In 1926 Dooyeweerd was appointed professor of legal philosophy at the Free University, and for the next two decades he devoted nearly all his energies to the development of Christian scholarship. In the area of philosophy his great trilogy, *De Wijsbegeerte der Wetsidee* (Philosophy of the Cosmonomic Idea), published in 1935-36, was an eloquent witness to the vastness of his vision which he elaborated with reference to several special sciences, especially political and legal theory, in numerous academic monographs.

Immediately after the war, however, the need to address the non-academic community was particularly urgent once again. During the war a spirit of unity and deeply felt comradeship, born of the need to entrust one's life to the next resistance fighter, had fostered hope among many that a lasting bond could be forged, not only when a common enemy was to be fought, but also when Holland was to be built up again. For many the question was existential: can we not "break through" the old, ideologically inspired oppositions and divisions within the nation? Should we not consider the Marxist notion of "class struggle" and the Calvinist notion of "antithesis" to be relics of a bygone era? Let us build as we battled – together!

Such was the appeal issued by the Dutch National Movement. Initially it met with eager response. Along with many a leading statesman, Queen Wilhelmina was very favorably disposed toward the movement's aspirations and hoped that the first free elections, to be held in the spring of 1946, would entrench the new ideal in the places of power. When Dooyeweerd began his series of articles, the principle of pluriform democracy was at stake. This principle safeguarded the presence of a Christian position in the public realm alongside the conservative, centrist, and radical positions of humanism. The Dutch National Movement favoured the elimination of the spiritual "antithesis" between Christianity and humanism in public life. In practice this would mean the replacement of the principle of pluriform democracy by the new community ideal of "personal socialism" which entailed decentralized government and supposedly was based on both humanist and Christian worldviews.

As it turned out, the principle of pluriform democracy, which constituted the basis for Holland's parliamentary system since the 1880s, prevailed during the 1946 elections. And it cannot be denied that Dooyeweerd's call to fundamental reflection, issued weekly in *Nieuw Nederland*, was a contributing factor.

In Dooyeweerd's view, those who propagated the unity of the people on the basis of a breakthrough of old lines of principled demarcation had been uprooted by the crisis of the western world in the twentieth century,

Translator's Preface (1979 edition)

an uprootedness which had become the more existential because of the horrors and atrocities of that terrible war. Consequently, they were unable to really come to grips with the question as to the *direction* postwar renewal would have to take. Dooyeweerd was convinced that this question could be answered only against the background of a fundamental reflection on, and reappropriation of, one's *roots*, the wellsprings and ultimate sources of inspiration that alone can confer meaning on action. To be radical one must go back to the roots of one's culture, to the sources of the communal ways of life in which individuals, institutions, and organizations live and move and have their being. This is what his articles were all about.

Herein lies their significance beyond that postwar period of hope and confusion, beyond the borders of the Low Countries. For it was in this situation that Dooyeweerd for the first time offered to a broad public the results of his investigations into the role of the *ground-motives* as the dynamic, community-establishing expressions of ultimate meaning in terms of which western civilization has been, and still is being, shaped. Three points are of outstanding importance here:

1. If the ground-motives indeed embody ultimate meaning, it is here that every battle of the spirits in the struggle for cultural direction reveals its true character, its *religious* nature. This means that the *antithesis* – even if the word itself is not particularly fortunate – refers to the intrinsic connection between religion and the whole of life so that there simply *are* lines of demarcation and crucial differences that are not "negotiable."
2. If the ground-motives are community-establishing driving forces, catalyzers of action, they constitute the hermeneutic keys for understanding and interpreting periods and patterns of history and culture. They speak to us of our roots, our presence, and our destination. This implies that the meaning of such incisive historical divergences can come to radical clarity, that there are criteria by which the spirits may be tested, and that authentic confrontation is possible.
3. If the ground-motives are spiritual powers that – often unawares – take hold of the hearts of men and women, they will indeed inspire all understanding, interpretation, and every other kind of action. This implies two possibilities. Either one engages in reflection on the ground-motives which leads to self-reflection and self-critique that gets at the heart of things, that reaches down to the most fundamental choice one must necessarily make, or one is swept along by supra-individual powers, perhaps in resignation or fed by false hope, toward illusionary goals. Moreover, if the most fundamental wellsprings of action are recognized for what they are – religious ground-motives – *open dialogue* is possible among adherents of di-

vergent convictions as equal partners in a discussion, all sharing in the awesome reality of a broken world, broken on account of what man has done and has failed to do.

Dooyeweerd's study of the ground-motives is not an example of historistic relativism. The *condition humaine* and our common responsibility for it demand open dialogue among equals, but such equality does not extend to the ultimate motivations by which people and cultures are driven. Structurally religious, man gives his heart to forces that prolong and intensify the brokenness of human life, powers called forth by man himself that tear him apart. But Dooyeweerd makes a fundamental distinction between apostate ground-motives and the biblical one. Apostate ground-motives display an *inherent dialectic*, that is, a "destructive principle" is at work at their very core. This destructive principle is a spirit of negation that stands over against *revelationally given* meaning as matrix of mankind's place and calling in creation. In this way Dooyeweerd offers a renewed and deepened understanding of the significance of the "antithesis" between the spirit of darkness and the living, healing power of the Word of God.

This book is a profound call to depth-level reflection on the dynamics of cultural formation. I hope that it will contribute to an increasing awareness of what is truly important in private and public life.

John Kraay
Free University of Amsterdam
Christmas 1978

Editorial Preface (1979 edition)

This book contains a collection of fifty-eight articles originally published by Herman Dooyeweerd in the weekly *Nieuw Nederland* between August 1945 and May 1948. Nearly all of this material was first issued in book form by J.A. Oosterhoff under the title *Vernieuwing en Bezinning om het reformatorisch grondmotief* (Renewal and Reflection concerning the Reformational Ground-Motive [Zutphen: J.B. van den Brink, 1959]).

Oosterhoff also included in the Dutch collection eighteen other articles which Dooyeweerd had published as a parallel series in *Nieuw Nederland*. These dealt with the industrial organization policies of the postwar Dutch government, the relation between industry and the state, the nature of the business enterprise, and the impact of historicism on Guillaume Groen van Prinsterer's thought. This material is highly significant for an understanding especially of Dooyeweerd's conception of industry in its relation to the state. However, since these articles were written in the context of immediate issues within the Dutch socio-economy, they fall outside the scope of the material made available here. And because of their considerably more technical character, they would require a quite elaborate footnote apparatus to introduce them to the Anglo-Saxon reader. Since they deal with permanent issues within an industrialized society, they should indeed be published in English, possibly in connection with all of the other material which Dooyeweerd wrote about industrial structure, labor organization and socio-economic policy between 1944 and 1955. Or they could be included in a more permanent edition of Dooyeweerd's journalistic efforts in *Nieuw Nederland* as part of the Collected Works. The possibility of an English edition of the Collected Works was discussed with Dooyeweerd shortly before his death in 1977 and is currently being pursued by the Dooyeweerd Publication Society established by an international group of scholars interested in this mammoth undertaking.

The decision to limit this translation to Dooyeweerd's treatment of the impact of the biblical, Greek, Roman Catholic, and humanist ground-motives upon western culture was first made by H. Evan Runner of Calvin College in Grand Rapids, Michigan. With his encouragement the members of the Groen van Prinsterer Society prepared an in-house version in the sixties. This served as the basis of John Kraay's translation, whose work was edited by Mark Vander Vennen, a graduate student in philosophy at Duquesne University in Pittsburgh. Beert C. Verstraete, a graduate in classics at the University of Toronto, kindly consented to translate the last sections, entitled "Estates and Classes" and "Basic Problems in Sociology," which were not included in the Oosterhoff edition of 1959. Unfortunately, even with this addition the final chapter does not complete the total argument which Dooyeweerd had planned to develop. This is due to the fact that quite unexpectedly he terminated his involvement in the publication of *Nieuw Nederland*.

The division of the material into the present eight chapters is different from Oosterhoff's division into three. His first chapter, entitled "Antithesis," contained the introduction and the first four chapters of this book His second chapter, entitled "Reformation and Accommodation," is nearly identical with chapter five. And his third Chapter, "Reformation and Humanism," embraced what is here published in the final three chapters. The new division, intended to make the material more accessible, is a result of the combined efforts of John Kraay, Mark Vander Vennen, and myself. The three of us are also responsible for the footnotes. The new title was chosen, after much searching, to reflect more adequately the content of the book.

Because this translation had gone through so many hands, I took it upon myself to check it in its entirety against the original, as I had promised professor Dooyeweerd. I hope that this book will contribute not only to an understanding of Dooyeweerd's thought, but to an assessment of the spiritual exhaustion of the West and a surrender to the revitalizing power of the Spirit of Christ.

Bernard Zylstra
Institute for Christian Studies, Toronto
Summer 1979

Glossary

[The following glossary of Dooyeweerd's technical terms and neologisms is reproduced and edited by Daniël F. M. Strauss, with the permission of its author, Albert M. Wolters, from C. T. McIntire, ed., *The Legacy of Herman Dooyeweerd: Reflections on Critical Philosophy in the Christian Tradition* (University Press of America, Lanham MD, 1985), 167–171.]

THIS GLOSSARY OF HERMAN DOOYEWEERD'S terms is an adapted version of the one published in L. Kalsbeek, *Contours of a Christian Philosophy* (Toronto: Wedge, 1975). It does not provide exhaustive technical definitions but gives hints and pointers for a better understanding. Entries marked with an asterisk are those terms which are used by Dooyeweerd in a way which is unusual in English-speaking philosophical contexts and are, therefore, a potential source of misunderstanding. Words or phrases in small caps and beginning with a capital letter refer to other entries in this glossary.

* **Analogy** (see LAW-SPHERE)– Collective name for a RETROCIPATION or an ANTICIPATION.
* **Anticipation**– An ANALOGY within one MODALITY referring to a later modality. An example is "efficiency," a meaning-moment which is found within the historical modality, but which points forward to the later economic modality. Contrast with RETROCIPATION.
* **Antinomy**– Literally "conflict of laws" (from Greek *anti,* "against," and *nomos,* "law"). A logical contradiction arising out of a failure to distinguish the different kinds of law valid in different MODALITIES. Since ontic laws do not conflict (*Principium Exclusae Antinomiae*), an antinomy is always a logical sign of ontological reductionism.
* **Antithesis**– Used by Dooyeweerd (following Abraham Kuyper) in a specifically religious sense to refer to the fundamental spiritual opposition between the kingdom of God and the kingdom of darkness. See Galatians 5:17. Since this is an opposition between regimes, not realms, it runs through every department of human life and culture, including philosophy and the academic enterprise as a whole, and through the heart of every believer as he or she struggles to live a life of undivided allegiance to God.

Aspect– A synonym for MODALITY.

Cosmonomic idea– Dooyeweerd's own English rendering of the Dutch term *wetsidee.* Occasionally equivalents are "transcendental ground idea" or "transcendental basic idea." The intention of this new term is to bring to expression that there exists an unbreakable coherence between God's *law* (nomos) and created reality (*cosmos*) factually subjected to God's law.

Dialectic– In Dooyeweerd's usage: an unresolvable tension, within a system or line of thought, between two logically irreconcilable polar positions. Such a dialectical tension is characteristic of each of the three non-Christian GROUND-MOTIVES which Dooyeweerd sees as having dominated western thought.

*Enkapsis (enkaptic)– A neologism borrowed by Dooyeweerd from the Swiss biologist Heidenhain, and derived from the Greek *enkaptein*, "to swallow up." The term refers to the structural interlacements which can exist between things, plants, animals, and societal structures which have their own internal structural principle and independent qualifying function. As such, enkapsis is to be clearly distinguished from the part-whole relation, in which there is a common internal structure and qualifying function.

Factual Side– General designation of whatever is *subjected* to the LAW-SIDE of creation (see SUBJECT-SIDE).

Founding Function– The earliest of the two modalities which characterize certain types of structural wholes. The other is called the GUIDING FUNCTION. For example, the founding function of the family is the biotic modality.

* Gegenstand– A German word for "object," used by Dooyeweerd as a technical term for a modality when abstracted from the coherence of time and opposed to the analytical function in the theoretical attitude of thought, thereby establishing the Gegenstand-relation. Gegenstand is therefore the technically precise word for the object of SCIENCE, while "object" itself is reserved for the objects of NAIVE EXPERIENCE.

Ground-motive– The Dutch term *grondmotief*, used by Dooyeweerd in the sense of fundamental motivation, driving force. He distinguished four basic ground-motives in the history of Western civilization:
(1) form and matter, which dominated pagan Greek philosophy; (2) nature and grace, which underlay medieval Christian synthesis thought; (3) nature and freedom, which has shaped the philosophies of modern times; and (4) creation, fall, and redemption, which lies at the root of a radical and integrally scriptural philosophy.

Guiding Function– The highest subject-function of a structural whole (e.g. stone, animal, business enterprise, or state). Except in the case of humans, this function is also said to QUALIFY the structural whole. It is called the guiding function because it "guides" or "leads" its earlier functions. For example, the guiding function of a plant is the biotic. The physical function of a plant (as studied, e.g., by biochemistry) is different from physical functioning elsewhere because of its being "guided" by the biotic. Also called "leading function."

Glossary

* **Heart**– The concentration point of human existence; the supratemporal focus of all human temporal functions; the religious root unity of humans. Dooyeweerd says that it was his rediscovery of the biblical idea of the heart as the central religious depth dimension of human multifaceted life which enabled him to wrestle free from neo-Kantianism and phenomenology. The Scriptures speak of this focal point also as "soul," "spirit," and "inner man." Philiosophical equivalents are Ego, I, I-ness, and Selfhood. It is the heart in this sense which survives death, and it is by the religious redirection of the heart in regeneration that all human temporal functions are renewed.

* **Immanence Philosophy**– A name for all non-Christian philosophy, which tries to find the ground and integration of reality *within* the created order. Unlike Christianity, which acknowledges a transcendent Creator above all things, immanence philosophy of necessity absolutizes some feature or aspect of creation itself.

* **Individuality-structure**– This term represents arguably one of the most difficult concepts in Dooyeweerd's philosophy. Coined in both Dutch and English by Dooyeweerd himself it has led sometimes to serious misunderstandings amongst scholars. Over the years there have been various attempts to come up with an alternate term, some of which are described below, but in the absence of a consensus it was decided to leave the term the way it is.

It is the general name or the characteristic law (order) of concrete things, as given by virtue of creation. Individuality-structures belong to the law-side of reality. Dooyeweerd uses the term individuality-structure to indicate the applicability of a structural order *for* the existence of *individual* entities. Thus the *structural laws* for the state, for marriage, for works of art, for mosquitoes, for sodium chloride, and so forth are called individuality-structures. The idea of an individual whole is determined by an individuality-structure which precedes the theoretical analysis of its modal functions. The identity of an individual whole is a relative unity in a multiplicity of functions. (See MODALITY.) Van Riessen prefers to call this law for entities an *identity-structure*, since as such it guarantees the persistent **identity** of all **entities** (*Wijsbegeerte,* [Kampen, 1970], 158). In his work (*Alive, An Enquiry into the Origin and Meaning of Life* [Vallecito, California: Ross House Books, 1984]), M. Verbrugge introduces his own distinct systematic account concerning the nature of (what he calls) *functors*, a word first introduced by Hendrik Hart for the dimension of individuality-structures (cf. Hart: *Understanding Our World, Towards an Integral Ontology* [New York, 1984], 445–446). As a substitute for the notion of an individuality-structure, Verbrugge advances the term: *idionomy* (cf. *Alive*, 42, 81ff., 91ff.). Of course this term may also cause misunderstanding if it is taken to mean that each individual creature (subject) has its *own unique* law. What is intended is that every *type of law* (*nomos*) is meant to delimit and determine unique subjects. In other words, however *specified* the universality of the law may be, it can never, in its bearing upon unique individual creatures, itself become something *uniquely individual*. Another way of grasping the meaning of Dooyeweerd's notion of an *individuality-structure* is, in following an oral suggestion by Roy Clouser (Zeist, August 1986), to call it a *type-law* (from Greek: *typonomy*). This simply means that all entities of a certain *type* conform to this law. The following perspective given by M.D. Stafleu elucidates this terminology in a *systematic way* (*Time and Again, A Systematic Analysis of the Foundations of Physics* [Toronto: Wedge Publishing Foundation, 1980], 6, 11): *typical laws* (type-laws/typonomies, such as the Coulomb law – applicable only to charged entities and the Pauli principle – applicable only to fermions) are special laws which apply to a limited class of entities only, whereas *modal laws* hold universally for all possible entities. D.F.M. Strauss ("Inleiding tot die Kosmologie." *SACUM*, [1980]) introduces the expression *entity structures*. The term **entity** comprises both the *individuality* and the *identity* of the thing concerned – therefore it accounts for the respective emphases found in Dooyeweerd's notion of *individuality-structures* and in Van Riessen's notion of *identity structures*. The following words of Dooyeweerd show that both the **individuality** and **identity** of an entity is determined by its individuality-structure: "In general we can establish that the factual temporal duration of a thing as an individual and identical whole is dependent on the preservation of its structure of individuality" (*A New Critique*, vol.3,79).

Irreducibility (irreducible)– Incapability of theoretical reduction. This is the negative way of referring to the unique distinctiveness of things and aspects which we find everywhere in creation and which theoretical thought must respect. Insofar as everything has its own peculiar created nature and character, it cannot be understood in terms of categories foreign to itself.

* **Law–** The notion of creational law is central to Dooyeweerd's philosophy. Everything in creation is subject to God's law for it, and accordingly law is the boundary between God and creation. Scriptural synonyms for law are "ordinance," "decree," "commandment," "word," and so on. Dooyeweerd stresses that law is not in opposition to, but the condition for true freedom. See also NORM and LAW-SIDE.

Law-Side– The created cosmos, for Dooyeweerd, has two correlative "sides": a law-side and a factual side (initially called: SUBJECT-SIDE). The former is simply the coherence of God's laws or ordinances for creation; the latter is the totality of created reality which is subject to those laws. It is important to note that the law-side always holds universally.

Law-Sphere (see MODAL STRUCTURE and MODALITY)– The circle of laws qualified by a unique, irreducible, and indefinable meaning-nucleus is known as a law-sphere. Within every law-sphere temporal reality has a modal function and in this function is subjected (French: *sujet*) to the laws of the modal spheres. Therefore every law-sphere has a law-side and a

Glossary

subject-side that are given only in unbreakable correlation with each other. (See DIAGRAM on p. 233.)

* **Meaning**– Dooyeweerd uses the word "meaning" in an unusual sense. By it he means the referential, non-self-sufficient character of created reality in that it points beyond itself to God as Origin. Dooyeweerd stresses that reality *is* meaning in this sense and that, therefore, it does not *have* meaning. "Meaning" is the Christian alternative to the metaphysical substance of immanence philosophy. "Meaning" becomes almost a synonym for "reality." Note the many compounds formed from it: meaning-nucleus, meaning-side, meaning-moment, meaning-fullness.

* **Meaning-nucleus**– The indefinable core meaning of a MODALITY.

Modality (See MODAL STRUCTURE and LAW-SPHERE)– One of the fifteen fundamental ways of being, distinguished by Dooyeweerd. As modes of being, they are sharply distinguished from the concrete things which function within them. Initially Dooyeweerd distinguished fourteen aspects only, but in 1950 he introduced the kinematical aspect of *uniform movement* between the spatial and the physical aspects. Modalities are also known as "modal functions," "modal aspects," or as "facets" of created reality. (See DIAGRAM on p. 233.)

Modal Structure (see MODALITY and LAW-SPHERE)– The peculiar constellation, in any given modality, of its meaning-moments (anticipatory, retrocipatory, nuclear). Contrast INDIVIDUALITY-STRUCTURE.

* **Naive experience**– Human experience insofar as it is not "theoretical" in Dooyeweerd's precise sense. "Naive" does not mean unsophisticated. Sometimes called "ordinary" or "everyday" experience. Dooyeweerd takes pains to emphasize that theory is embedded in this everyday experience and must not violate it.

Norm (normative)– Postpsychical laws, that is, modal laws for the analytical through pistical law-spheres (see LAW-SPHERE and DIAGRAM on p. 233). These laws are norms because they need to be positivized (see POSITIVIZE) and can be violated, in distinction from the "natural laws" of the pre-analytical spheres which are obeyed involuntarily (e.g., in a digestive process).

* **Nuclear-moment**– A synonym for MEANING-NUCLEUS and LAW-SPHERE, used to designate the indefinable core meaning of a MODALITY or aspect of created reality.

* **Object**– Something qualified by an object function and thus correlated to a subject function. A work of art, for instance, is qualified by its correlation to the human subjective function of aesthetic appreciation. Similarly, the elements of a sacrament are pistical objects.

Opening process– The process by which latent modal anticipations are "opened" or actualized. The modal meaning is then said to be "deepened."

It is this process which makes possible the cultural development (differentiation) of society from a primitive ("closed," undifferentiated) stage. For example, by the opening or disclosure of the ethical anticipation in the juridical aspect, the modal meaning of the legal aspect is deepened and society can move from the principle of "an eye for an eye" to the consideration of extenuating circumstances in the administration of justice.

* **Philosophy**– In Dooyeweerd's precise systematic terminology, philosophy is the encyclopedic science, that is, its proper task is the theoretical investigation of the overall systematic integration of the various scientific disciplines and their fields of inquiry. Dooyeweerd also uses the term in a more inclusive sense, especially when he points out that all philosophy is rooted in a pretheoretical religious commitment and that some philosophical conception, in turn, lies at the root of all scientific scholarship.

Positivize– A word coined to translate the Dutch word *positiveren*, which means to make positive in the sense of being actually valid in a given time or place. For example, positive law is the legislation which is in force in a given country at a particular time; it is contrasted with the *legal principles* which lawmakers must positivize as legislation. In a general sense, it refers to the responsible implementation of all normative principles in human life as embodied, for example, in state legislation, economic policy, ethical guidelines, and so on.

Qualify– The GUIDING FUNCTION of a thing is said to qualify it in the sense of characterizing it. In this sense a plant is said to be qualified by the biotic and a state by the juridical [aspects].

* **Radical**– Dooyeweerd frequently uses this term with an implicit reference to the Greek meaning of *radix = root*. This usage must not be confused with the political connotation of the term *radical* in English. In other works Dooyeweerd sometimes paraphrases his use of the term radical with the phrase: *penetrating to the root of created reality*.

* **Religion (religious)**– For Dooyeweerd, religion is not an area or sphere of life but the all-encompassing and direction-giving root of it. It is service of God (or a substitute no-god) in every domain of human endeavor. As such, it is to be sharply distinguished from religious faith, which is but one of the many acts and attitudes of human existence. Religion is an affair of the HEART and so directs all human functions. Dooyeweerd says religion is "the innate impulse of the human selfhood to direct itself toward the *true* or toward a *pretended* absolute Origin of all temporal diversity of meaning" (*A New Critique*, vol.1, 57).

* **Retrocipation**– A feature in one MODALITY which refers to, is reminiscent of, an earlier one, yet retaining the modal qualification of the aspect in which it is found. The "extension" of a concept, for example, is a kind of logical space: it is a strictly logical affair, and yet it harks back to the spatial modality in its original sense. See ANTICIPATION.

Glossary

* **Science**– Two things are noted about Dooyeweerd's use of the term "science." In the first place, as a translation of the Dutch word *wetenschap* (analogous to the German word *Wissenschaft*), it embraces all scholarly study – not only the natural sciences but also the social sciences and the humanities, including theology and philosophy. In the second place, science is always, strictly speaking, a matter of modal abstraction, that is, of analytically lifting an aspect out of the temporal coherence in which it is found and examining it in the Gegenstand-relation. But in this investigation it does not focus its theoretical attention upon the modal structure of such an aspect itself; rather, it focuses on the coherence of the actual phenomena which function within that structure. Modal abstraction as such must be distinguished from NAIVE EXPERIENCE. In the first sense, therefore, "science" has a wider application in Dooyeweerd than is usual in English-speaking countries, but in the second sense it has a more restricted, technical meaning.

Sphere Sovereignty– A translation of Kuyper's phrase *souvereiniteit in eigen kring*, by which he meant that the various distinct spheres of human authority (such as family, church, school, and business enterprise) each have their own responsibility and decision-making power which may not be usurped by those in authority in another sphere, for example, the state. Dooyeweerd retains this usage but also extends it to mean the IRREDUCIBILITY of the modal aspects. This is the ontical principle on which the societal principle is based since each of the societal "spheres" mentioned is qualified by a different irreducible modality.

* **Subject**– Used in two senses by Dooyeweerd: (1) "subject" as distinguished from LAW, (2) "subject" as distinguished from OBJECT. The latter sense is roughly equivalent to common usage; the former is unusual and ambiguous. Since all things are "subject" to LAW, objects are also subjects in the first sense. Dooyeweerd's matured conception, however, does not show this ambiguity. By distinguishing between the *law-side* and the *factual side* of creation, both subject and object (sense (2)) are part of the factual side.

Subject-Side– The correlate of LAW-SIDE, preferably called the factual side. Another feature of the factual subject-side is that it is only here that individuality is found.

Substratum– The aggregate of modalities *preceding* a given aspect in the modal order. The arithmetic, spatial, kinematic, and physical, for example, together form the substratum for the biotic. They are also the necessary foundation upon which the biotic rests, and without which it cannot exist. See SUPERSTRATUM (and the DIAGRAM on p. 233).

Superstratum– The aggregate of modalities *following* a given aspect in the modal order. For example, the pistical, ethical, juridical and aesthetic together constitute the superstratum of the economic. See SUBSTRATUM.

* **Synthesis**– The combination, in a single philosophical conception, of characteristic themes from both pagan philosophy and biblical religion. It is this feature of the Christian intellectual tradition, present since patristic times, with which Dooyeweerd wants to make a radical break. Epistemologically seen, the term *synthesis* is used to designate the way in which a multiplicity of features is integrated within the unity of a concept. The re-union of the logical aspect of the theoretical act of thought with its non-logical "Gegenstand" is called an inter-modal meaning-synthesis.

* **Time**– In Dooyeweerd, a general ontological principle of intermodal continuity, with far wider application than our common notion of time, which is equated by him with the physical manifestation of this general cosmic time. It is, therefore, not coordinate with space. All created things, except the human HEART, are in time. At the law-side time expresses itself as time-order and at the factual side (including subject-subject and subject-object relations) as time duration.

Transcendental– A technical term from the philosophy of Kant denoting the a priori structural conditions which make human experience (specifically human knowledge and theoretical thought) possible. As such it is to be sharply distinguished from the term "transcendent." Furthermore, the basic (transcendental) Idea of a philosophy presupposes the transcendent and central sphere of consciousness (the human HEART). This constitutes the *second* meaning in which Dooyeweerd uses the term transcendental: through its transcendental ground-Idea, philosophy points beyond itself to its ultimate religious foundation transcending the realm of thought.

Glossary

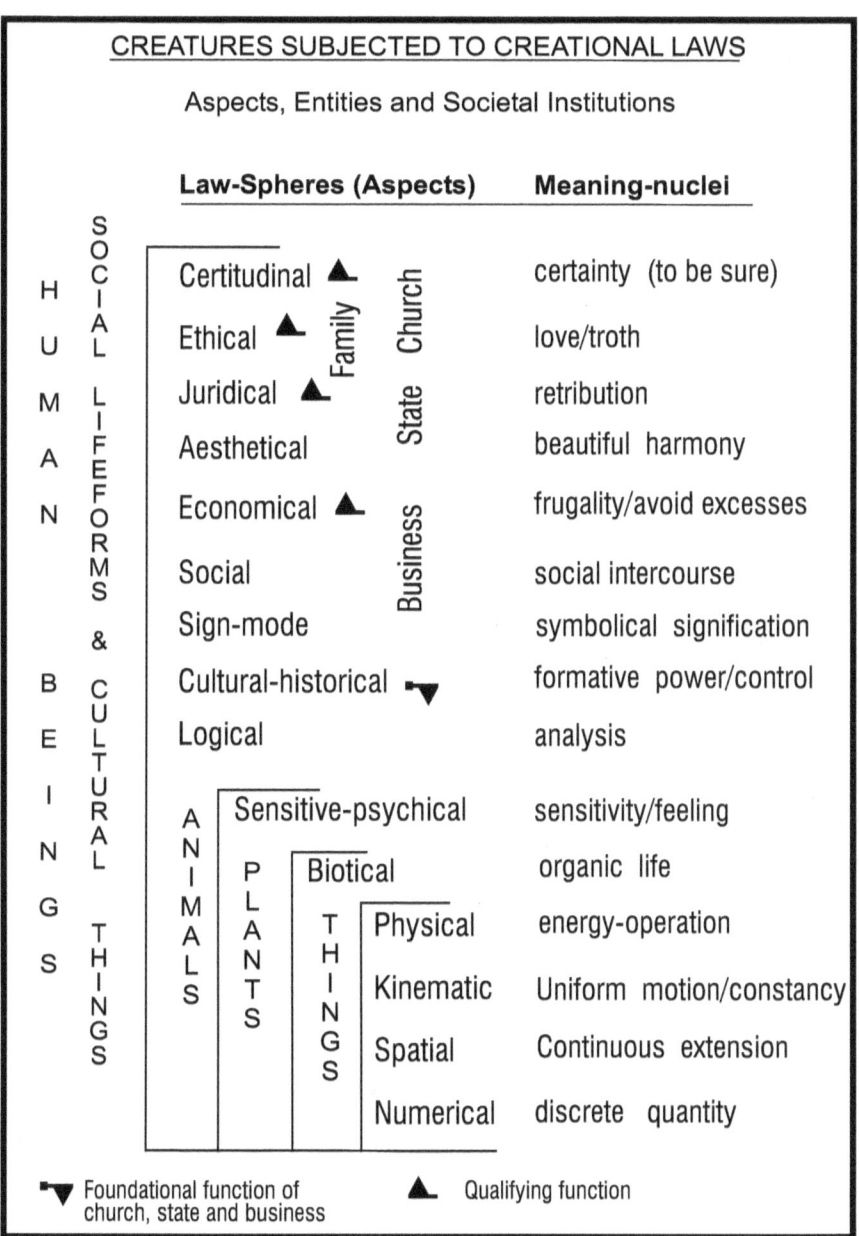

Diagram and choice of terms by D.F.M. Strauss.

Index of Persons

A
Abraham 3, 5, 43, 49, 55, 70, 92, 100, 181, 219-220, 225
Aengenent 135
Aeschylus 29
Agricola 150
Alexander the Great 22
Anaximander 16
Apollo 17, 20
Aquinas 118, 122, 133, 137, 151, 158, 194
Aristotle 16, 22, 29, 34-35, 115, 117-120, 122, 126, 134, 141, 152
Augustine 33, 114-116, 134
Augustus 23

B
Ballanche 186
Barth 60-61, 68, 93, 139-141, 143, 145-146
Bodin 157-158, 194
Bonald 186
Brunner 68, 93, 143, 145-146

C
Caligula 23
Calvin 84-85, 129, 166, 219-220, 223
Cassirer 104
Clovis 79
Codrington 103
Comte 191, 198, 202, 209-210
Constantine the Great 28
Copernicus 151, 153
Cromwell 155, 173

D
Descartes 154-156
Dionysus 17, 20, 22-23

Dooyeweerd 19, 26, 46-47, 66, 78, 86, 124, 217, 219-232
Durkheim 101

E
Erasmus 150-151

F
Fichte 177, 210

G
Galileo 151, 155, 191
Gierke 78
Goethe 17, 42, 56, 102, 179
Gogarten 143
Groen van Prinsterer ix, 3, 5, 58, 64, 70, 162, 187, 219, 223
Grotius 150, 157-158, 161, 194

H
Haller 187
Hegel 7, 13, 89, 203-204, 210
Hesiod 17, 19
Hitler 27, 79
Hobbes 154-156, 161, 163-164, 170, 173, 194, 197
Homer 18
Huizinga 73
Hume 160

J
Job 60

K
Kalsbeek 217, 225
Kant 37, 171-173, 175-177, 179, 203, 210, 227, 232, 238
Koenraadt 128
Kors 136

Index

Kuyper vi, ix, 3, 5, 43, 49, 55-56, 70, 92-93, 124, 181, 219, 225, 231

L
Leo XIII 122, 133
Leonardo da Vinci 68
Locke 160-162, 164-165, 167-168, 194-195, 202
Louis XI 199
Luther vii, 51, 139-143, 146, 150, 187, 238

M
Machiavelli 150, 162
Maistre 186
Marcuse 52
Marx 2, 11, 49, 196-198, 202, 205, 220
Mekkes 165
Melanchthon 142
Melanesians 103
Montesquieu 165-167

N
Napoleon 51, 87, 179, 184
Newton 16, 151, 191
Nietzsche 11
Nilsson 19

O
Ockham 137-141
Osiris 105

P
Pascal 107
Paul 29, 37, 96, 98, 120-122, 140, 228
Pesch 128

Pius XI 122, 125, 129, 132, 135-136
Plato 7, 34-35, 116
Pufendorff 194

Q
Quesnay 202

R
Ricardo 197
Rickert 210
Rousseau 74, 160-162, 165-166, 168-171

S
Saint-Simon 198-202, 209-210
Sassen 136
Satan 4, 37-38, 47, 61
Savigny 190
Say 203
Schelling 187, 210
Schlegel 177
Sertillanges 133
Smith 197, 203, 217
Spann 128
Spencer 209
Stahl vi, 52, 55, 67
Stein 203

T
Thorbecke 58
Tiberius 23
Tönnies 203

W
Weber 206, 215
William I 69
William of Orange 165

Index of Subjects

A

absolutism 28, 49, 125, 127, 170
absolutization 13, 29, 38, 56, 58, 88, 105, 112, 170, 172, 180, 184, 190
analogy 19, 94-98
Anangkē 16-18, 28-29, 36, 101, 111, 144
ançien régime 54, 57, 162
antithesis xi, 1-8, 11-15, 28-29, 31-32, 35, 38-39, 41, 47-48, 50, 66, 73, 84-85, 88, 93-94, 99, 108-109, 134-136, 139-140, 143-144, 170, 182, 219-222
Anti-revolutionary
 – Party ix, 70, 219
 – political thought 55
 – thought 67
apostasy 3, 12, 30, 32, 36-38, 68, 91-92, 100-102, 104-105, 108, 122
aspects of reality 31, 33, 41-45, 47-48, 58, 60, 65-66, 70-72, 75, 83, 86, 89-90, 93, 95, 99, 101, 104, 172, 211-213, 215-216
authority 1, 3, 22-28, 53-55, 57, 69-70, 78, 80, 87, 97, 107-108, 118, 123-124, 132-133, 135-137, 142, 145, 151-152, 156-159, 161-164, 166, 170-171, 173, 185, 190, 194, 199, 231
autonomy 53-58, 87-88, 112, 115, 117, 120, 124, 128, 131-134, 150-152, 156, 160-162, 164-165, 168, 170-172, 175-178, 204, 210, 216

B

balance of powers 9
bankers 199-200
Barthianism 60, 139, 146
behavior 70-71, 208-210
Bible 29, 55, 59, 63
biological school 209
Body of Christ 113, 130
bolshevism 11
Bourbons 198
bourgeoisie 200

C

Calvinism 84-85, 129, 219
causality 159, 209-211, 213
Christopher Group 136
church 3, 10, 24, 28, 32, 45, 48-49, 55-56, 61, 64, 76-79, 81-82, 86, 90-91, 96-97, 106-107, 109, 111, 113-114, 116-117, 119, 124, 127, 129-139, 142, 144-145, 149-152, 154, 157, 185-186, 193-194, 201, 207, 214-215, 231, 235
church fathers 96, 114, 133, 139, 150
civil society 164-165, 195-197, 202-204
civitas terrena 108
class
 – concept 201-205
 – conflict 197-198, 200
classes 198-202, 204, 207
coherence 18, 42-46, 48-49, 58-59, 86, 90, 94-95, 97, 99-100, 105-106, 151, 159-160, 190-192, 200, 214, 216, 226, 228, 231
common
 – good 27, 53, 55, 57-58, 123-125, 127, 164, 185
 – grace 27, 37-39, 60, 108, 146
Communist Manifesto 202, 205
community ix, 1-2, 9, 21-22, 24-28, 30-31, 37, 39, 41, 48, 54, 57, 63, 75-80, 83, 85, 87-89, 101, 104, 109, 114, 123-132, 142-143, 162, 176-182, 184-186, 190, 192-194, 200-201, 204, 219-221, 239
confessions 32, 48
contemplation 21
conversion 41, 101, 114, 214
Counter-Reformation 10
counter-revolution 70

Index

creation
- motive 28-29, 43, 46, 60-61, 63-64, 66, 68-69, 71, 80, 109-110, 118-119, 123-124, 126, 140-141, 143, 145, 151, 170, 180
- order 29, 31, 48, 56, 60, 65-66, 70-73, 75-76, 80, 82, 89-90, 101-102, 109, 119, 130, 146, 151, 153, 156, 172-173, 216
- ordinances 38, 60, 139, 145-146

Crusades 199
cultural mandate 66, 68, 72
culture xi, 4, 8-11, 14-29, 32, 37-39, 41-42, 44, 49, 51-52, 65-68, 72, 74, 76-78, 80-87, 90-91, 98-101, 103-108, 111-113, 116-117, 120, 125, 137, 139, 142-146, 149-150, 156, 160-161, 172, 175, 179, 183, 185-186, 190, 212-213, 219, 221-223, 225, 237
cynics 21

D

Das Kapital 196
decentralization 50-51, 87, 236
deity 16, 95, 101, 103, 112, 119-120
democracy 22, 67, 74, 88, 162, 165-170, 173, 220
dialectical theology 143, 145-147
dichotomy 35
differentiation 25, 54, 58, 76, 78, 80-83, 85-86, 88, 99, 104, 106, 156-157, 162, 185, 196, 201, 230
direction 6, 10-11, 13, 21, 35, 38, 54, 59-60, 69, 73-74, 82, 86, 91-92, 99-101, 103, 105, 111, 114-115, 120-122, 143, 145, 150, 175, 177, 179, 181-185, 187, 189, 192, 200, 202, 221, 227, 230
disclosure 86, 88-89, 98-101, 103-105, 107-108, 185, 230
dogma 2, 63, 89, 97, 115, 134-135, 138, 154, 187, 206-208
dualism 36-37, 86, 108, 113, 116, 119, 124, 137, 141-143, 145-146, 170, 177, 180, 185-186, 193
Dutch National Movement 1-2, 4, 7, 84, 136, 220

E

economics 4, 52, 71, 107, 128, 190-191, 195, 197, 202-204, 214
Egypt 105
elite 166, 168-169, 198
emancipation 150-151, 158
empire 10, 22-23, 25-28, 49
encyclicals 122
Enlightenment 10, 74, 86, 106-108, 155, 158, 160, 171, 175-176, 184, 186-187, 191-193, 204
entrepreneur 196-198, 200, 202
equality 21-22, 26, 54, 158, 160-166, 168, 170, 173, 179, 185, 187, 191, 197-198, 222
estates 57, 69-70, 164, 198, 201, 203-205, 207
ethics 36, 116, 128, 176-177, 190
evolution ix, 52-55, 57, 64-65, 67, 70, 74, 87, 91, 107-108, 127, 151, 153, 155, 162-165, 168, 170, 173, 175, 178-179, 183-187, 189-191, 193, 196, 198, 200, 202, 205, 209-211, 219
exegesis 96, 150

F

faith 2, 8-10, 14-17, 27-28, 33-34, 41-43, 46-47, 63-64, 71, 81, 83, 85-86, 91-108, 113-116, 120-121, 134, 138-142, 144-145, 150-151, 156, 170-172, 187, 210, 216, 230
familia 24-27, 44, 76, 78, 80, 103, 121, 175, 180-181, 183, 187
Faust 17, 42, 47, 57, 102
feudalism 19, 168, 196
folklore 86
formation 3, ix, 1, 10-11, 14, 16, 28, 38, 59, 66-69, 71-72, 74-76, 79, 83-84, 86, 89, 97, 103, 107-108, 112, 115-116, 123, 127, 136, 139, 141-142, 145, 149-150, 156-157, 172, 199-200, 205, 207, 219, 222-224
Frankish kingdom 79
Franks 199
free love 177

freedom motive 152-153, 155, 158, 160-162, 165-166, 168, 170-173, 175, 178-179, 182, 184, 192-194, 200, 210
French Revolution 43, 50-51, 53-54, 57, 64-65, 70, 73-74, 87, 162, 165, 168, 170, 175, 178-179, 183-186, 189, 191, 193, 196, 198, 200, 202, 205
Führer principle 79-80

G

Geisteswissenschaften 210
genius 52, 85, 176-177, 179
Germanic culture 77, 86
government 1, 23, 50-51, 54-55, 58, 69-70, 81, 87-89, 107, 123, 127, 129, 132, 138, 141, 156-157, 161-164, 166, 170, 181, 185, 194, 196, 198-200, 219-220, 223, 237
ground-motives xi, 8-9, 11, 14-15, 32-33, 35-36, 38-39, 41, 43, 47, 57, 60, 97, 99, 111-112, 116, 137, 139, 143, 145, 147, 152, 156, 226
guilds 53, 57, 78, 80, 186, 196
guilt 3, 26, 36, 39

I

ideal type 215
immortality 20, 32-35, 44, 105
interlinkages 180, 200-201

H

heart 3-4, 12, 23, 29-37, 41, 43, 46-47, 60, 64, 78, 90-93, 95-96, 98, 100-102, 109, 116, 118, 120-122, 130, 161, 167, 199, 208, 221-222, 225, 227
Historical School 58, 69, 73, 75, 186-187, 190-193, 200, 205, 209-210
historicism 43, 47, 50, 52, 55, 58, 63-64, 66-67, 71, 74, 86-87, 97, 108, 183-184, 186-187, 190-193, 209, 211, 223
Holy
– Roman Empire 10, 22
– Spirit 12, 15, 28, 30, 34, 38, 91, 96, 98, 113, 121

I

idealism 179, 189, 200, 203, 209-211

ideology 11, 74, 109, 178-180, 182, 186, 189, 204
imperium 22
individual 1, 3-5, 9, 16-19, 22-23, 25, 27, 30, 32-34, 38, 44-45, 51, 53, 58, 67, 69, 72-76, 83-88, 104, 107-108, 111, 117, 121, 123, 125-129, 132, 144, 156, 158-159, 161, 163-169, 173, 175-186, 190, 192-193, 195-197, 200, 203-205, 209-210, 213-216, 221, 227-228, 231
individualism 86, 108, 177, 180, 185-186
individualistic 87, 107, 158, 166, 175-176, 178-179, 182-183, 185-186, 196-197, 200, 204-205, 209
individuality 51, 83-85, 104, 176-180, 182, 184, 186, 193, 204, 210, 215-216, 227-228, 231
individualization 58, 83, 104
industrialization 197, 202
irrationalism 177, 182, 192
irreducibility 44, 46, 66
ius
– *gentium* 25-28, 80
– *civile* 23-25

K

Kingdom of God 95, 108, 130

L

law 17, 24-27, 30, 36-37, 41, 43-44, 46, 49, 51-54, 59-60, 66-67, 69-73, 75-77, 80-81, 89-90, 98, 101, 106-107, 117, 121-124, 126, 131, 138-142, 146, 150-151, 153, 155, 157-165, 167-173, 175-186, 189-195, 197-200, 202, 204, 207, 209-211, 215, 219, 225-232, 238-239
labor 22, 38, 67, 81, 87, 125, 136-137, 143, 164, 196-198, 203, 208, 214, 217, 223
liberalism 164-168, 173, 198
Logos 113
love 1, 18, 29-30, 37, 47, 49, 68, 90, 94, 116, 140, 142, 146, 150, 177
Lutherans 50, 187

M

magic 3, 23, 25, 94-95, 105
mana belief 103
marriage 60, 124-126, 129, 131, 146, 176-177, 201, 206, 214, 227
mechanistic worldview 172
mechanization 197, 203
medieval society 70, 78, 80, 149, 157, 186, 194
Melanesians 103
metaphysics 115, 204
modal aspects 214-215, 229, 231
modernism 107
Moira 17-18, 28, 144
monarchy 163, 165, 194, 199, 207
motion 1, 7-8, 12, 30-31, 33-34, 41-42, 46-47, 59, 65, 81, 98-99, 101, 109, 120, 136, 151, 153-155, 172, 183, 211-212
Mount Olympus 17

N

national socialism 11, 26-27, 52, 67, 71, 79-80, 83, 125, 143, 186
natural law 26, 51, 69-70, 75, 117, 121, 123, 126, 131, 156, 158, 161-162, 168, 173, 175, 179, 194-195, 202, 210, 229
nazism 11, 52, 74, 87, 185
neo-Kantian 210, 227
neutrality of science 172
New Guinea 77
norms 1, 61, 69-70, 73-75, 82, 96, 105, 108, 135, 171, 179, 186, 203, 206-208, 229

O

object function 92, 229
Olympian gods 17-18, 21, 28, 34, 67, 111, 144
Orphic school 20

P

papacy 28, 145
Papuan tribe 77
parliament 138, 164-168, 181, 199, 220
pater familias 24-27, 78

personality ideal 151, 153, 171-172, 175-179, 187, 203-204
philosophy 7-8, 18, 20-21, 26, 28, 32, 42, 53, 64, 92-93, 113, 133-134, 141-142, 154, 156, 187, 189, 206, 210, 214, 220, 223, 225-232
physico-chemical 44, 46, 92, 211-212
Physiocrats 195-196
poison 43, 86, 212
polis 9, 19, 21, 26, 89, 196
political theory 59, 127, 157, 164, 173, 189, 193-195, 219, 238
power 2, 9-12, 15-16, 19, 22-25, 27-28, 30, 36, 39, 44, 47, 49, 52, 54, 58, 60-61, 63, 67-69, 71-72, 74-79, 81-82, 84-91, 96-97, 102, 104-114, 116, 118-119, 129, 133, 136, 139, 141, 143-144, 146, 149, 151-152, 156-157, 162, 164-171, 173, 177, 181, 195, 197, 199-200, 208, 210, 215, 220-222, 224, 231, 235
principle xi, 1, 4-5, 10, 13, 17-22, 26-29, 32-37, 54-56, 58-60, 63-64, 67-68, 70-71, 73-75, 78-80, 82, 84-88, 90, 98, 101-102, 106-107, 112, 115-117, 119-120, 122, 124-129, 132, 134-136, 138, 141, 158, 162, 165-168, 170, 173, 175, 181, 184-186, 189, 197-198, 205-206, 213-214, 219-220, 222, 226, 228, 230-232
progress 74, 86, 107-108, 185, 205-206
proletariat 197
Protestantism 10, 139, 145, 157
providence 52, 183, 187, 192
psychological 9, 159, 210
psychology 32-34, 42, 210, 214
public interest 57, 127, 170, 198
public law 26, 158, 162
Puritan Revolution 163

R

race 1, 21, 60, 74, 83, 86, 126-127, 131, 150, 180-181, 185
rationalism 86, 108, 176-177, 182, 184, 186-187, 191-192
reason 18-19, 33-34, 36-38, 44, 53, 57, 73, 78, 81, 92, 99, 117-121, 126, 129,

133-134, 136-138, 141-142, 151-153, 155, 158, 161, 163, 167, 169, 171, 178, 199, 206
Rechtsstaat 107
redemption 12, 15, 28, 32-33, 35-38, 41, 59-60, 68, 88, 102, 108, 110, 113-114, 117-118, 121, 131, 139-140, 143, 145, 147, 150, 156, 170, 180, 187, 194, 214, 226
reformation 115-116, 141, 171, 205
religion 2, 5, 8-11, 14-21, 23, 28-29, 32, 35, 38-39, 41-44, 47-49, 55, 58, 64, 66-68, 76, 83-84, 87, 91, 97, 99, 101, 103-104, 107-109, 111-112, 114-117, 119-120, 134-135, 137, 139, 141-142, 144, 149-153, 156, 160-161, 187, 191, 193, 221, 230-231
republic 23, 162-164, 166, 185, 187
res publica 9, 24-25, 53-54, 80, 162-163, 166, 169, 185, 198
Restoration period 51, 70, 162, 175, 184, 186, 189-192
Roman
 – Catholic Church 10, 77, 80-82, 118-119, 130-132, 137, 145
 – Catholicism 10-11, 14-15, 116, 119, 128-132, 134, 140-141, 143-145, 149, 156, 194
Romanticism 51, 176-179, 189, 192-193, 209-210
root-community of humankind 21, 48, 130, 181
rule of law 107, 165

S

sacraments 98, 129, 133, 142
scholasticism 21, 93, 115, 117-118, 134, 137, 142, 146, 149-151, 158
science ideal 106, 151-156, 160, 168, 171-173, 175-176, 178, 182-184, 191-192, 200, 204
secularization 158
self-knowledge 8, 33, 35, 103, 112, 131
sense perception 21, 93, 214-215
sin vii, ix, xi, 2-3, 5, 8, 11-13, 15, 19-23, 29-31, 33, 35-39, 41, 44-45, 48-49, 55,
57, 59-61, 63-65, 69, 72-74, 76, 78, 81-82, 84, 87, 90, 92-93, 99, 102-105, 107, 109-112, 114, 116-120, 122-123, 127-128, 130, 133, 137-138, 140-144, 146, 149-150, 153, 155-157, 162-163, 165-166, 169, 172, 180, 182-183, 189-192, 196, 198-199, 201-203, 208-209, 211, 214, 216-217, 220, 222-223, 225-227, 230-231
social contract 159, 161, 164, 169, 176, 185, 190
socialism 1-2, 11, 27, 50, 52, 67, 71, 73, 79-80, 83, 86, 89, 125, 143, 186, 220, 238
sociology 42, 184, 189-193, 195, 197-200, 202-209, 211, 213-216
solidarism 128
sophists 19, 21
soul 34-37, 44, 46, 72, 81, 91-92, 98, 105, 112, 115-119, 122, 129-133, 136, 142, 144, 154-155, 227
sphere sovereignty 22, 27, 43-46, 48-51, 55-59, 63, 67, 82, 87-88, 90, 106, 124-127, 129, 132, 170, 181, 185, 219
state of nature 161, 169, 197
Stuarts 163-164
Sturm und Drang 176
subject-function 213, 226, 229
subject-object relation 213, 232
subsidiarity 125-127, 129
substance 20, 31, 34, 115, 117, 126, 154, 212, 229, 239
Superman 11
synthesis 2, 7-8, 11-15, 29, 50, 115-116, 118, 137, 139, 142, 145-146, 149, 175, 192, 226, 232

T

theology 12, 32, 34-35, 42, 92, 97, 99, 113-115, 120-121, 134, 143, 145-147, 187, 231, 236
theoria 20
theory 6, 8, 12-14, 32, 42, 51, 55, 64, 97-98, 113-115, 125-129, 152, 157, 160, 164, 166-167, 173, 175, 178, 180-181, 189, 193-195, 202-205, 209, 214, 219-220, 229, 238

Index

Thomism 126-127

time ix, 1-3, 7-11, 14, 16-21, 24, 27, 32-34, 38, 43-45, 48-52, 54-57, 59-60, 63, 67, 73, 78, 81, 83-84, 86, 88, 91, 93-95, 97, 100, 109, 116, 130, 139, 142, 146, 149, 157-159, 163, 171, 175, 181, 183-184, 187, 192, 195-196, 201, 203, 208, 210-211, 219, 221, 226-227, 229-230, 232, 239

totalitarianism 129

tradition 2-3, 10, 52-53, 72-75, 85-86, 105, 107, 141-142, 151, 163, 167, 182-184, 186, 189-192, 219-220, 232

U

universalism ix, 128, 178, 180-182, 184, 186, 192

V

values 43, 63, 204, 210
Volk 51-52, 75-76, 79, 83, 87, 182
Volksgeist 51, 75, 182
volonté générale 170

W

Word of God 12, 36, 55, 59, 97-98, 100, 108-109, 143, 145-146, 181, 222
Word-revelation 28, 34-35, 59-60, 66, 96-100, 102, 214

www.ingramcontent.com/pod-product-compliance
Lightning Source LLC
Chambersburg PA
CBHW032032290426
44110CB00012B/770